STUNTMAN!

STUNTMAN!

★ ★ ★

MY CAR-CRASHING, PLANE-JUMPING, BONE-BREAKING, DEATH-DEFYING HOLLYWOOD LIFE

HAL NEEDHAM

LITTLE, BROWN AND COMPANY

NEW YORK   BOSTON   LONDON

Little, Brown and Company
Hachette Book Group
237 Park Avenue, New York, NY 10017
www.hachettebookgroup.com

First Edition: February 2011

Little, Brown and Company is a division of Hachette Book Group, Inc. The Little, Brown name and logo are trademarks of Hachette Book Group, Inc.

The publisher is not responsible for websites (or their content) that are not owned by the publisher.

Library of Congress Cataloging-in-Publication Data
Needham, Hal.
    Stuntman! : my car-crashing, plane-jumping, bone-breaking, death-defying Hollywood life / Hal Needham. — 1st ed.
        p. cm.
    Includes index.
    ISBN 978-0-316-07899-3
    1. Needham, Hal.   2. Stunt performers—United States—
Biography.   3. Actors—United States—Biography.   4. Directors—
United States—Biography.   I. Title.
    PN1998.3.N3835A3 2011
    791.430'28092—dc22
    [B]   2010021821

10   9   8   7   6   5   4   3   2   1

RRD-IN

Printed in the United States of America

THIS BOOK IS DEDICATED
TO MY MOM, EDITH NEEDHAM.

Contents

STUNTMAN!

Previews

Thirty Feet High, Upside Down and Going Backward

The explosion must have been second only to the A-bomb. A cannon placed in the floorboard and loaded with four black-powder bombs shot the four-door Chevy thirty feet in the air and folded it in half. When I opened my eyes in midflight, I was upside down and going backward. I knew this wasn't going as planned and at any moment there was going to be one helluva wreck. The car landed on its roof, which caved in, jamming the doors. But the big problem was that I wasn't breathing.

I saw that the back window had blown out from the impact, so I made my way to it. Gasping for air, I crawled out from under the trunk of the pancaked car. At that moment the boys working with me on the stunt came skidding to a stop. I heard one say, "Holy shit, he's alive!"

The hospital confirmed that I had a broken back, six broken ribs, and a punctured lung. I counted the missing teeth myself: three. John Wayne would have to finish the movie without me...

Murder? Suicide? Burt Reynolds?

After spending eleven days in the hospital, I walked into the house I was sharing with Burt Reynolds all humped over, because my ribs couldn't find their connecting points. Burt told me that if I ever intended to amount to anything I would have to straighten up. Even knowing how much those broken ribs were going to hurt, I couldn't keep from laughing. I thanked him with a middle-finger salute and went upstairs.

Burt never missed a chance to throw in a funny line, but you'd think he'd have been more sympathetic seeing as how I helped him dodge a possible murder rap during the filming of *The Man Who Loved Cat Dancing*. I was the stunt coordinator and doubling Burt in the movie, and he was starring with Sarah Miles, who was married to *A Man for All Seasons* screenwriter Robert Bolt at the time. About halfway through the shoot, Sarah's business manager, David Whiting, came to visit her on location in Gila Bend, Arizona. Burt's birthday was coming up, so I had decided to rent a hall and celebrate with some barbecue, a little music, and a lot of booze. The Sunday morning I was preparing for the party, a crew member told me that David's dead body had been found the previous night facedown near a pool of blood in Sarah Miles's room.

When Burt showed up at the hall, I repeated what I'd heard. He asked what I was going to do about the party. I thought about it for a second and answered, "I'm sure not going to invite the dead man." Right or wrong, I forged ahead with the party. Needless to say, it wasn't much of a success, as everybody stood around drinking and gossiping about whether it was suicide or murder.

The next morning the air was full of suspicion. Sitting by the pool on a rare day off, I started hearing rumors that the sheriff was going to arrest Burt for murder—something about some supposed love triangle. I raced out to the set to tell Burt and the director,

Richard Sarafian, what was happening. We met in Burt's motor home. When Burt heard an APB might be put out on him, he was in shock. Sarafian was concerned about what his star was going to do. I suggested Burt go to Utah, the film's next location, so he could buy some time to hire legal counsel and stay out of the slammer while the law attempted to extradite him to Arizona. Burt agreed. How would he get there? I told him to lie down in the back of his motor home and hang on. I knew the way to Utah...and as it turned out, our great escape was unnecessary as Burt was never charged...

Cannonballing Coast to Coast in Thirty-two Hours

There was another time we blew across the state line, keeping our eyes peeled for the police. I was behind the wheel of a modified Dodge van that had its interior ripped out and was semi-equipped to look like an ambulance. It had red emergency lights on the roof and "TransCon MediVac" painted on the side. I had stuffed a full-blown 440 wedge engine under the hood and added two extra gas tanks capable of carrying ninety gallons. I'd also mounted three filler spouts, one for each tank, to be able to fill them quickly. It was the perfect vehicle for our team—me, the great car journalist Brock Yates, his pretty brunette wife, Pam, and Dr. Lyle Royer, whom I had met in a bar on the Sunset Strip—to compete with in the Cannonball Run.

The race had been run a number of times. The drivers would disguise themselves and their vehicles to be less conspicuous—as if that were possible, racing from coast to coast at a hundred-plus miles an hour. The vehicle covering the distance in the shortest amount of time was the winner, and the prize was a trophy and bragging rights until the next race. The only rule they had was that there were no rules. The first car in the cross-country race left the starting line in Darien, Connecticut, at 9 p.m., followed every fifteen minutes by the next in line. We left at 1:45 a.m. and headed west, with Brock driving. The traffic was bumper-to-bumper. I told Brock we couldn't win at this pace, so I hit our red lights. Now I knew how Jesus (or was it Moses?) felt when he parted the Red Sea. The cars ahead moved to the side of the road, and we left New York City in our wake.

Around 4 a.m. we were blowing through New Jersey, gobbling up miles in record time. I looked in the mirror and saw headlights way, way back there. Brock told me to back off to about eighty and see if they got any closer. Sure enough, the car closed the gap and turned on its red lights. We pulled over.

Brock and I, both dressed in orange-and-white ambulance attendants' jackets, got out and walked back to meet the police. One officer asked, "Where are you heading? It's a long way to a hospital in that direction."

Brock casually replied, "California."

"Why?" the officer asked.

"That's where the patient has to go," I said.

The officer looked confused. "Why California?" he asked.

"You'll have to ask the doctor. We're just drivers," Brock said.

Brock and I led the way to the ambulance door and opened it. Pam lay strapped to a gurney with an oxygen mask on and IV needles taped to her arm. The Doc, who was wearing a white coat, handed the officer a clipboard with a UCLA Medical Center form filled out. The officer looked down at it, obviously confused by the jargon. Explained the Doc, "She has a lung disease."

The officer appeared suspicious. "Why didn't you fly her?"

"She couldn't tolerate the altitude," the Doc said impatiently. "We can't even take the northern route...too high. Have to head to the south."

We could see them mulling over the dilemma. If they delayed us and something happened to the patient, it would be on their heads—which is what Brock and I were counting on. Finally one said: "Okay, go ahead, but keep your speed down. Emergency or not, you're going way too fast. You're endangering half the state."

After they left, we jumped in the van and Brock turned to Lyle and said, "Nice going, Doc," as I mashed the gas and asked that engine for all it had.

And the idea for a movie was born: What if we put Burt Reynolds, Dom DeLuise, and Jack Elam as the Doc in the van—with Farrah Fawcett as the patient—and had them race across the country on the big screen against Cannonballers Terry Bradshaw and Mel Tillis in a stock car, Roger Moore doing James Bond in an Aston Martin, Dean Martin and Sammy Davis, Jr., dressed as Catholic priests in my Ferrari, Jackie Chan in a rocket-powered Subaru, a couple of good-lookin' ladies in a Lamborghini, and anyone else willing to challenge the law…

Bootlegging Coors from Texas to Hotlanta

High speed played a part in the *Smokey and the Bandit* movies, as did Jackie Gleason (Sheriff Buford T. Justice), but to the day he died I don't think he ever knew my name. When things were hunky-dory, he called me "Pally," and when he was unhappy, it was "Mr. Director." While I was preparing to shoot the first *Smokey*, Jackie called and said he had a few questions about the movie and wondered if I could come over to his hotel to discuss things. An hour later I rang his doorbell, wondering how this was going to work out. The Jackie Gleason we all knew answered the door dressed in slacks and a sports jacket with a red carnation in the lapel. I stuck out my hand and introduced myself.

Invited in, I took a seat, and we made small talk for a few minutes. Then I told him I had been working all day and sure could use a drink. He apologized, and we moved to the bar. He fixed the drinks, and we toasted to a good shoot. I told him how much I'd enjoyed watching him on *The Honeymooners*. I think he had a story about every episode, and we drank a toast to each one. That's a lot of episodes. Finally I told Jackie I had to get up early for the first day of shooting. As I headed for the door he said, "Now, don't you be late." I promised I wouldn't and said goodnight. On the way back to my hotel, I wondered what he'd wanted to talk to me about, because not one word had been said about *Smokey*.

The next morning I arrived on the set and found Jackie sitting in his chair, legs crossed, wearing the same clothes as the night before. He might not have taken his clothes off, but he had removed his shoes, because now they were on the wrong feet. As I approached he said, "Hi, Pally," raised his coffee in a salute, and tipped over backward. He got up laughing and said it was time for him to get dressed and made up. As I got to know him better, I learned that all he wanted was some company and a drinking partner...

NASCAR, the Skoal-Bandit, and Voodoo

When I started my NASCAR team, I made Burt Reynolds my partner and named the team the Skoal-Bandit because of the popularity of *Smokey and the Bandit*. No race car had ever had its own name, and it turned out to be a stroke of genius. By 1984 the Skoal-Bandit team was on fire. Our driver, Harry Gant, was winning races and scoring lots of top tens. He was running in the championship race against his two main competitors, Dale Earnhardt and Terry Labonte. I hatched a plan to get Skoal some PR.

I called a press conference in a tent, where I had two toy race cars sitting on a table, one that looked like Dale's and one like Terry's. Incense was burning, and atmospheric smoke floated out from beneath the table. I proceeded to stick pins into the cars. The story made all the race magazines and newspapers—because Earnhardt's engine blew up halfway through the next race. Personally, I didn't think my voodoo act had anything to do with his engine blowing. The following weekend our truck was parked right next to Dale's. When he saw me, he said, "Don't leave." He went into his truck, returned with two shock absorbers, and formed them into a cross, saying, "I got you covered, Needham!" And then he laughed.

The PR was so outstanding that I came up with a new voodoo plan. I hired an actor from Atlanta, flew him to Charlotte, and dressed him in a top hat and tails. He wasn't just any actor; he was a black Shakespearean actor. I told him that as I walked through the garage area, he should follow six feet behind me. When I stopped at Dale's car, I wanted him to move in close and stare at it. Then we would do the same thing when we came to Terry's car. He did exactly what I asked. As we passed Richard Petty's car, his crew chief, Dale Inman, was sliding under Richard's car just as he caught a glimpse of my voodoo doctor. He immediately slid back out and stared at the guy. By the time we reached the other end of the garage area, the speakers were blaring "Hal Needham! Report to the NASCAR trailer!"

The officials in the trailer looked at me as if I was crazy. Then one of them told me, "If you don't get that guy out of here, there might be a riot." I thanked the actor, rushed him into a limo, and put him on the next flight back to Atlanta. Though my well-being might've been in jeopardy, the PR was bigger than ever before...

Speed of Sound: 739.666 MPH

A toy company contacted me about making a Hal Needham Stunt Doll and asked me to stage a PR stunt to launch it. I was the son of a sharecropper with eight years of education. What a shock it would be to people I grew up with back in the hills of Arkansas to see a Hal Needham doll. The toy company had just dumped Evel Knievel, and they wanted me to do something spectacular to make my name better known among young boys. That was all I needed to hear. Boys like macho, and they like speed. Bill Fredrick, who had designed a rocket-powered truck I used for a river jump in a GM commercial (my first broken back), was building a car to break the sound barrier with a land vehicle. All he needed was a little cash to finish the car. I talked to him, and he agreed I could drive the car if the toy company, Gabriel, would supply the money to finish the car and fund the necessary runs. A deal was struck with CBS to cover the run on *CBS Sports Spectacular*. Wow. Big publicity if I broke the sound barrier. I told the toy company the plan, and they bought in.

A few months later we were at Mud Lake in Tonopah, Nevada, ready to break the sound barrier—more than 700 miles per hour. We would make a few slow runs to check out the car and, not incidentally, me. On the line for the first run, I listened as the countdown went from ten to one. I hit the throttle. Wow. What a kick that thing had. It was a peroxide rocket that developed full power in five milliseconds. Thank God we had the pressure up only about 20 percent, because the car still hit the speed traps at over 250 mph. It scared ol' Hal just a tad.

By 10 a.m. the car was back on the line, refueled and ready for run number two—at a higher pressure to feed more fuel into the catalyst, which would mean more speed. This time I was better prepared for the jolt of energy leaving the start line. I hit the pedal and was launched across the lake. Things zipped by pretty fast, and at the end of the run I was told I had been clocked at 357 mph.

I thought we were going in leaps and bounds toward our objective of 700 mph. CBS, on the other hand, was worried that it was going to take too long and wanted more speed faster or they would have to pull up stakes and leave. The toy company wasn't going to like this: no TV show, no PR. We had to do something.

I walked over to Bill and told him we had to go for it. "Boost the pressure," I said. "Let's show them some real speed!"...

Hooper and Blowing Up Half of Alabama

When people see my movies, I want to get their adrenaline flowing; if I don't, I haven't done my job. *Hooper* was the story of a stuntman, so I wanted to put in every stunt I could dream up—a motorcycle sliding under a moving semi, car jumps, fire, fights, high falls. In the final scene a city is hit by a major earthquake, causing panic in the streets as Burt Reynolds and Jan-Michael Vincent race a Trans Am through the chaos to a final rocket-propelled jump. This would be the master shot of all master shots. I had thirteen cameras placed all around the area, with a major stunt set up to happen right in front of each one of them—and half of Alabama being blown up in the background. The final camera would be positioned in a chopper with me, because that was the only seat in the house where you could see the whole thing unfold...

1

Sharecropper's Son

As a sharecropper's son living in the hills of Arkansas during the Great Depression and using a mule's ass as a compass to guide me up and down cotton rows, I never figured I would write a book about my life. But considering what I've accomplished, a lot of people told me to commit it to paper. So here goes.

They say ignorance is bliss, and I agree. How do you know you're poor if that's the way you've always lived? If your neighbors live the same lifestyle you do, then it must be the norm. Our home was average for a sharecropper's family of seven, a two-room log house that had a fireplace for heating and a woodstove for cooking and warming bathwater. Growing up, I'd never heard of water being piped into a house. We had to carry every drop we used from a mountain spring five hundred yards down the hill. At six years of age, carrying two one-gallon buckets of water uphill, it felt like a mile. The toilet was two holes in the ground in a small shack about fifty feet from the house. The only light at night came from two kerosene lamps we used sparingly. That meant no favorite books being read at bedtime, but that didn't really matter because we couldn't afford to buy books anyway. Kerosene cost money, of which we had very little. My family's yearly income averaged $400.

Our transportation was a wagon pulled by a team of mules—

or walking. The only place to go was to town, which consisted of two buildings: a combination grocery store, post office, and gas station, and the cotton gin next door. Socializing with your neighbors didn't happen. At the end of the day you were so tired, all you wanted to do was eat supper and go to bed. Besides, it was four or five miles to the nearest neighbor's house.

One family that lived about nine miles from us was apparently rich. My stepdad, Corbett, had been there one time and told us of their wealth. He said they had a five-room house, lots of hogs, and milk cows. Their cotton field was so big they had to hire help to pick all the cotton. They also had a car. Now that really got my curiosity up. I had never seen a car, only pictures of one. But we never had the time or a reason to travel in that direction, so my curiosity would have to wait.

Each morning while Mom was cooking breakfast, Corbett, my sister Edwonia, my brother Armin, and I would pick wild berries and fruit. We always planted a huge garden. As the tomatoes, sweet corn, potatoes, okra, and green beans ripened, Mom would can them to get us through the winter. With no electricity for refrigeration, we also had to can all our meat, which came from the two hogs we butchered each fall. By the time the snow fell, Mom had canned around three thousand quarts of food, all on that little wood-burning stove.

Rabbits and squirrels were also a big part of our food supply. My brother and I had a dozen rabbit traps. At night we would bait them with corn and set them, and the next morning before daylight we would "run the traps" to check our luck. If we caught a rabbit, that meant we would have rabbit, biscuits, molasses, and gravy for breakfast. If not, it would be biscuits, molasses, and gravy.

In the afternoons my brother and I would hunt squirrels with a .22-caliber rifle. Accuracy was prized. My stepdad didn't want to hear that we had missed a shot, because that meant no squirrel for dinner and one less shell that had cost him half a cent. Squirrels are very sneaky. They can hide in a tree so that it's impossible to see them. When you approach, they scurry around to the opposite side. So my brother and I would tie a piece of string to a bush and then walk to the other side of the tree. We would wait quietly for a few seconds. Then by pulling the string, we'd shake the bush real hard and watch the top of the tree. Sure enough, the squirrel would come around to our side and bingo!—squirrel for dinner. My brother and I always hoped for two or three squirrels, because one didn't go very far with seven stomachs to fill.

Another source of food was fish. We lived thirty feet from the Red River. Sometimes mom would tell me to catch perch for dinner. I used a cane pole with a cork and baited the line with a worm. Perch are about the size of your hand, so it takes about four per person to make a meal. Seven times four equals twenty-eight perch, which usually took two to three hours to catch. We also fished with a trotline, which is a heavy line attached to a tree, stretched across the river, and tied to another tree, with hooks tied at three-foot intervals. Not knowing the fish's appetite for the evening, we gave them a choice. We baited one hook with a worm, the next with a fat caterpillar, the next a grasshopper, and the last with a small tree frog. We would run the line every three or four hours throughout the night and note which kind of bait was missing. That told us what looked appetizing to the fish, so we would rebait the hooks with their preferred food.

Blue channel catfish were the best eating, averaging between one and a half and four pounds. With a little luck, we could catch dinner for three or four nights. But I always hated it in the middle of the night when I heard Corbett yelling, "Wake up! It's time to run the line!"

The weeks were long, and though Sunday wasn't a day of rest for us, we would quit working a few hours early—not because God rested on the seventh day, but because we were bone tired.

One Sunday, Corbett said he sure wished he had a newspaper to see what was happening in the world. I saw an opportunity to step up and do a good deed, so I volunteered to walk to town to buy the paper. It was only four miles, because I would take the shortcut through the woods instead of sticking to the road. It was agreed that I could make the trip as long as I didn't lollygag around the store and got home before dark. Newspapers in our area weren't printed daily or weekly but monthly. If you bought last month's paper, it was half price. Corbett said last month's issue would be fine; that way we could save a nickel. He gave me a dime in case there weren't any month-old papers and I had to buy the current one.

Dime in hand, I headed through the woods toward town. There wasn't a trail to follow, but I had walked to town with Corbett a number of times, so I felt confident I would recognize various trees, creeks, and hills. On the walk my mind would wander into fantasyland, and then I'd snap back to reality and look for the landmarks to guide me. Once I reached town and bought a month-old paper, I got to talking to the store owners. They had two boys about my age, and I joined them outside in a game of marbles. We were laughing and giggling and having a ball. After several games their father came out and suggested it was time for me to head home.

I knew I had played too long and that darkness was approaching fast. I grabbed the paper and hit the road at a dead run. As I reached the turnoff to the shortcut, I hesitated. The road would be easier to follow, but I knew it made the trip two miles longer. I decided to take the shortcut through the woods. At first I had no problem, but as it got darker the landmarks were harder to recognize. My heart pounding, I saw the bogeyman in every shadow and behind every tree. My mind and eyes were playing tricks on me, but I knew I couldn't panic. I had to find the landmarks that would lead me home.

Just when I thought I was lost for sure, I heard a dove call. It was time to man up, and no matter what, show no sign of fear. I knew that sound was my brother and sister looking for me. When we were calling each other, we would cup our hands and blow through them, which sounded just like a dove.

I answered their calls and homed in on the direction they were coming from. When we met up, I asked without the slightest quiver in my voice what they were doing out there. They said Mom and Corbett were worried that I might have gotten lost. At home I kept up my brave front and told them I had just been taking my time, but I'm not sure if they believed me.

During the winter the Salvation Army would bring a big truck of groceries and used clothing to town. Mom and I would stand in line to get a few pounds of beans, some lard, and a sack of flour. Best of all, they would give each child a piece of hard candy. I learned from experience not to bite into it, as it would be gone in no time. Instead, I would let it melt in my mouth to make it last longer.

My mom made biscuits and gravy using the flour and lard they gave us and the milk from our one milk cow. If the cow was dry, mom used water for the gravy. It wasn't as good, but it was food. Believe me, we never had any leftovers. Mom mixed only enough batter so each of us could have two biscuits. For lunch and dinner we'd have beans and corn bread. If there was no meat to flavor the beans, she would use a hunk of lard and some salt and pepper. We raised our own corn so we'd have enough cornmeal to get us through the winter. When the beans ran out, we had corn bread and buttermilk for both lunch and dinner. We would crumble the corn bread into a bowl, pour buttermilk on it, add some salt and pepper, and call it a meal. I was too young to realize how important the donated flour, beans, and lard were at the time.

I don't know how we would have survived without the help of the Salvation Army. Not only did they give us food, they occasionally gave us used clothing. It didn't matter what size it was, someone in the family could wear it. If not, Mom would alter it so it fit… kinda. I remember one time, Mom and I stood in line for an hour or more. It was bone-chilling cold, and I was shaking. After the lady behind the counter gave us our goodies and we started to leave, she said, "Just a second," and disappeared through a door. She returned with a coat and handed it to me. "Try this on," she told me. It was a bit too big but warm, and I grew into the coat before it wore out. I will never forget the tone of my mother's voice thanking her.

Making a living and keeping food on the table were our priorities; education took a backseat. If and when we attended school, we had to walk about four miles. We went to school November through February, and sometimes into March, depending on the weather. Once winter broke we would plow, plant our crops, and cultivate them until the middle of July. We'd go back to school for a few weeks while the crops matured and then drop out again at harvesttime. September and October we spent picking cotton, gathering berries, canning food, and cutting firewood for the winter. Before we knew it November had arrived and it was time to go back to school.

My brother Armin and I were hired as the school janitors. Our job was to arrive at school an hour early, sweep the floor, carry in firewood, and build a fire in the potbelly stove. The money was good: $2.50 a month. But there was a problem. Many days our farm chores outweighed the necessity of going to school. But we still had to walk the eight miles to and from school to do our job, which made us change our minds about being janitors. We asked to be replaced but were told that nobody else wanted the job, so we would have to continue. We came up with an idea. The next morning we built a fire in the stove and placed a handful of .22-caliber shells deep in the ashes. The kids said that when the first shell exploded, it blew the stove door open, sending smoke and ashes all over the place. It scared them, but after two or three shells went off they figured out what was happening and it became funny. Armin and I were fired.

Strange as it sounds, we looked forward to going back to school, because it was a lot easier than the work we had to do at home. I had one teacher who either really liked me or felt sorry for me because we were so poor. Many days at lunchtime she would give me part of her meal, saying it was more than she could eat. As I look back, I think she brought more than she needed, knowing I wouldn't turn down her offer. I later found out she had wanted to adopt me. Poor or not, my mom would have no part of it. I often wonder where I might have ended up if Mom had said yes.

In 2004, a few months before my mom died at the age of ninety-seven, she told me that when she was pregnant with me, she knew her first marriage was coming to an end. One more mouth to feed would only add to her problems; maybe an abortion would be best. She lived in Memphis, Tennessee, at the time, and her downstairs neighbors talked her out of it, telling her, "Edith, you never know. This might be the child that will always be there for you." The neighbors' last name was Brett, so my mom named me Harold Brett Needham. I was happy to take care of her until the day she died.

You might say my stunt career started early. One day when I was eight years old, my brother and I were sent to town to pick up some commercial fertilizer. A neighbor who lived five miles down the road asked us if we could take his wagon and bring back a load of fertilizer for him, too. He told us he sure would appreciate it. So off to town we went.

I was driving the family wagon and my brother was driving the neighbor's. After loading up, we headed home. I began wondering which team was the fastest, so my brother and I decided to find out with a little race. The mules weren't exactly Thorough-breds, but they ran pretty good. The only problem was going to be the sharp turn up ahead. Who would slow down first? Answer: neither one of us. I was on the outside of the turn. Just as I was pulling ahead, my wheels caught a rut, sending the wagon side-ways and causing it to flip over. I was thrown off and landed hard, though nothing was broken. I lay on the ground and watched my team of mules head for home as fast as they could run, dragging the wagon, which was disintegrating piece by piece.

My brother stopped for me. I jumped in his wagon and chased after my team. A short distance later we found the mules grazing as if nothing had happened. I unhooked them from the wrecked wagon, mounted one, and led the other home.

I knew I was in for some kind of whipping from my mom, as my stepdad never laid a hand on us. Telling a little white lie wouldn't work because the evidence at the scene told the whole story, so I fessed up and took my medicine. My mom gave me the whipping, and then she cried, both because she gave me the whipping and because she knew how much it would cost to repair the wagon and buy more fertilizer. It hurt more to see Mom cry than the whipping did.

My stepdad was a thief, a hustler, and a crook, but he had to be to feed seven people during the Depression as a sharecropper. No one was lower than a sharecropper. Here's how it worked. A farmer had an extra house—if you could call it a house. It was usually a log cabin with two rooms and holes in the walls that had to be filled with mud to keep the cold out. The roof always leaked, which meant you had pots sitting all over the place to catch the drips. The house came with four or five acres of farm-land. The sharecropper would move into the house and cultivate the land. He could keep everything from the garden, but he had to split all money from the sale of the cotton sixty–forty—with the sharecropper getting the sixty.

But my stepdad worked out a way to keep all of the money. Before the crop was harvested, he would go to another part of the county and make a deal with a different farmer to sharecrop the following year. The day he collected the money from the cotton gin, he'd come home and load our few pieces of furniture onto the wagon. He'd tie the cultivator behind the wagon along with our milk cow and throw us kids on top. As soon as darkness fell it was adios, farmer! And we were off to our next home...with all of the cash.

That was the way we existed until 1941. I was ten years old when World War II broke out. My stepdad went to St. Louis, Missouri, to work in a defense factory and seek his fortune. He promised to send for the family as soon as he had a place for us to live and a couple of extra bucks. In the first letter we received, Corbett enclosed two train tickets so my older brother, Armin, and my sister Edwonia could go to St. Louis. He told us he could get them jobs, and that would help pay for Mom, me, my little sister, Gwen, and my baby brother, Jim, to join them. The plan worked. In just two months we boarded the train to St. Louis. It was packed with servicemen, and there were no seats. As my mother stood in the aisle holding my baby brother, a young soldier saw her and gave up his seat. I hung on to the back of Mom's seat as the train rocked and rolled along.

After a couple of hours I decided the floor would make a good seat, and a short time later the sandman threw sand in my eyes and out I went. Then someone shook me. I looked up to see a young soldier. He said he was tired of sitting and wanted to stretch his legs. Would I hold his seat? Willing to help the military in any way I could, I took his seat and fell back asleep. It was one in the morning when we arrived in St. Louis and my mom

woke me. We exited the train with our cardboard boxes and burlap bags, a sight that invited plenty of stares from people in the
station. My brain would not accept the message my eyes were
sending: there were lights by the millions, trains everywhere, and
too many people to count.

How he did it I didn't know, but Corbett made his way through
all those people toward us. Boarding a streetcar, we headed for our
new home. I found an empty seat and sat by the window in utter
amazement as the lights, houses, cars, and people went by in a blur.
Twenty minutes later we got off at Grand and Olive Streets. More
lights, department stores, even movie theaters. Wow, what a place
to live! Then I was told we were transferring to a bus, which would
require another twenty-minute ride to the house. I asked, "Just how
big *is* this city?" Corbett and my mom thought that was funny.

From the bus stop, it was only two doors down to our new
home in a two-story brick building. We lived upstairs. The only
problem was that the toilet was in the basement—but that was
better than the two-holer back in Arkansas. And it flushed, so
you didn't have to hold your breath. We had four rooms: a kitchen,
a dining room, and two bedrooms. I suggested we might even be
able to rent one out but was quickly voted down. In the basement,
along with the toilet and shower, was a furnace. Every day a truck
came by selling coal by the bushel—no more woodcutting! Oh
yeah, we also had running water in the kitchen and a four-burner
gas cookstove. What more could a boy ask for?

That first night in bed, I lay there trying to imagine what this
new life would be like.

The next morning after breakfast Corbett gave me a nickel
and told me to go to the store up the street and ask for an Eskimo
Pie. I asked what that was, but got no answer and was told to run
along. I walked out our door, turned left, went a hundred feet
to the first street, turned right, and crossed at the intersection.
There was the store.

I went in and made my purchase. Ice cream bar in hand, I left the store. Uh oh, I thought, I'm lost. I was completely turned around. Sitting down on the curb, I ate the Eskimo Pie, which beat the hell out of any homemade ice cream we ever tried to make. Then I waited for something good to happen. After a few minutes my mom stuck her head out the window and called my name. Well, I'll be! *That's* where I live.

Getting to school could have been a real problem because it was five blocks away, but the good thing was I could stand at my front door and see the building. My sister took me the first day, and I'd never seen that many kids in my life. My school in Arkansas only had one room for all eight grades and no more than twenty kids total. Most years there would be three or four grades without students. In St. Louis I must've had thirty kids in my class alone.

One thing I learned in Arkansas was how to work, so it didn't take me long to land a job at a neighborhood grocery. I would stock shelves, sweep the floor, and make deliveries from three o'clock until six, which was closing time. My pay was fifty cents a day. Another job I had was setting pins in a bowling alley. In those days, when the bowling ball hit the pins, they fell into a pit. After the ball and pins came to a rest, the pinsetter would jump into the pit, put the ball in the return ramp, and send it back to the bowler. He would then pick up the pins and place them in the rack to be set for the next player. We were paid ten cents for a complete game. If you were fast and didn't mind working your tail off, you could set two lanes at once. On a good night I could make five bucks.

There was a slight element of danger to the job. All the bowlers knew that the signal to throw the next ball was when the pinsetter jumped up on the back of the pit wall and lifted his legs. But every once in a while, I would be in the pit working and look up to see a ball and pins flying at me. To let the bowlers know that was a no-no, I would spit in the finger holes of the ball and send it back to them. They always got the message.

I worked hard, but when a buddy of mine told me I could get a job at Sportsman's Park, the stadium where the St. Louis Cardinals and Browns played their home games, I applied. They hired me to sell soda pop, and I earned twenty cents for every twelve sodas I sold, bringing my take to five or six dollars a day! I began work an hour before the game started and prayed that they didn't go into extra innings, since it was a lot of walking up and down stairs carrying two buckets of soda. Nobody had to rock me to sleep when I got home; I was plumb tuckered out. The good part was that I got to keep everything I made. Mom and Corbett worked in a defense plant, so I didn't have to contribute my money to support the family.

For the first time in my life I had money to invest. I was only thirteen years old, but it was big-time to me. My mom suggested I buy war bonds that the government was selling to fund our troops. For $17.50 you could buy a bond that paid $25 at maturity. Even though I wasn't very good at math, I knew that was a good deal.

One day that summer Mom told me to get dressed, I had to go meet somebody. I asked who, and she replied, "Your dad wants to see you." I thought, why? I didn't know my birth dad, and he sure hadn't put any food on the table up to now. What was to be gained by this reunion?

At my aunt's house I met dear old Dad. He was six feet one, a good-looking man with wavy hair and a lady-killer smile. There was no hugging or crying—hell, I didn't know this man. The conversation was limited to "How old are you now?" What a dumb question; he should know that answer. "How's school?" I told him fine, even though it wasn't. We had lunch, and I went home. It was a long four hours.

Dad had remarried and owned a neighborhood bar. His wife, Mae, was really nice to me the few times I spent the weekend with them. Dad thought a big day for me was to go barhopping while he introduced me to all his drinking buddies. Back at his place, he would tend bar at night. I had the run of the place until about ten o'clock, when Mae would tell me it was time to go to bed. When Dad got up late Sunday, he would drive me home. Big deal. What about a ball game?

He knew I worked at the ballpark selling soda pop. I was always reciting the batting averages of every player on the team—who was hot with the bat and who was in a slump—and it was obvious I was a fan. I thought how nice it would be if he'd buy a couple of tickets so I could sit and really enjoy a game. But he just chose to buy drinks for all his friends as we barhopped around the neighborhood.

It was interesting to watch as he would introduce me to someone who would say, "I didn't know you had a son." He would always come back with "I got two sons and a daughter." There were always questions like "Where have they been? I've never heard you talk about them." I always waited for those answers.

School in St. Louis was difficult for me. In Arkansas I had finished the fifth grade, but in the big city I had no idea what they were talking about in their fifth grade. I just showed up every day and sat there. A few years later I graduated from the eighth grade—but just barely. The following fall, diploma in hand, I headed for high school. About a month into ninth grade my English teacher, dear Miss O'Brien, pulled me aside. "Hal, you're not learning anything in school. You might as well not be here," she said. I told her I agreed and thanked her for her advice.

That was the end of my formal education.

To say the least, my mom was quite upset. She cried and told me I would never amount to anything without an education. It always hurt me to see my mother cry. I promised her I would get a job and work as hard as I could to climb the ladder of success. I had eight years of education, and all I had ever heard growing up was: "You can't do that; you're too small. You can't do that; you're not smart enough." But you know something? I just never listened to those folks.

2

The Making of a Stuntman

I had no idea what I was going to do once I left school behind. I looked through the want ads and eventually found a job climbing trees for a tree service. Little did I know that this job would be a building block in my career as a stuntman. The job paid $1.05 an hour, and it was full time. I worked fifty-four hours a week, and my take-home came to about $45. Heights didn't bother me, so I took to the trees like a squirrel. As a matter of fact, that became my nickname.

It looked as if this ladder-to-success thing might take a long time, but I kept my promise to my mom and worked hard. I stuck with it for three years, and they made me a foreman and gave me a raise to $1.50 an hour. Problem was, after becoming a foreman there was no more ladder to climb. The next-highest-paying job in that company was to own it, so I decided to move on.

One day I saw one of those Uncle Sam posters, where he's pointing at you and saying "I Want *You*." In the background paratroopers were floating through the sky. The Korean War was in full swing, and I decided this was a job for Needham. Whip North Korea. I could probably do it by myself. I arrived at the recruiting office early the next morning to enlist. Three days later, I was on my way to basic training at Fort Riley, Kansas. I was young and tough and loved the challenges they put me through. Sixteen weeks later, I was sent to Fort Benning, Georgia, for paratrooper school. I couldn't wait. After all, heights didn't bother me, and they guaranteed that my chute would work. What's to fear?

After finishing jump school, the cadre told me I was the toughest thing that ever wore a pair of jump boots. With jump wings on my chest and bravery in my heart, I ventured across the state line to a bar in Phenix City, Alabama, where a five foot ten truck driver proved them wrong. As my buddies helped me out of the bar, I told them he'd sucker punched me. That's my story, and I'm sticking to it.

The army then shipped me to Fort Bragg, North Carolina, to be a part of the 82nd Airborne, America's Guard of Honor. That was great, but what about Korea? I also took arctic training at Fort Drum, New York, desert training in Texas, and went on so many other maneuvers in North Carolina that I couldn't count them. I soldiered hard and made platoon sergeant.

Again I asked, "What about North Korea?" My company commander told me that there was only one regimental combat team of troopers in Korea, and they had graduates of jump school, as well as 16,000 members of the 82nd Airborne at Fort Bragg and another 16,000 from the 101st Airborne at Breckenridge, Kentucky, to draw on for replacements. Since they had made only one combat jump, with few casualties, there was little demand for replacements. My chances of going to North Korea were slim to none.

I was thinking if I'm not going to fight, why am I training so hard? I decided to find something else of interest to do. I volunteered for every army school I qualified for: leadership school, NCO (Noncommissioned Officers) school, chemical warfare, light and heavy weapons, and Ranger training. But what intrigued me most was a request for volunteer NCOs with fifty jumps or more to test a new parachute. It may seem a little risky to jump with an untested chute, but if it failed to deploy, you knew your reserve chute had been used for years, thereby giving you better than a fifty-fifty chance. Good enough for me.

Most often when the Airborne started a training maneuver, it began with a simulated combat jump. On one maneuver, as we boarded the C-119, I was surprised to see my battalion commander climb aboard. I was the jumpmaster, and I knew I had to mind my p's and q's. I noticed one of the new men, fresh out of jump school, shaking violently, as if he had the chills. I asked him what was wrong, and he said he was scared. I told him that there were forty-three other guys who felt the same way. He told me he wasn't afraid to jump, but they had given him a 60-millimeter mortar to jump with.

Since this was only a maneuver, I didn't think it was worth taking the chance of causing this trooper to have a problem. I told him to take the mortar off and have the plane crew give it to the ground troops when they picked up the next load of jumpers. The colonel wanted to know what was happening, and I told him.

"Sergeant, your company will need that mortar when they land," the colonel instructed me.

I thought, is he kidding? This is play war, not real war. He suggested that I give the scared trooper my rifle so that I could jump with the mortar, and then we could exchange them once we landed. Fine with me.

As I hooked the mortar onto my harness and strapped it to my legs, I realized it was packed too long (the scared trooper was six inches taller than me), and so it dragged on the floor when I stood up. I couldn't walk with it on, and for sure wouldn't be able to jump up and out the way I had been taught to exit the plane. I would have to stand in the door and roll out headfirst—definitely the most dangerous way to exit the plane. The green jump light came on, and I rolled out.

The next thing I knew, I was wrapped up in my shroud lines.

My parachute had no chance to open. I was rolling and tumbling through the air. Scared—but calm enough to look for a way to save my life—I pulled the rip cord on my reserve. Then all hell really broke loose. As I tried to throw the reserve parachute away from my body so it would open, it kept tangling up in my shroud lines. That's the last thing I remember.

When I woke up on the ground, I thought I was being barbecued. There's a rule that if a man is hurt, you throw a smoke grenade near him so the medics will know someone needs help. They must have thought I needed a lot of help, because there were ten smoke grenades burning around me.

After I lay there a couple of minutes covered in parachute silk, I sat up and pulled the chute off my head just as the medics arrived.

"Lie down, man, you should be dead," one of the medics said. "We have to take you to the hospital."

"I think I'm okay."

It turned out I was. The doctor couldn't find as much as a bruise on me. Still, he sent me back to the barracks and ordered that I not go back into the field. When the troops returned, they had numerous stories about what had happened during my jump as I rolled and tumbled through the air wrapped in my reserve chute. Most important, they told me my reserve opened partially about a hundred feet above the ground. Everybody believed the mortar I had strapped on had flown up and knocked me unconscious.

Payday in the army was the first of the month, and by the fifteenth most of us were broke. That gave us fifteen evenings to polish our brass and spit shine our boots. Sometimes on weekends, to make a buck, I would pull KP (kitchen police, washing pots and pans in the mess hall) for someone who had an extra ten dollars and no desire to clean pots. The same was true for pulling guard duty.

Another way to pick up an extra buck was sewing: GI-issued uniforms never fit. Therefore, all the troopers wanted their uniforms tailored and would take them to the post dry cleaner for alterations. One night at the Combat Club, after about six beers, my buddy Reid and I decided to go into the tailoring business. Even though neither of us had any experience, we figured we could learn how to do it cheaper than the cleaners and would get lots of business. We knew a civilian couple; the husband was the chairman of a big company, and his wife—not out of necessity—was a great seamstress. She agreed to show Reid and me how to tailor a uniform. The chairman thought it was so hilarious that he volunteered to loan us the money to buy a sewing machine, and his wife gave us permission to work out of their home. Reid and I would pin the uniforms for tailoring during the week and on weekends do the sewing under the wife's watchful eye. We charged half the price asked by the cleaners at the fort. We didn't get rich, but we had more money than most of the troops.

The most sought-after extra-income job was one that needed a considerable amount of start-up money. Here's how it worked. Say a soldier got a three-day pass or just wanted to go to town and blow off some steam but he was broke. He would find someone with cash and borrow money, promising to pay back the loan plus 50 percent interest. Loaners had to make sure they got paid back the moment the borrowers came out of the pay room (the captain's office). It was not unusual to see eight or ten guys waiting as the borrowers came out and the loaners demanded their money.

One weekend Reid and I were telling our civilian friends what easy money this was, and the husband suggested he supply the financing. Reid and I would loan out and collect the money and split the profits fifty–fifty with our financier. What a deal. Back at Fort Bragg, Reid and I let it be known that we had money to lend. Business boomed. The first month my take was more than I got paid. Word spread that we had plenty of money, and soon we were loaning out two to three thousand a month.

Then the captain threw a wrench into the gearbox. Each month before we got paid, the captain gave a payday talk: don't get in trouble, don't go AWOL, don't catch the clap, and so on. This time he announced that he would no longer tolerate a line of loan sharks outside his office collecting money on payday. As he went out the front door, I went out the back and caught him. I explained that Reid and I had loaned three thousand dollars that month, and if we didn't collect it as the troops came out of his office, we wouldn't get paid back. I promised that if he would let me collect this month, I would quit lending money. He agreed to this one time, but never again. I thanked him and took my position at his door to collect my money for the last time. That evening when dividing up the profits with our civilian financier, we told him the story and thanked him for his help. I knew it was back to KP, guard duty, and tailoring uniforms.

A couple of months passed, until one evening I was in my room when I heard someone call the barracks to attention. Knowing an officer had entered, I got up to see who and why. It was the captain. He said, "At ease" and came directly to me, asking to speak to me in private, in my room. "Sergeant, do you have any money?" he asked. I told him I had less than fifty dollars. He wanted to know if I could come up with five hundred dollars that night. I assured him I could, within the hour. He told me he would be waiting in his office and left.

Reid and I drove to our financier and told him we were back in business, but we thought it would be best not to charge the captain interest. I returned to the captain's office and handed him the envelope with his cash inside, saluted, and left. I'd brought back an extra thousand and started loaning it immediately. The following payday as the captain counted out my pay, he just laid an extra five hundred dollars on top. Not a word was said. From that day on the captain borrowed money from me on a regular basis and allowed me to stand in front of his office to collect on my loans.

You know, as a soldier, I thought I would see combat, and when this proved not to be true, I began to think that a career in the military was not for me. After three years I decided it was about time to get out of the army and head back to St. Lou. About thirty days before my discharge the captain called me into his office and gave me the re-up speech that all NCOs got from their company commanders. He told me he would soon be putting another rocker (stripe) on my arm, and he ran down all the benefits of the military—medical, retirement, not to mention three hots and a cot.

"Captain, I have one major complaint," I said. "It's the C rations we have to eat while we're in the field. I fed a can to a dog, and he went around for a week licking his ass trying to get the taste out of his mouth."

The captain wished me well, and thirty days later I was on my way home.

I returned to St. Louis in June 1954 and looked over my resume—eight years of formal education, three years in the tree-trimming business, and the skills I had learned in the army. I knew I wasn't qualified to be a brain surgeon, and I figured I would have to do something dangerous to make money. I considered becoming a smoke jumper, but when I found out that smoke jumping didn't pay enough relative to the risk, I decided the best thing to do was go back to climbing trees. My former employer welcomed me with open arms. Why not? Anybody with the nickname "Squirrel" *should* be a tree climber. Things went along okay in the beginning, but it wasn't long before I grew restless.

One hot and sticky afternoon, I hit the ground after trimming a gigantic elm tree. My clothes were soaked with sweat. I sat down next to the pool for a well-deserved cigarette, and the lady of the house came out in a huff. "Young man," she lectured me, "if you insist on getting in my pool to cool off, at least you could take off those filthy boots." Though I hadn't been in the pool and didn't plan on jumping in, I apologized and promised that next time I would remove my boots.

As she stormed away, I thought about my buddy Bob Brooks. He had been to California twice and kept telling me it was the land of milk and honey, with cool ocean breezes and beautiful women in bikinis. He was always begging me to go with him to the land of opportunity. Now seemed like as good a time as any. Besides, while I was in the service, my mother had moved to Santa Ana to be close to my sister Edwonia and her husband, who was in the navy and stationed in nearby Long Beach. I finished my smoke, walked over to my crew, and asked if anyone wanted to buy my climbing gear. One of them said, "They may call you Squirrel, but you still need your gear, unless you're going to do something else." I told them I was indeed going to do something else: I was going to California. Between them, they bought all my gear. I called Brooks and told him I was in. I packed three pairs of jeans, a half dozen T-shirts, a razor, and a toothbrush, and we hit the road early the next morning.

The trip wasn't easy. We figured we had enough money, but after replacing two blown tires and a fuel pump we got concerned about running low. We decided sleeping in the car would be necessary. Then a speeding ticket from the Texas highway patrol cut our food money in half; hot dogs and hamburgers would have to do.

I arrived in Santa Ana at ten at night, and it took a while to find my mother's house. Mom was surprised to see me, to say the least, but happy. I think. We sat around and talked for hours. Brooks and I took a financial inventory. I had less than $10 and he had about $40. We made an executive decision: find a job in a hurry!

The next morning I took a walk. One block from my mom's house I spotted a truck parked in a driveway. On the door was a sign that brought tears to my eyes: "The Tree Specialist." Even though it was Sunday, I knocked on the door of the house. A big man named Earl Edney opened the door and asked what he could do for me. "If that's your truck out here, you could give me a job," I said. I told him how good I was in the trees and that my nickname was Squirrel. I added that I was flat broke. He told me to be there in the morning at six-thirty.

Within a couple of days it was clear that the kids Earl had working for him didn't have the faintest idea how to get things done. Earl would go around and bid on jobs, and these kids would try doing the work. They weren't very organized or very good, so it took days to finish a small job. After a couple of weeks Earl realized there was some money to be made if he had a hot foreman as a partner. So we teamed up, bought a couple of used trucks and some new equipment, and hired four more men.

I may have been twenty-three, but I had not experienced much in the way of culture. I thought everyone who ate out went to coffee shops. Hamburgers, sandwiches, and soup were the norm, until one day I saw a bar with the sign Now Serving Lunch. I went in to check it out. At the counter the bartender handed me a menu. I ordered meat loaf, mashed potatoes, and gravy. She asked what kind of bread I wanted. Not knowing any other kind, I answered, "White." Then she asked what kind of salad dressing I wanted. Not knowing what she was talking about, I told her it didn't matter. When the bartender returned and set the salad in front of me, I didn't know what to do with it. I had never had a salad. Do I eat it, throw it on the floor, or just look at it stupidly? When she brought the meat loaf, she asked if she should take the salad away. I thought might as well; then I won't have to worry about what to do with it. Over the next few days I found out that a salad was an appetizer served before a meal.

As half owner of The Tree Specialist I thought I had found my future, until one day at a root-beer stand I met another ex-paratrooper, Cliff Rose, who was trying to break into

Hollywood as a stuntman. Cliff had an agent, and he had done a couple of episodes of the TV show *You Asked for It*. They liked his work, and it turned out there was a show coming up for which he'd need a second stuntman. Would I be interested? The thought of me on TV was too much to say no to. I would be rich and famous. I immediately said yes, then as an afterthought asked, "By the way, what are we going to do?"

Cliff explained the stunt. He would be riding a very fast horse, running at about 30 miles per hour. His buddy, Don Lykins, would be flying a Cessna 150 about 58 mph. I would be out on the wheel of the airplane, and as we flew over him, I would jump from the plane and knock him off the horse.

"Are you kidding me?" I said. Jumping eighteen feet at 58 mph? But then I thought "rich and famous" and decided it was a hell of a plan.

What Cliff had neglected to tell me was that this whole thing was his idea. *You Asked for It* was a request show; the audience would write in and ask to see any number of crazy things. Cliff had already performed several legitimate write-in requests for stunts, and had dreamed up this idea and written his own request because he wanted the job.

A week before the shoot date, Cliff and I picked a quarter horse, because they're known for their quick burst of speed. The thing we didn't know was whether, when the plane flew eight or ten feet over his head, this horse would spook, duck off to the side, or start bucking. The only way to find out was to give it a try.

Lykins borrowed a plane and met us at the location. He flew past, dipping his wings to tell us he was ready. We had previously agreed he would fly above Cliff about a hundred feet the first time, then drop to fifty feet the second time, and then descend ten feet each flyover. If all went well, we'd be ready to do the stunt. Not only did the plane not scare the horse, but after a couple of passes the horse considered it a challenge to a race. As the plane approached, he would spin, turn, and rear up in anticipation. When Cliff turned him loose, that was his signal that the race was on.

The big day arrived, and so did my mom. She wanted to see this happen — for that matter, so did I. She didn't seem nearly as concerned as I was. Of course, she didn't know much about heights, speed, airplanes, or horses. I was beginning to think I had let "my alligator mouth overload my jaybird ass."

The radio crackled with the news that everything was ready, and I boarded the plane. Lykins took off and made a pass over the TV production company, where someone was waving a green flag. A little farther in the distance I saw Cliff on the horse. He waved to signal that he was ready. Lykins flew a few hundred yards and turned back for our run. He was flying so low and slow that the stall warning was beeping, signaling that the plane was about to fall out of the sky. My mind was made up that if Lykins lost control of the plane, he was going to crash by himself, because I was bailing out. The only way to control the altitude was with the throttle, a maneuver called "hanging it on the prop." He couldn't see Cliff or the horse because the nose of the plane was too high. That's where I came in.

Squatting on the wheel, I was to hand-signal Lykins left or right, up or down. He was hanging it on the prop pretty good. He was a fool to rely on me, and I was an idiot for being on that wheel. Trust me, this is not a stunt you want to practice. You only have a split second to decide when to jump. As we approached, my mind was racing. I knew I had to do it right the first time. I was watching Cliff on the horse, and he was looking good. Now! I sailed through the air and hit Cliff, and then the ground hit me.

I stood up and looked at Cliff. He was okay. I then looked at the director, who signaled for Cliff and me to come over. I thought congratulations were in order; instead, he said we would have to do it again, because we had overshot our mark by a hundred feet and it would appear very small on-screen and maybe even out of focus. My mom was always a lady who spoke her mind. In a few choice words she accused the director of trying to kill her son. I silently agreed with her but knew I had to tempt fate one more time.

If you think I was nervous the first time, the second was far worse. I now knew how tough it was going to be. If I missed, there was a possibility my family might be walking slow and singing low at the cemetery. I got lucky and nailed it. The second one was perfect. The director was happy and so was my mom. Me, I was just delighted it was over.

The next few days were tough. Walking was difficult. Returning to my day job climbing trees was almost impossible, but I managed. About the time the soreness wore off, Cliff came to me with another job. This time it would be for the big screen.

Warner Bros. was making a movie based on the life of Charles Lindbergh called *The Spirit of St. Louis,* starring Jimmy Stewart and directed by Billy Wilder. The production was going to shoot a barnstorming sequence with two old biplanes, and they needed two stuntmen. All the stuntmen had to do was stand on the top wings while the pilot did loops and spins, hang upside down on a ladder under the plane during low passes over the spectators and cameras, transfer from the top of the upper wing of one plane to a grab bar on the underside of the lower wing of another plane flying just above. Oh yeah, and both men had to jump at the same time with five parachutes each. After one parachute opened, the stuntman would release it and open the next one until all five had been deployed. The plane would be only 2,500 feet high. Any jumper will tell you that's not enough altitude to open five parachutes and land safely.

Count me in.

I will never forget my first day on a movie set. The production had set up grandstands, ticket booths, and a variety of other attractions to give this large vacant field the look of a 1920s fairground. I would guess they had about 2,000 extras and about 150 crew members at the location. I had no idea it took this many people to make a movie. I had never seen a movie star up close until Jimmy Stewart walked onto the set. I was in awe. Imagine me, a country boy, just ten feet from one of the biggest stars in the world.

I snapped back to reality when a bullhorn called for the stuntmen to report to the area where the biplanes were parked. Before we took off the production manager asked what we were going to charge for the stunt. Having no idea what would be appropriate but wanting to get all we could, we suggested $2,000 each time we did the stunt. Billy Wilder was standing close by and overheard the conversation. "For two thousand, I'll do the stunt," the director shot back.

Cliff and I looked at each other, thinking he had to be kidding. Surely a man of his talent and celebrity, the director of such films as *Stalag 17, Double Indemnity,* and *The Seven Year Itch,* wouldn't risk his life to save the studio a few thousand dollars. Or would he?

Wilder walked over to one of the planes, climbed on top of the wing, and strapped himself to the safety bar. The planes were landing and taking off on a field rather than a paved runway. If one or both wheels hit a hole, there was a chance the plane would flip upside down, so standing on top was not the ideal place to be. Cliff and I had chosen to take off and land seated in the cockpit, which meant we had to climb to the top wing in flight, without a parachute. Between and on top of the wings were wire braces that we intended to use as handholds as we climbed up. We suggested to Mr. Wilder that he do the same, but the idea didn't appeal to him. From his perch atop the wing, Wilder signaled to the pilot "Let's go!"

The plane bounced across the field and got airborne. The pilot made a couple of passes overhead and landed. Wilder climbed down with a twinkle in his eye that said we knew we weren't getting $2,000. "Now, how much do you want for the stunt?" he asked. Cliff and I agreed that $1,000 would be just fine. Billy Wilder had cut our earnings in half for that particular stunt, but we had many others to do and felt sure he wouldn't want to try any of those. He would not be strapped to a safety bar, and one mistake could be fatal.

We did the stunt six times before Wilder had all the shots he needed. It was more money than I ever imagined I'd make in a single day. That night I thought it had all been a dream. Cliff and I talked about the stunts yet to be filmed and calculated how much we could possibly make. With the combination of the excitement and the money, I couldn't wait to get back to the set.

Early the following morning, Cliff and I showed up and were told that the next stunt would involve Cliff standing on top of the upper wing and me hanging upside down by my ankles from a rope ladder underneath the plane. Hanging from the ladder was nothing; it was climbing down to it that was the most dangerous.

The old single-engine biplane had two cockpits. The pilot would sit in the rear and fly the plane, while Cliff and I would be jammed in the front. Once airborne, Cliff would climb out and up onto the top wing. I would climb out and down to the axle where the rope ladder was attached, and then climb down the ladder. On the bottom rung of the ladder were two rope loops, known as a circus hitch. I had to place one loop around each ankle and then lower myself into an upside-down hang.

If you have ever been on a movie set, you know they are never ready when they're supposed to be. But I didn't know that. We flew around for ten minutes or more with me hanging upside down. I didn't know whether the shot was over and I should climb back up into the cockpit, or just watch the world go by upside down. I finally twisted around and looked up at the pilot, who motioned for me to stay put and then pointed to his watch and held up two fingers.

About five minutes later we made two low passes over the crowd and cameras. The pilot dipped the wings a couple of times to get my attention. When I looked up, he motioned for me to climb back into the cockpit. I pulled myself up and sat on the bottom rung of the ladder so I could remove the circus hitch. After hanging upside down for so long, I was dizzy and waited for my head to clear. I hoped the world would soon come back into focus. I finally made my way up to the axle and unhooked the ladder. Carrying it with me, I climbed back up to the cockpit.

After we landed the pilot said that I sat on the ladder so long that he thought maybe I had gotten scared and was frozen in place. He was trying to figure out how he was going to land the plane with me sitting on the bottom rung of the ladder, fifteen feet below the wheels, without killing me.

Cliff and I worked for six weeks on *The Spirit of St. Louis* and did all the stunts. We repeated most of them three or four times, which was great, because we were paid each time we did the stunt. The final tally showed that I earned more money in six weeks than I had made the previous year climbing trees. The vote was in. I'd sell the tree business to my partner. Look out, Hollywood, here I come! For the first time in my life, I had a goal: to become a Hollywood stuntman.

3

Bullshit Doesn't Photograph

What I didn't know was that the stunt business at that time was more or less run by ten or twelve stunt coordinators, or boss stuntmen. If they didn't know you, you didn't work, unless it was a specialty job like *The Spirit of St. Louis*. Well, they didn't know me, so for nine months I didn't work.

I began looking at my options. I could go climb a tree or apply for a Screen Extras Guild (SEG) card. At that time, SEG members were paid $15.05 per day, better known as "fifteen and a nick." The requirements were minimal: walk and breathe. Even I could do that. This would also allow me to be present on movie sets, where I could learn the business. When the stuntmen worked, I could meet them. Not being bashful, I would damn sure tell them who I was and what I could do.

The first stuntman I approached was Chuck Roberson, who was working on a set where I was an extra. Chuck doubled John Wayne and worked all the time. He was one of the top ten stuntmen in Hollywood, and for sure his friendship could be a big boost to my future. I introduced myself and told him of my dream to be a stuntman. To my surprise, he told me that he had heard my name mentioned a number of times. He knew about my work on *The Spirit of St. Louis* and assured me that if he ever got a call to walk around on an airplane wing, I would be the first person he would call to replace him.

Chuck was known for helping young stuntmen. Before the end of the day, he invited me over to his house and told me that he would help me in any way he could. Two days later I knocked on his door and took him up on his offer. He told me that my timing was perfect. He had two jobs the following day and offered me his place on one of them, a movie called *Timbuktu.* Needless to say, I didn't sleep much that night.

When I arrived on the set, eight other stuntmen were planning stunts for a battle scene in and around a fort. As they talked about who was going to do what, they left me out of the conversation. After a while the stunt coordinator turned to me and said, "Chuck," knowing full well that Chuck had sent me as his replacement. Then he said, "No, it's not Chuck. What is your name?"

I said it slowly and deliberately, so they would remember: "It's Hal Needham."

In a mocking way he said, "Hal, which stunt are you capable of doing?"

"Whatever you want me to do," I shot back.

He pointed to a tower forty feet high on the fort wall and asked if I could do a high fall from there.

"I don't see why not," I said confidently. Everybody looked at me as if to say, "Yeah, in a pig's eye." The stunt coordinator told me to go to wardrobe and tell them I was the guard doing the high fall out of the tower.

All decked out in my army uniform, I returned to the set only to be questioned about my ability to do the stunt. With the door open, I gave them a rundown of my paratrooper days, tree-climbing ability, athleticism, and so on. When I was finished, one of the stuntmen looked at me. "Bullshit doesn't photograph, Needham," he said. They all laughed.

When it came time for my stunt, I had their undivided attention. I also had a surprise for them. At that time, everyone doing a high fall always came off headfirst, so they could see the landing pad. In those days there were no air bags. The landing pad was made up of cardboard boxes stacked six to ten feet high, with mattresses on top. Sixty feet was about the limit for a high fall if you wanted to work another day. I wanted to do something different, to give a new look to high falls so I wouldn't look like some cliff diver in Acapulco. I had been practicing for a couple of months and decided now was the time to show off my new move. I'd "take" the imaginary gunshot, spin around, and come off backward.

The director called "Action!" Around I went, backward, and fell forty feet. As I landed the entire cast and crew broke into applause. Every one of the stuntmen came to me and complimented me on one hell of a high fall.

Chuck Roberson and I became friends. When he moved to an oceanfront property in Ventura, I rented his house. On weekends I turned it into a stuntman's practice facility. The stuntmen and I worked with stunt horses, did high falls out of a tree in the backyard, and practiced motorcycle stunts and fight routines. Chuck would drop by and watch. He also took a lot of ribbing about me being his protégé. One afternoon he told a group of veteran stuntmen that Hal Needham and a bunch of young guys who wanted to be stuntmen practiced every weekend at his house, and he invited them to go over and watch. Better yet, he told them, go over and practice with these young guys, because you might learn something. That statement turned some heads and eventually landed me some small jobs.

In the meantime it was back to work as an extra for fifteen and a nick. Working as an extra was my introduction to legendary director John Ford, who had a couple of rules. One: never whistle on the set. Two: pay attention when you heard "Danny Boy" being played on the accordion, because that was the cue for Mr. Ford's entrance. To tell you the truth, the first time this happened

I didn't even know what the hell was going on. Everybody, including me, was in awe of him.

We were shooting on a soundstage at Paramount, and the scene was a cowboy camp, with ten extras playing cowboys. Before we shot the scene, Ford instructed us to act and do what cowboys do around the camp. Another extra, Jerry Gatlin, and I decided to gather some firewood. Behind a big rock that was part of the set we found an enormous log. It was all we could do to drag it; forget about carrying it. When the assistant director called "Background action," Gatlin and I dragged the log from behind the boulder into the campsite. I glanced over at Ford who, I swear, picked up his eye patch to see if this was really happening. He didn't say a word, but he got even. Ford shot the scene multiple times at various camera angles, and Gatlin and I had to drag that log in every shot. I don't know if it was my imagination, but Ford seemed to smile every time we did another take.

One day I got a call to be at the airport the next morning to fly to Big Bear Lake to work as an extra on *Have Gun — Will Travel*, a Western TV series starring Richard Boone as the gentleman gunfighter Paladin. A buddy of mine, Lenny Geer, and I went out that night and had a few, which sure didn't make the flight into the mountains in a small plane a pleasure.

The episode, called "Haunted Trees," was about a sawmill and treetoppers. (I *told* you climbing trees would eventually give me the break I needed.) Lenny and I were sitting in the shade nursing our self-inflicted wounds and watching two stuntmen attempt to climb a big pine. One of them was Boone's stunt double. They didn't have a clue.

As Lenny and I watched, I commented a little too loud that those guys didn't know how to climb a tree. A voice from behind said, "And I suppose you do." I shot back, "You can bet your house on that, son." I recognized the guy as the production manager.

He told me to follow him. We headed down to the set, where

he instructed the prop man to fix me up with climbing gear. I put the spurs on, cinched the safety belt, and asked, "What now?"

"Let's see how good you are," he said.

With the safety line held in my hand rather than hooked to my belt, I ran at the tree, jumped about three feet in the air, sank both spurs into the trunk while simultaneously flipping the safety line around the tree with one hand and grabbing it on the other side with the other. I literally ran up the tree about forty feet. Then, in reverse action, I was back on the ground in a matter of seconds. The two stuntmen who were supposed to do the climbing were looking for a place to hide. Richard Boone and the director, Andrew V. McLaglen, came over.

"How'd you learn that?" Boone asked.

I told him that I had trimmed trees for a living before I started in the movie industry. With that, the director turned to the wardrobe guys and told them, "Put him in the clothes." (That means the "double" clothes.)

I was going to double Richard Boone in one of the top-rated television shows in America. But there was one small problem: Boone was six two, 210 pounds, and I was five eleven, 175. The wardrobe department used a lot of safety pins to try to make the costume fit. Boone thought it was hilarious.

When the director yelled "Action!" I ran up that pine as fast as I could. He quickly hollered "Cut," and down I came. As I hit the ground, he walked up and told me that half speed would be fine. After all, Paladin was a gunfighter, not a lumberjack. We reshot the scene, and everybody was happy, especially me.

After we wrapped, we had to walk a hundred yards to the vehicles that would take us back to the motel. I was walking behind Andy McLaglen and Richard Boone and overheard Andy tell Boone something to the effect that maybe they should keep "that kid" until they finished. Boone agreed. I spoke up and told them I would be happy to stay and that my name wasn't Kid, it was Hal Needham. Boone smiled. "We now know two things about him," he said. "He can climb trees, and he isn't bashful."

The next day on the set there was nothing for me to do. Oh well, that's moviemaking. On the plane home, Boone came back and asked if I could do a fight scene. I told him I could, and that I was good. Chuckling, he turned to the assistant director and told him to bring me in on Monday as one of the fighters in the bar. Things were looking up. I was upgraded from an extra to a stunt-man, put on a stunt check, and paid an adjustment for hazardous duty for climbing a tree. I would receive my second stunt check Monday for the fight scene.

After a long weekend, I showed up early Monday morning. Lunchtime came and went, with no fight scene. However, I was picking up on bits and pieces of a problem between Boone and his stuntman double. The problem ended when Boone fired him just before the fight scene, but now Boone and Andy were concerned about setting up the fight routine. I personally didn't see a problem; after all, they had me. I approached the director and told him I could set up the fight. Andy said he would let me know and walked over to talk to Boone. A few minutes passed, and Boone came over and asked if I really thought I could stage the fight. "Not a problem," I said. "It's as easy as climbing a tree." Boone chuckled again as if to say, why did I ask?

At fight time I was ready. I had gotten my hands on the script and come up with what I thought was a better routine than the screenwriter's. My ideas made Boone look much more heroic—and he wouldn't need a stunt double. He could do the fight himself. After I walked him through my version, he nodded and said, "Let's do it."

It went off like clockwork. Boone smiled and winked at me. With my ear to the ground, I heard him and Andy talking about who to get to double Boone the following day. So I approached and made Boone a proposition. "If you got enough pins to pin that wardrobe one more time, I would love the opportunity to really show you what I can do," I said. "If you like what you see, I'm available for future work. If you don't like what you see, you don't have to pay me."

Boone looked right through me, and I thought I had gone a step too far. "You're a lot smaller than me, but with this black costume it may not be noticeable," he finally said. He turned to the wardrobe man and told him to cut down one of his Paladin suits to fit me. Then he paused. "No..." he said. My heart sank. "Cut down two, for safety's sake."

I was walking on clouds. No, I was flying over them.

The next morning I was standing on a rock thirty feet above the ground and eighteen feet above the top of a stagecoach, on which I was supposed to land as the coach raced beneath me. The coach roof was only about four feet wide and six feet long. From where I stood, it looked like a postage stamp. Andy asked if I was ready. I replied with bravado, "If you're waitin' on me, you're backin' up."

The driver took the coach back to its starting spot. The camera rolled and Andy called "Action!" At that moment I couldn't tell the difference between the noise of my heart thumping and the horses' hooves pounding as they approached. When the moment was right, I sailed through the air and landed right in the middle of the coach roof—which caved in, leaving me waist deep in the passenger compartment.

To save the shot, Andy decided to get a close-up of Boone just as his character landed. He would draw his gun and order the driver to stop. Fine by me. I could use the money if I had to do it again, but I would rather live to fight another day, or even later that day.

All I had to do on the next stunt was jump out of the coach as it passed the camera. Andy called "Action!," but the driver came in so slowly I didn't jump. Andy called "Cut!" We turned around and went back. Andy asked why I hadn't jumped, and I explained that I thought something was wrong because we were going so slow. When Boone asked how fast I wanted to go, I told the driver to turn the horses loose! Boone roared with his infectious laugh. Later I found out why. Two weeks before, his stuntman had to do the same stunt. He too didn't jump the first time, but when they asked him why, he said the coach was going too fast. Another mark on the plus side for ol' Hal.

On the second take the coach was flying. I jumped off and landed right in front of the camera. As I got up, I was looking at a smiling Andy and Boone.

For the last stunt of the day, Paladin had to dive from a hayloft and take out the bad guy walking guard duty below. For some reason the screenwriter wanted Boone to leap out holding two armfuls of hay. Okay, but why? I talked to the stuntman guard and told him I would dive headfirst and hit him pretty hard in order to stop my upper body, and let my feet hit first so I wouldn't nose-dive into the ground. He didn't have a problem with that. Other than the hay blocking my sight line and blinding me as I dove out of the loft, it worked perfectly, no thanks to the writer.

My big day on *Have Gun* was over. I was sitting on the porch of the ranch house where we were shooting when Boone approached. He said he had told wardrobe to cut down some more Paladin outfits for me, and he assumed that would be okay. He also told me that he had instructed the production department to make sure I got a copy of the following week's script so I could break down the stunts. Then he added one last thing. "I know I don't have to say this, but if you have an idea that you think will make a scene better, I'd like to hear it." With that he stuck out his hand and said, "Welcome aboard."

Not only was I Richard Boone's stunt double, but I also became the stunt coordinator for *Have Gun — Will Travel*. I would now decide which stuntmen to hire and what they would do. At first on *Have Gun*, the company, to save money, would take me on location as an extra, and when I doubled Boone or did a stunt, they would upgrade my contract to stuntman status. It was cheap on their part and degrading to me.

One day as we were preparing to go on location the following week, the production manager came by and said, "Hal, we'll do the usual, take you on a SEG contract and convert you to a stunt contract when you do a stunt."

"Wait a minute," I said. "I've been on the show doubling Boone for eight months. He has a lot of stunts to do while on location, so give me a little dignity and put me on a stuntman contract."

He came back with "No chance. Same deal as before."

I reached for my wallet, took out my SEG membership card, held it up in front of him, tore it into little pieces, and said, "I'm no longer a member of the SEG." The production manager shook his head. "We'll just have to replace you," he threatened and walked away.

I thought, now you've done it, Needham; you blew a good job. Maybe so, but I wasn't going to back down. Later that day I was talking to Boone. He said we'd have some fun on location, and that I would make a lot of money with all the stunts I had to do. I told him I wasn't going, because the production manager and I didn't see eye to eye on what contract I should be on and that he was replacing me. "Really," Boone said.

They called Boone to the camera for the scene. With the entire crew watching, Boone told them that *Have Gun* would have a new star on location starting next week because he and Hal weren't going. Then he did the scene as though nothing was wrong. Afterward the production manager motioned me over. Boone was watching. As I approached, he said, "You'll regret that move."

"Maybe, but we now know who doubles Boone and who's the stunt coordinator on the show, don't we?" I said.

The production manager stormed off. Boone came over and asked if he should pack for location. I said, "Unless they hire a new star, and if they do, then I'm not going." Boone told me it was damn decent of me to look out for him like that and walked away. I never worked as an extra again.

Nobody was more important to my career than Richard Boone. For six years I worked on thirty-nine episodes a year of *Have Gun — Will Travel*. It was a great opportunity for me to hire all those stuntmen who were stunt coordinators on other shows but didn't know me, and an opportunity for me to showcase my talents and be creative with Boone's blessing. Shooting thirty-nine episodes a year was enough to show every stuntman who Hal Needham was and what he could do. Those stuntmen not only worked for me, they hired me to work for them.

Have Gun — Will Travel was a very popular series, and Boone made numerous appearances on variety shows. One day he asked if I'd like to go to New York and stage a fight with him on *The Ed Sullivan Show*. I had never been to New York, and doing a fight on *Sullivan* sounded like a blast. He told me to pick another stuntman to go with us, so he could fight two bad guys. I chose Chuck Couch, a friend of mine who was fearless.

I was about to learn how the other half lived. I flew first class for the first time, and the free drinks and dinner were perks I could get used to in a hurry. Landing in New York, we took a limo to the Plaza, the biggest and finest hotel I have ever seen, much less stayed in. An entire family could have lived in my room.

Boone called and suggested we have dinner in his room. It wasn't a room; it was a suite, and a big one. Boone mixed Chuck and me drinks and handed us the menu. I couldn't pronounce half the items listed. Noticing my dilemma, Boone suggested that he order for me. He asked if I liked oysters on the half shell.

I told him that I didn't know; I'd never eaten oysters. When dinner arrived, Boone showed me how to eat them. They fit my taste buds perfectly.

The next day we went to the studio and rehearsed for the live broadcast. Boone, Chuck, and I would do a big fight, and as I tried to escape, Boone would shoot me and I'd do a high fall from a balcony onto a card table. When we ran it for real, Ed Sullivan and the audience loved it. When the taping was over, Boone had the limo take us to a fancy restaurant. A lady at the next table was wearing a very stylish hat. Boone caught her eye and lifted his drink in salute, pointing to his head. I began thinking that if I hung out with him, I might learn how to be a gentleman.

After a round of drinks, the waiter handed us menus and told us about the dinner specials. Of course I had no idea what he was describing. I looked at the menu and spotted two things I recognized. When it came time for me to order, I said I would have a dozen blue points on the half shell, a T-bone medium-well, and a salad with blue cheese.

Boone chuckled. "For a country boy, you catch on fast."

4

Don't Be Afraid to Take a Chance to Make a Big Impression

The Alamo was a big John Wayne movie that I didn't work on. The production needed twenty-eight stuntmen on location for four months, and because the movie was being produced by Wayne's company and directed by the Duke himself, it was understood that his longtime stunt coordinator, Cliff Lyons, would be running the show. Though I was well known, I had never worked for Cliff.

Deciding to go see Cliff at his office, I was kept waiting for half an hour—not a good sign. Once face to face, I told him how much I would like to be one of the stuntmen he was taking, that I would make a good hand, and that I was versatile and could do all the horse stunts, high falls, and fights that I knew were in the script. Cliff was never one to hold back his thoughts. He said he didn't know my work and felt he should take people he was familiar with. My pride was hurt, to say the least. I knew I was more talented than many of the guys he was taking. I also knew I had no chance of changing his mind.

I was living on La Tuna Canyon Road, which was also known as Stuntman Canyon because so many of us lived there. The day all the stuntmen were heading out to the *Alamo* location, I stood in the front yard and waved as each one passed by. I wasn't working that day, so I went in the house feeling sorry for myself. By late afternoon I'd gotten more phone calls than ever before in one day wanting to know my availability. Then it struck me. With twenty-eight of the top stuntmen gone, there was going to be a lot of work in Hollywood. In the following four months I worked two and three different jobs each day; in fact, I set my all-time record of five shows in one day.

You're probably wondering how a guy could do five shows in one day. First of all, they were all TV series I'd previously worked on. Because they knew me, I was able to get them to move their schedules around for my stunts. Second, the first two jobs were on the Paramount lot and the next three were at Universal. Production always wants you on the set two to three hours before you actually work, so they would say, "Your call is 7 a.m." I would look at my schedule and know I couldn't be there at 7, but I could make a 9 a.m. call, guaranteed. They would say, "Okay, but no later."

So here's how my day went. At 7 a.m. I was on *Bonanza.* I never doubled any of the leads, but I would often get a call to double one of the bad guys getting beat up or killed. Such was the case this morning. It was a fight scene, with me getting the whupping of a lifetime. (It's always better to double the good guys, because you don't have to hit the ground as much.) We did the master shot with the doubles. It was five blows to my face and a chair over my head, and the scene ended. Next they shot a few close-ups of the stars, and by 8:30 I was finished. Perfect timing.

My 9 a.m. call, also at Paramount, was on *Have Gun — Will Travel.* Obviously, I had pull on the show, because I was both the show's stunt coordinator and Boone's stunt double. However, today I would be doubling a guy playing a heavy getting shot off his horse, which is known as a saddle fall. By 10 they were ready to shoot my scene. At 10:30 I was on my way to Universal to get shot and fall from the top of a stagecoach on the TV series *Lara-mie*. One of the stars was Bobby Fuller, a very good friend of mine. He was an athlete and a good horsebacker (rider) who loved to do as much of his own action as the studio would allow. Whenever he had a fight scene to do, Bobby would always request that I dou-ble the actor he was fighting—no matter if he was short or tall—because we worked well together. He also loved the fact that it was obvious on camera that he and not a double was doing the fight.

I told Bobby about my tight schedule. I needed to be on the set of another Universal series, *The Virginian*, by 3. Bobby used his influence, and they shot my stagecoach fall early in the day. He also got the transportation department to give me a ride, and I arrived on the *Virginian* set a half hour early. The assistant direc-tor was happy to see me because the company was slightly ahead of schedule. By the time I got dressed they were ready to film me crashing through a saloon plate-glass window. It was only 4 p.m.; I was running ahead of schedule. My next call was a night shoot. It being summertime, it wouldn't be dark for three or four hours. Good, I had time to eat!

At 8 p.m. I was ready to do my high fall from the roof of a four-story building. The company had a problem, however. One of the actors was sick and hadn't shown up. The schedule had to be shuf-fled around, and I was told to hang loose; it would be a while before they needed me. It was 3 a.m. when they finally told me to get into position. I did my high fall and was told it was a wrap. Driving home I thought, what a waste. Had I known there was going to be such a long delay, I might have been able to work in one more job.

I may have been busy, but I was shocked when I later found out that the stuntmen who worked on *The Alamo* knew they could have made more money at home, because they would go for weeks at a time while the dialogue scenes were being shot without doing a stunt.

*   *   *

When Chuck Roberson left for *The Alamo*, he took two falling horses. One was Cocaine—a great falling horse—and one was named Hondo. Chuck had brought the latter home from the movie *Hondo* and had been "training" him. On the movie, numerous stuntmen tried to fall Hondo, but each time he would just keep making big circles but never go down. Not good. Chuck swore he was getting rid of that no-good SOB.

When he arrived home, not only did he have Cocaine and Hondo, but he had also bought a local no-name horse that was put to use in the movie's background. He thought it had the right stuff to be a falling horse.

Home for Chuck's horses was the big barn on the property of the house I was renting from him. The place had a lot of sand washes for training and exercising. Sand washes are good for two reasons. First, when you ride a horse in deep sand, a mile is equal to five miles on hard dirt. Second, the sand was deep enough that you could fall the horse anywhere, anytime. On movie sets we would bring in a ten-ton truckload of sand for the horses to land in. Here, the whole wash was a landing area.

Chuck told me that the no-name horse had all the traits to be a good stunt horse. The more I rode him, the more I could see what he meant. The horse had a great disposition and smarts, and he was gentle. But he did have one bad habit: if you rode him next to anything—a fence, horse trailer, or building—he would move close enough that he would mash your leg between his belly and the object, at the same time trying to knock you off. Pulling the rein on the opposite side only made things worse. He would move in tighter and go faster. This could be a big problem on a movie set. Hondo had a different kind of personality. He was seven-eighths Thoroughbred, which meant he had fire. He wasn't afraid of anything—explosions, gunfire—he would charge right through it.

Chuck told me he was going to be too busy to train No Name

and asked if I would like to buy him. We agreed on a price. By the way, he offered, since Hondo had made him look like a fool on *The Alamo,* if I wanted him, I could have him for nothing. He added that he would definitely need more training. For the next eight months I spent every spare minute training both horses to rear, jump, and fall.

I didn't work on *The Alamo,* but in the end it was pretty good to me. I made lots of money while all those stuntmen were gone and ended up with two of the greatest stunt horses in the movie industry: Hondo and No Name, which I christened Alamo.

I had plenty of work, some of it thanks to my stuntman buddy Ronnie Rondell. When I say Ronnie was a stuntman, I mean he was second to none. He also had a great contact: his father was a bigwig at Universal Studios and had the power to hire stuntmen. Need I say more? Ronnie and I were always the first to be hired. Universal had twenty or so TV series shooting year-round. One was a pilot called *Riverboat,* starring Darren McGavin and a newcomer. I got a call to work on it, and in wardrobe, they threw a costume at me and told me to look for someone dressed like me — he was the newcomer I would be doubling.

I looked around the set and spotted a guy my size dressed like me who looked a lot like Marlon Brando. I walked over and introduced myself. His name was Burt Reynolds. We exchanged a few niceties, and I moved on. When it was time to do the fight scene in which I'd double Burt, the other stuntmen and I laid out the routine under the watchful eye of the director — and unbeknown to me, Burt himself. As I was going over the details, Burt came over and suggested he do his own fight. That way the director wouldn't have to shoot any close-ups.

The director thought that was a splendid idea. I'd heard this story before, an actor doing his own stunts. What did I have to lose? I would be paid no matter who did the fight, because I was on a stunt contract and I'd set it up. I walked Burt through the routine a couple of times, and he said he was ready. Sure, I told myself, he's ready, and so am I—to watch a Chinese fire drill. When the director called "Action" chairs started flying, punches were thrown, tables overturned. The set looked like a tornado had blown through. The director yelled "Cut!" and everybody got up. I didn't see any broken noses, fat lips, or cracked teeth. Well, I'll be, I thought. He really got lucky. It all came off beautifully.

Burt came over and thanked me for letting him do the fight. "Don't thank me," I said, "you did a great job." Burt was very athletic and capable of doing a lot of stunts. But when the going got really tough, that was where I came in. By that I mean any stunt where Burt might get seriously hurt—dangerous stunts such as rolling a car or doing a high fall or a full-burn fire scene. (Movie and television studios have production insurance in place that would forbid Burt, or any other actor for that matter, to be put in harm's way. If the star gets hurt, the production shuts down.)

During *Riverboat* Burt and I became good friends. On weekends he would come over to my house where the stuntmen were working out. I had cut the limbs off a big tree and put a net underneath it so we could practice high falls. Burt always wanted to join in, though he would never go quite as high as we would. He went on to do several TV series and to bare almost everything in the centerfold of *Cosmopolitan*. With his lead role in *Deliverance* he became a movie star, and later became the number-one box office star in the world. This would turn out to be very good for my career.

One day I read in the industry trade papers that a company was getting ready to shoot a movie called *Paratroop Command*. This was a feature, and it was right up my alley. Being a war film, it had to have a lot of explosions and most likely a lot of action. If they needed some parachute jumps, I had the experience. My thinking was that obviously they needed me on this film. The paper listed the producer as Stanley Shpetner, whom I didn't know, and gave the production company's address. Uninvited, I walked into Shpetner's office and told his secretary I would like to see him. I explained that I was a stuntman and an ex-paratrooper. She buzzed him on the speaker box and relayed my information. After a pause he said, "Tell Mr. Needham I will see him. But I want him to come through the door as if he were in combat, searching house to house for the enemy." She turned off the speaker and with a sweeping gesture pointed to the door.

Lucky for him I didn't have a grenade, as I might have tossed it in first. Instead, I backed up as far as possible and ran at the door as fast as I could. I hit the door with my shoulder. The top hinge broke, leaving the door askew as I flew through the opening and landed on my stomach. Pretending to aim a rifle, I scanned the room, then stood, stuck out my hand, and introduced myself.

"I wish I'd had a camera rolling, because that was pretty spectacular from where I was sitting," he said, adding, "If I had that much damage for each person I hired, I wouldn't have an office." That was all he said about the door. We talked for half an hour. He described some of the stunts he'd need and asked if I felt I could do them. I told him that with enough money and time, anything was possible. Then he gave me the bad news. This was a low-budget film, and he had only three weeks to shoot it. I told him that it just so happened I could work it into my schedule.

I got the job and found out Stan was telling the truth. It was a very low budget film, and we had to improvise a lot. The director wanted me to do a fall out of a tree about twenty-five feet high. There wasn't a fall pad within twenty miles of our set, so I made my own. I cut a stack of oak limbs, piled them up, and put a tarp over them. Then I stretched the tarp tight and staked down the corners. Not an ideal landing pad, but it worked. My stuntman buddy Cliff Rose (from *Spirit of St. Louis* and *You Asked for It*) and I did almost every stunt in the movie. Stan Shpetner and I became good friends. He produced more films, some with larger budgets, and I worked on all of them.

Although I was doubling Richard Boone on *Have Gun* and Burt Reynolds on *Riverboat,* I still managed to work on two or three other shows a week. It was a good thing I had all that work, because around this time I took on a ready-made family. While I was working on *Spirit of St. Louis,* I had met Arlene Wheeler, a waitress at Knott's Berry Farm. We dated, but I was establishing myself as a stuntman and I didn't want to get married unless I could support her. She also had three children: a daughter, Debbie, eight, and two sons, Danny, six, and David, five.

With steady work on *Have Gun — Will Travel,* I felt comfortable about getting married. We had the ceremony at the house I was renting from Chuck Roberson; Richard Boone was my best man. Arlene's kids lived with us. Their biological father, Richard, had moved in with his mother after he and Arlene divorced. They lived some fifty miles from our house. Every couple of weeks his mother would pick up the kids on a Friday and bring them back Sunday afternoon. Everybody was happy with the arrangement.

As my career prospered, Arlene and I bought a three-bedroom home on a half acre in Lakeview Terrace with enough land to build a corral for my two horses and a swimming pool for the kids. I also bought a Shetland pony and a surrey for the kids to play with. When I raced motorcycles in the desert, the kids always wanted to go with me. I bought a motor home so we'd have a place to sleep out there, as well as a motorcycle for each of them. All was going well.

Then, one Sunday during the summer, the kids didn't return from visiting their father. Arlene called to see what was going on and was told that Richard had decided the kids should live with him, so he wouldn't be bringing them home today.

Arlene panicked. I tried to calm her with the assurance that we would get them back through the courts. Richard was a hothead who owned guns. One time he had accidentally shot off his foot while drunk, so I decided it was better not to aggravate the situation. We hired a lawyer, and a hearing date was set.

The judge listened to both sides of the story. Our lawyer showed him my financial statement and photos of our home. The judge saw no reason why the children shouldn't be with their mother and ordered that, because Richard was so concerned about them, he should financially contribute to their welfare. He was to pay sixty dollars a month and could have the kids visit him as long as it didn't interfere with their education. I told the judge this was fine by me. However, I asked for one stipulation: the first month he failed to pay child support, he would forfeit his visitation privileges. The judge agreed. The money was nothing, but I knew Richard wouldn't pay, and I was right. He never sent a dime. But because Arlene liked the kids' grandmother, she allowed her to take the kids occasionally, as long as she promised to bring them back.

I worked so many jobs in those days that Arlene used a calendar to keep track of who owed me what. I would come home at night and she'd ask which shows I had worked on and how much I'd made. She'd write the information on the calendar, and when the check came crossed it off. That was the only way to keep track. Of course the boys would look at that calendar and talk about all the money I was making. One day Danny and David announced that they wanted to be stuntmen. Fine by me, but they needed some training. I called Stevie, a friend who had a stable, and told her I was sending the boys over. I explained they wanted to be stuntmen, so they needed to learn about horses. She was tough as nails, and she understood what I was saying. When the boys walked into the barn, she handed each of them a shovel and told them to clean the stalls. Needless to say, the glamour quickly evaporated.

My birth dad, Howard, was the furthest thing from my mind. After I had entered the military, I'd lost all contact. Was it his fault or mine? I'd say both. I guess there just wasn't a reason to stay in touch. One day I got a call from a stranger with some information about him.

The caller asked if I was Hal Needham and I told him that I was. He informed me that he had found a suitcase in a parking facility in downtown L.A. and that my name and phone number were on a piece of paper inside it. He asked if Howard Needham was any kin. I told him that would be my dad. He gave me his address so I could retrieve the suitcase.

I drove to an upper-middle-class neighborhood in Sherman Oaks and was greeted at the caller's door by a well-dressed man in his fifties. I could tell he was embarrassed as he handed me the suitcase. The bag's exterior forewarned me what I might find inside, though I didn't open it in front of the man. I thanked him and left. A couple of blocks away I pulled into a gas station and looked inside. There were half a dozen pairs of dirty socks and underwear, two rolled-up stained shirts, one pair of filthy pants, and a piece of paper with my name and phone number scribbled on it. Also inside was the paperwork for Dad's Social Security checks, which listed my uncle's address and phone number in St. Louis.

I didn't have to be Sherlock Holmes to figure out my dad was homeless and probably on the streets of downtown L.A. I threw the suitcase and clothes in a Dumpster and went home. I told Arlene the story and said I intended to go downtown and see if I could find him. Then I called my uncle in St. Louis. He told me Dad's Social Security checks came to him and that Dad let him know where to forward them. The last few he had sent to an address in L.A., which he gave me. I asked him if Dad called to give him my number and have him phone me.

First thing the next morning I drove to the address, but the house was empty. Cobwebs covered everything but the mailbox. I thought maybe Dad knew when the checks were coming and camped out by the mailbox to pick them up. I headed downtown to search for him. It seemed hopeless, but I checked a few of the flophouses, and sure enough, I found two where he'd spent the night, one of them only a couple of days earlier. He was somewhere near here.

I spent five days driving around skid row looking and asking questions. One afternoon, while driving through downtown, I looked up ahead and, from the back, recognizing his hair and his walk, knew that I had found him. I pulled over and as he passed called out, "Hey, Dad."

He stopped and looked at me. I knew he was confused, so I said, "Dad, it's me, Hal, your son."

He came over and leaned on the open window and asked, "What are you doing down here?"

"Looking for you," I said. "Don't just stand there, get in."

He did, and after a few seconds I pulled out. He asked where we were going, and I told him home. He asked if I was married, and I said yes and that I had three kids. He knew he wasn't exactly dressed to go visiting and meeting people. He said, "I can't meet your family looking like this."

I told him I had a plan. We stopped at a YMCA, where he showered. I then bought him a suitcase and a wardrobe to fill it and some clothes to wear. When people say the clothes make the man, there's a lot to that. Within a couple of hours he'd gone from looking like a homeless person to an average citizen. I could see he felt better already.

I called Arlene and told her we were on our way home. As I pulled into the driveway he didn't say a word. I introduced him to

Arlene and the kids and showed him to his room. He came out a few minutes later and seemed very uneasy. I suggested we have a drink as Arlene cooked dinner. We made small talk, had another drink, and then Arlene called "Come and get it." During dinner the kids did most of the talking. Afterward I showed him around the place, the pool and my two falling horses in the corral behind the house. His comments were minimal. The one thing we didn't talk about was his situation. I told him to make himself at home and turned in for the night.

At breakfast I told him public transportation was limited. It was a mile to the nearest bus stop. Arlene and I both worked and needed two cars, but I gave him four hundred dollars of spending money and suggested that he could call a cab if he wanted to go somewhere. He said that would be fine. The kids went to school and Arlene and I went to work.

On days when Arlene and I didn't work or got home early, we lent him our car so he could get out of the house, but I could see he was getting claustrophobic. Things went on this way for a month. One day I came home and found a note saying he was going to San Rafael to see my sister Edwonia. He thanked Arlene and me and signed the note "Howard." I never saw him again.

Edwonia called to let me know he had arrived at her house and was staying with her. Some months later she called to say she'd put him in an assisted living home, and asked if I could pick up the cost. I did until he died. I didn't attend the funeral. The reason was that I had a long talk with mom. It seemed that dad chose to spend his money on booze, nightlife, and other women rather than on his family. As soon as I was born, she packed up and left. He never once tried to contact her to offer any support. I didn't feel obligated to go to the funeral. I never had a dad.

My feature career began to take off thanks to Andy McLaglen, whom I had gotten to know while working on *Have Gun — Will*

Travel. Andy and Richard Boone were pals, so Andy had directed about half of the *Have Gun* episodes. Andy, who stood six feet four and weighed well over two hundred pounds, loved to tease me. He would say, "Little Hal is going to fall off his horse right here," or "Can Little Hal do this without getting hurt?" Andy must have worn a size 14 shoe. He could step on your foot and make it look like an accident while apologizing *so* sincerely. But if he stepped on your foot, you were considered to be one of his circle of friends.

He pulled all kinds of jokes on me. One time I was doubling Boone, and I had to climb a mountain. It was a big mountain, so I asked Andy how far he wanted me to go. "Not far," he said, and added that he would cut when he had enough footage for the scene. I took my starting position and Andy hollered "Action!" I climbed for several minutes and began to wonder whether the whole show consisted of Boone climbing the mountain. After another three or four minutes I was completely out of breath. I stopped, knowing Andy couldn't possibly need any more climbing footage. I turned toward camera and saw that everybody was in the lunch line. I climbed down and got in the chow line. As I passed Andy, who was already eating, he said, "Did Little Hal get lost?" Andy couldn't make me mad, because he was a good guy—and he made me a pile of money.

Just my luck, Andy became a major feature director. He went on to direct some big-budget films, including *McLintock!*, *Shenandoah*, *The Way West*, *The Undefeated*, *Hellfighters*, *The Devil's Brigade*, and *Bandolero!*, and I worked on all of them. *Shenandoah* had a scene that required some country boy expertise. The script read: *"In the calm before the battle, a cow goes walking across the field between the Rebels and the Yankees."* As the cow crosses the field, a Rebel lieutenant asks a sergeant (played by me), "Is that a Yankee cow or is that a Rebel cow?" I answer, "It looks like a Yankee cow to me, sir." He says, "Sergeant, you have my permission to retrieve that Yankee cow." The sergeant places a white flag on his saber and moves out to retrieve the cow. He tries to get the cow to the Rebel side, but despite his efforts it turns and runs toward and through the Yankee lines. It happens just before the Yankee army's troops do battle with the Rebels who are facing them about two hundred yards across the field.

This provided me with a challenge. I went to the local wranglers and asked if any of them had a cow that had just come fresh. For all you city slickers, that means "had a calf lately." One of them said he had had three in the past two days. I told him I wanted all three mommas and their babies. I knew any one of them would work, but a couple of backups couldn't hurt.

The next morning the troops were in place. They shot the dialogue, and then it was showtime. "Send the cow across!" someone yelled. Are you kidding? The cow hadn't seen the script and didn't know its cue, but Hal had, and everything was ready. Four wranglers were holding the momma cow as another wrangler carried the calf across the field between the two lines, along the path that we wanted the cow to follow. It took four wranglers to hold the cow, because she wanted to follow her baby. When they rolled the cameras, the cow was turned loose.

As I rode out to retrieve the cow for the Rebel troops, I met her midfield and she nearly knocked my horse down trying to reach her calf. I managed to keep her at bay for a few seconds, and then she shot past me and went directly to her baby. (In the editing room, they would cut the film before the cow got past me and cut to the troops hollering on my behalf.) We then filmed the second part: put the cow, her calf, and me in the middle of the field and have the wrangler take the calf to the Yankee side. Roll the camera, and turn the cow loose. She got past my best effort to stop her and headed straight for the Yankee lines, nearly upending a Yankee cannon getting to her baby. As I retreated to the Rebel lines, the battle sequence began.

As a stunt coordinator, I always found a way to make a scene more exciting, and Andy was always willing to listen to my ideas. While shooting *The Rare Breed,* starring Jimmy Stewart, Maureen O'Hara, Juliet Mills, and Don Galloway, Andy asked me to restage a scene where Maureen and Juliet, riding in a buckboard, are escorted up a narrow canyon by Stewart and Galloway, who are on horseback. Earlier in the story Stewart had fought and embarrassed Jack Elam, who played the heavy and was now seeking revenge. Elam's opportunity came as Stewart led his party up the canyon toward a herd of oncoming longhorn cattle. At walking speed the cattle presented no problem, but Jack's idea of revenge was to stampede the cattle head-on into Stewart and his party.

In the buckboard scene the script called for Stewart to see the stampede coming and lead everyone into an alcove. The cattle would run by, but there would be no exciting payoff to the scene. Andy wanted to make the scene more exciting and dangerous, and show Stewart as a hero for saving the ladies. That night I wrote my version of what I thought could get the job done. The next day I gave it to Andy. He loved it and passed it on to the studio so they could position the scene into our shooting schedule and make the necessary budget changes.

I was immediately called to the office of Marshall Green, head of production. Looking across his huge desk, he told me that this new scene read as if it had been written by me, not Andy. He thought it was great but had some problems. Besides the fact that it would cost big bucks, how could it be shot without killing somebody?

My scene read like this: Stewart would be riding point, a hundred yards in front of Galloway, who was a hundred yards ahead of Maureen and Juliet in the buckboard. When Stewart saw the stampede, he would turn around and race back, warning them of the oncoming danger. Galloway would also turn around and race back, then transfer from his horse to the buckboard with the ladies, take control of their horse, and attempt to outrun the stampeding cattle. With the cattle closing in, the buckboard would hit a rock, flip over, and Galloway would be jerked out and horse-dragged through the canyon. At that moment, Stewart would arrive at the wreck. With no path to safety, Stewart would position the ladies underneath the buckboard for protection and then climb under himself. Last but not least, as the stampeding cattle approached, I wanted to run fifty head of cattle over the top of the buckboard, with the actors actually underneath it.

I explained to Green that I would double Galloway for the transfer, so I would be driving and have control of the horse when we wrecked the buckboard. Because I was dragged out of the scene, Jimmy Stewart would be left with the heroics of saving the ladies. My plan to protect the actors under the buckboard was to put a half inch of metal plating on the floorboard and sides. I would brace it up with wooden 4 × 4s and fasten cables attached to metal stakes to all four corners. I guaranteed him it wouldn't budge even if all fifty cattle were on top of the buckboard at the same time.

Green listened to the plan, then said there were only a few stuntmen he would give the green light to on something this complicated and dangerous, and I happened to be one of them. But, he emphasized, if anything went wrong, I'd be on his shit list for a long time.

The scene came off perfectly. Nobody got hurt, and everybody loved the way it looked. I had to hand it to Maureen O'Hara, Jimmy Stewart, and Juliet Mills. As the cattle stampeded over the top of the buckboard, you could tell it was the actors and not their doubles under there, with cattle feet pounding the ground just inches from their faces.

Everything went so well that at the end of the shoot Marshall Green handed me an envelope. It was the first time I'd received a bonus check, and believe me, it's not the norm for production managers to hand out bonuses. It's their job to save money.

Screenwriters sometimes write action scenes that don't necessarily fit the story or that might be impossible or too expensive to do. Not that writers aren't smart—many of them just don't know what's doable when it comes to stunts. As a stunt coordinator or second unit director, I would read the action scenes and see if I thought I could make them more interesting and fit the story line a little better. Sometimes they took my suggestions, sometimes they didn't. But that didn't stop me.

Later in my career I took a different kind of a gamble on *The Longest Yard*, which starred Burt Reynolds. The only action sequence was the movie's opening scene, where Burt has a disagreement with his rich girlfriend, storms out of the house, and speeds away in her Citroën Maserati. The screenwriter had written a long police chase, with Burt being arrested at the end. I was hired to direct the sequence and double Burt, and the scene was going to be shot in Savannah, Georgia. The director, Robert Aldrich, told me to pay no attention to the script and use my imagination. He wanted me to film an exciting car chase and do something at the end that would draw attention to Burt, so that in the next scene Burt could be confronted and arrested by the police. He added: "But *whatever* you do, don't wreck the Citroën." First, the car was expensive, and second, someone wanted to buy it after the shoot, provided it wasn't damaged. He wished me luck, and I was on my way to Savannah.

I found some interesting locations, the best being an unusual drawbridge. Instead of breaking in the center and lifting up like most drawbridges, this bridge broke on each end and lifted the center section up flat. I decided to have two police cars chase me in the Citroën onto the part of the bridge that lifted, then have the bridge operator start raising the span with all three of us on it, at which time I would lock up my brakes and let the two police cars skid past me. I would then put my car in reverse and back off the bridge, which by this point would be eight or ten feet high. As I landed, I would throw the car into a 180-degree reverse spin and speed away. (That maneuver pretty well took care of the sale of the car, as it wound up with a wrinkled-up rear end—not looking real cherry, but still drivable.)

I also found a spot to do something that would attract attention: a pier twenty feet above the water. My idea: why not have Burt stop on the pier, get out to look it over, reach inside the car, put it in gear, and run it off the end? That would be an attention-getter. To make sure I didn't lose the car, I hooked a cable to the frame and fastened the other end to the end of the pier. Once the car went underwater, I'd have a crane standing by that would hook onto the cable and lift the car out of its watery grave.

We did the shot, pulled the car out, and sat it on the pier. Everything went according to my plan. We sent the film back to the studio so they could see my idea for an attention-getting car chase climax. The call came the next day. The director thought it was a great idea, better than he had imagined, but the production manager wanted to talk to me. It's a great shot, he said, but how could you do this? The person who was going to buy the car had changed his mind after seeing it deep-sixed in saltwater. I told him not to fret. I'd sold the car for the same price, on the spot. When word got around town about the shot we were going to do, a local man approached and asked what I was going to do with the car after I gave it a bath. I told him someone in Hollywood was going to buy it, and he said he'd match that price; that way I wouldn't have to haul it back to California. I told him he had a deal. When I relayed this information to the production manager, he said that in addition to lining up a great shot, I was also a good businessman. I guess you just have to follow your instincts.

You also have to lay it all on the line. Say I'm getting ready to do a big stunt—a stunt in which I could end up crippled or even get killed. I have confidence in my ability. I know that if I do the stunt and come out unscathed, my reputation will soar. It will be the talk of Hollywood. The next time a spectacular stunt is called for, my phone will be ringing. That's how you make a big impression.

5

If You're Booked to Burn,
You Can't Drown

One day while shooting a TV show in downtown L.A., I was asked to make a jump from a fire-escape balcony across an alley to another balcony one floor lower. After looking at it, I felt confident I could jump the width of the alley, which was about twelve feet, because I would be jumping down instead of straight across. The problem was, the balcony I was supposed to land on was only four and a half feet wide. If I hit the railing, I would add some numbers to my broken-bone count. There was no doubt that I had to clear that railing and, being five floors up, hope my momentum would carry me over it and onto the balcony. If it didn't, I wouldn't just need an ambulance—a hearse might be more in order.

I made a corporate decision. It would be better to shoehorn myself between the railing and the brick wall. That way, if I erred, I'd err on the long side and ricochet off the wall. At least I would land on the balcony, which would eliminate a ride in the hearse. Before doing the stunt, I asked that they keep the ambulance close by.

Soon word had spread that some fool was about to commit suicide, and both ends of the alley were packed with spectators.

Every window along the alley had two or three heads sticking out, as the people seemed anxious to witness the splatter of my body on the cobblestones below. Now I knew how the Christians felt in the arena with the lions. These people weren't calling for blood or death, but if it happened, they didn't want to miss it. A lot of people must have been late for work that day, because it took us a couple of hours to get set up. But believe me, not a soul left.

One final look from my perch (standing on the railing) brought another element into play: the balcony *above* my landing zone. I've been told I have a hard head, but if I struck it on the balcony above, I was sure to come out second best. Don't send the hearse away just yet. The cameras were in place; my audience awaited. They rolled the cameras. My heart was beating so fast and loud that I wasn't sure I would be able to hear the director call "Action." I was glad he had a bullhorn, because I heard him loud and clear.

With every muscle in my body I launched myself through the air, trying to get my body into the perfect position to hit my target. I cleared the railing and hit the brick wall—and out went my lights. When they came back on, my audience was still applauding. Yep, the brick wall had won that round. With a knot on my head, I was helped down the stairs to the street. Exiting the building, I heard the director and my audience cheering, "Great stunt! Way to go!" and I was on my way to the X-ray department. People were right—I do have a hard head, because there were no fractures.

All in a day's work.

There were two things the stuntmen I worked with agreed on: it was dangerous, and it was definitely not boring. Some stunts relied on more than just the stuntman doing his job, and every now and then things didn't go as planned. On one movie I was stationed in a German guard tower, firing down on the attacking

Americans when a soldier threw a grenade, blowing up the tower and me out of it. The special effects team had rigged an explosion in the tower and put a metal plate between the blast and me to keep any debris from hitting me.

As the director lined up the shot, the effects team put a large flat pan of gasoline in the tower. It looked safe to me. Besides, I was on the other side of the protective plate. They rolled the camera but something went wrong with it, and the scene had to be reset. I walked out of the tower and stood on the compound wall. The gas fumes were pretty strong. Fifteen minutes later all was repaired and ready, and they rolled the camera. As soon as the explosion went off, I knew I was in trouble. The gasoline hadn't exploded but the fumes had, blinding me for a split second. I couldn't see my catch pads, but I knew where they were, so out I went. I hit my pads okay, but the skin on my face and hands was curling up and blistering. The reason for the explosion was simple. If you take a fifty-five gallon drum, cut the top off, fill it with gas, and light it with a match, it will burn until it's empty. Now fill an enclosed drum half full of gas and leave it set a few minutes—but whatever you do, don't take out the bunghole cap and use a match to see how much gas is in it, because that momma is going to explode big-time. It's the fumes that explode and ignite the gas.

To some extent, that was what happened with the guard tower. It was pretty well boxed in by a roof and four walls. While the camera was being repaired, the fumes became so strong that when the explosion went off, it ignited them. The flash not only blinded me momentarily, it also cooked me a little. I'll take half of the blame. In my case, it was inexperience and a lack of knowledge. But you learn by your mistakes. I can't blame the effects man; he had years of experience, but he also had a director screaming "Let's go!" He later apologized. We were pretty good friends, so I knew he meant it. Over a drink that night he said if

I ever had a doubt about how something was rigged, not to be bashful, but ask. I learned my lesson well, and from that day forward, I always did.

Special effects men as a whole are very good. From setting explosives to bullet hits, they do all the rigging necessary for the stuntmen to do their thing. Working as a team, special effects and stuntmen can pull off some pretty amazing gags, which is the term stuntmen use for stunts. But effects men, like everybody else, sometimes make mistakes.

On the first feature film I coordinated, called *Little Shepherd of Kingdom Come,* with my pal Andy McLaglen at the helm, I was working with the special effects team to create a Civil War battle scene. The Rebs had a lookout tower about twenty-five feet high. Ronnie Rondell and I were positioned in the tower as lookouts when the Yankees fired their first cannon shot, which was supposed to hit the tower and blow it down. Ronnie and I would do high falls into some pads camouflaged with pine needles.

Here's how it was rigged and what was supposed to happen. The tower stood on four six-by-six legs. The two front legs had a giant hinge on them so the tower would fall in a straight line. The two back legs had explosive primer cord wrapped around them to cut them and allow two cables on the front to pull the tower over—at which time Ronnie and I would simulate being blown out of the tower and do our high falls.

As a new stunt coordinator, I tried to tread lightly when seeking information, even though the outcome might have something to do with whether or not I continued to breathe. The hinges and cables looked fine, but I asked the effects man about the primer cord. He told me he didn't have time to explain the fundamentals of powder, and walked off. He sounded confident. I guessed I would have to settle for that. Ronnie and I took our positions in the tower. They rolled the camera, and Andy called "Action!" A

Yankee cannon on the other side of the field belched fire and smoke. A few seconds passed to give the cannonball time to reach the tower. Then it happened. The tower exploded big-time.

But instead of falling straight, the way it was planned, the tower twisted away from my pads. Rondell was standing by the opening at the top of the ladder. Being as agile as he was, he jumped and hit his pads. I was now trapped in the tower and knew I was in a world of hurt if I didn't get out of there. Using every muscle in my body, I broke through the two-by-four railing and headed for the ground. I landed flat on my back. We later figured the only thing that saved me from more serious injury was about a foot of pine needles on the ground. When I regained consciousness, I was lying in the back of a station wagon. Arlene was with me. I asked her where we were, and she told me what had happened. At the hospital they told me I was going to live. I sure didn't feel like it. They released me later that afternoon, and I went back to the motel and tried to rest.

When I woke the next morning, it was all Arlene and I could do to get me out of bed. Everything hurt. On the set, the effects man walked by where I was sitting and completely unapologetically asked how I felt. I told him he was lucky I couldn't get up right then because he had an ass-kicking coming.

The effects man didn't say anything, but I must have put some fear in him, because he backed off a little too far on the powder for the next stunt. In it, Rondell was supposed to jump up onto an ammunition wagon at the same second he screamed at the wagon's team of horses to go. Special effects would set off an explosion and blow up the wagon. Ronnie was concerned after the tower explosion that he might be launched into space.

We approached the effects man and demanded that he show us the placement of the explosion and the protection Rondell would have. He showed us the bomb and said it would blow the cover off the wagon. It would have a lot of flames and smoke, but not too much power. He then showed us a quarter-inch-thick metal plate he would place between the bomb and Rondell so no shrapnel would hit him. Rondell and I walked away to talk and decided it looked pretty safe.

We got ready to shoot the stunt. In the background, the Civil War was in full swing, with men shooting and falling. Rondell leaped into the seat of the ammunition wagon and screamed at the horses. Effects triggered the explosion. Not only did the explosion not blow the cover off the wagon, it barely set it on fire. It was so weak that Rondell knew something was wrong and didn't bother to do his fall. As a matter of fact, the explosion didn't even scare the horses hooked to the wagon.

Andy McLaglen was hot under the collar and let it be known. The set people put a new cover on the wagon and effects rerigged the explosion. Rondell and I watched the amount of black powder being poured into the container and decided the effects man was more afraid of the director than of my threats. The situation didn't look good. Rondell said he would stay low and hope the metal plate would protect him. They rolled the cameras and called "Action" as Rondell hollered at the team. *Boom!* The wagon cover and the wooden bows that held it in place disappeared up into the trees, the sideboard on the wagon became toothpicks, and for damn sure nobody had to cue Rondell to do his fall. The horses also left the scene in a hurry. The only thing that worked perfectly was the metal shield between Rondell and the explosion. Shield or no shield, when the force of the explosion hit Rondell he looked like Superman as he flew through the air.

To get work and stay in the know, everybody in the industry read *The Hollywood Reporter* and *Daily Variety,* known as the trades. Every Friday both papers listed movies in preproduction, giving the movie's title, stars, director, and department heads, including the stunt coordinator. *Kings of the Sun* was one of these listings.

The story of the Mayan Indians' struggle against the invading Spaniards, the movie starred Yul Brynner and was directed by J. Lee Thompson. Chuck Hayward was the stunt coordinator. I read no further. I'd never worked with or for Chuck, even though Westerns were his forte.

But I soon had a call from Ronnie Rondell telling me that Hayward had hired him for the movie. I said, "Ronnie, I know you're good, but horses are not your specialty."

"There's not a horse on the show," he said. "The action is big battle scenes, high falls, fire gags, and sword fights."

"Be safe and make a lot of money," I replied.

The following day the phone rang. "Hal, this is Chuck Hayward," the caller said. "I'm doing a show in Mexico that's right up your alley. Can you get away for six to eight weeks?" I was in shock but answered, "When and where?"

On the plane to Mazatlán, I could see Hayward was taking athletes like Rondell and me, not the usual stuntmen he'd worked with on many John Wayne Westerns. The following day Chuck took us to the set to plan the battle and all the stunts. The studio had built a Mayan village of grass huts and a seventy-foot pyramid completely fenced-in for protection. As the Spaniards attacked from the ocean, they would have to run through walls of flames that the Maya had preset. The Spaniards' costumes — similar to a kilt with a chest plate, leaving the arms and legs bare — were not good for fire stunts.

The pile of logs that was used to create the wall of flame was enhanced by diesel fuel fed through pipes hidden in the logs. Under pressure, the fuel would rise fifteen feet into the air. If a person were to run through the flames, raw, unburned fuel would be falling on him. Another problem was that we would be running uphill in the sand, which made jumping the logs impossible. The only way over was to hit them with one foot. After one look at the flames and raw fuel, the stuntmen had a meeting. We decided to ask for less diesel fuel to be sprayed. The assistant director, who had a tough-guy self-image, said the stunt was "nothing" and told us that if we didn't want to do it, he would have the Mexican extras do it. But the Mexicans wanted no part of his plan. Following much discussion and negotiating of the price, some of us agreed to do the stunt.

They lit the fire, and we ran toward the burning logs. Some came through in pretty good shape. A couple of guys fell into the flames but scrambled out. Still, everyone ended up with blisters on their arms and legs from the burning fuel. When the director wanted us to do it again, we raised the price.

On another stunt, I was a lookout on top of a rock about fifteen feet high, and I got a spear in the back, which sent me flying from my perch face-first into my fall pads. It was no big deal, except for the fact that the camera would follow my fall and focus on two actors with a page of dialogue. The actors screwed up the dialogue eleven times, which meant I had to do the fall twelve times. They were apologetic, but they also didn't know I got paid every time I did the fall.

Ronnie Rondell did the toughest stunt on the movie. He played a lookout standing on a four-by-four-foot platform atop a forty-foot pole that was to be set on fire and rigged to fall onto one of the thatched-roof huts, which had catch pads inside for him to land on. The pole was wrapped in burlap and soaked with diesel fuel. When lit at ground level, the flames would rise up the pole close to Ronnie, and then effects would trip the pole to fall. At best, it was scary to watch. After the stunt was over, Ronnie said the heat rising from the fuel-soaked burlap was tough to handle; he could hardly wait for the pole to fall, regardless of the outcome.

The majority of the battle took place on the pyramid, which had one big drawback. After the framework had been covered in plywood, the carpenters sprayed gunite on the plywood to make it look like earth. The material used on the walls of swimming pools, gunite is like sandpaper magnified a thousand times. If you wore a costume that covered your arms and legs, it was no problem, but ours offered no protection, so every time we did a fall we had to see the nurse to have our wounds cared for. A few days into the battle we were all covered in scabs.

Next, the director wanted some of the stuntmen to be shot with arrows to motivate their high falls. We had a stuntman on the movie named Richard Farnsworth, who was an amateur archer. (Years later, he was nominated for an Academy Award for his performance in *The Straight Story*.) Dick was asked how he felt about shooting arrows at the stuntmen with the camera rolling. He said he was willing to shoot the arrows, but he added that it would be a good idea to ask the stuntmen if they were willing to let him shoot at them. After all, forget movie magic and fakery: instead of the usual rubber tips, these were going to be real hunting arrows with steel tips. Several of us had seen Dick shoot and decided to give it a go. We would wear a foot-square metal plate covered with two inches of balsa wood under the front of our costumes and hope Dick hit the target.

On Sunday, the day before we would put our lives in Dick's hands, we were on the beach bodysurfing and enjoying the sight of bikini-clad locals parading up and down the sand. Not far from us Dick had set up an archery target with a foot-square target on it, the same size he would have to hit when shooting at us. Dick practiced for a couple of hours. About half of his arrows hit the target; the other half always seemed to be four or five inches lower — which would hit our crotch area. The more he missed, the closer we watched. After far too many misses, we had a talk with him and suggested that maybe this whole thing was a bad idea. He laughed, picked up his bow, and fired twenty arrows dead-center into the target. We looked at one another and knew we'd been had. Dick gathered up his equipment and said, "I'll see you tomorrow."

Next day on the set, though, things would be different. Dick would not be standing on terra firma; he'd be standing on a very shaky fifteen-foot platform. And instead of shooting at stationary archery targets, he'd be shooting us in the heat of battle.

That was but one of the problems. While building the pyramid they also built scaffolding along the front and one side made of tree limbs four to ten inches in diameter. That's where the stuntmen would struggle to keep their balance while sword fighting and waiting for Dick to launch his arrows. Two stuntmen would be doing battle. One would stab his opponent, who would do a high fall. The other would turn, stop for a split second as if looking for a new opponent (you looked, but the only thing moving was your head, because you knew that arrow was deadly), and that's when Dick would fire. When the arrow hit, he'd do his high fall.

Everything was working perfectly. We must have done a dozen scenes like that. Then J. Lee Thompson decided to make a change. Dick had been firing his arrows from his off-camera platform, which meant he could have the arrow already notched in the string, drawn back, and aimed, so all he had to do was release. But now Thompson wanted Dick actually in the frame. This meant he would be balancing on one of those small limbs while notching, drawing, aiming, and shooting.

Not knowing how long it would take Dick to fire the arrow, the stuntmen changed the routine for the combatants. We put a metal plate under our costumes in both front *and* back. This way, when Dick was ready he could just let the arrow fly regardless of what the combatants were doing. Actually, it worked out well. No two shots looked the same. Oh yeah—when Dick was off-camera, the stuntmen were paid a hundred bucks every time we took an arrow. With him on-camera, trying to keep his balance and hoping not to slip as he fired, we raised the price to two hundred a shot!

Between the sword fights, fire stunts, high falls, and Dick's arrow strikes, we staged a hell of a battle on *Kings of the Sun*. Though slightly burnt, bruised, and nicked by our swords, our checking accounts were bulging as we said good-bye to Mazatlán.

Let's talk about accidents—only this time it wasn't me who ended up in the hospital. I was the stunt coordinator on *The Way West*, directed by Andy McLaglen and starring Kirk Douglas, Robert Mitchum, Richard Widmark, Lola Albright, and Sally Field, among others. It was a story of a wagon train traveling from St. Joseph, Missouri, to Oregon. We had twenty wagons, fifty head of loose horses, and a small herd of cattle, and all of them had to be used in every exterior scene in the movie. In those days movie companies didn't use walkie-talkies to communicate on exterior locations. All the wagons, cattle, and horses had to line up for each shot. That was my job. After being told by the director what he wanted, I would ride up and down the wagon train telling each wagon what to do. When I got to the last wagon, which had a green flag in it on a long pole, I would tell the driver to wave the flag to let camera know we were ready. In response, they would wave a white flag, signaling to everyone that the camera was rolling, followed by a green flag, which meant action.

Many times as I reached the last wagon, I would see a red flag waving. That was my signal to come to camera. Most likely the director wanted to change something. As fast as my horse could run, I headed back for my new orders. I would listen to the director and then, asking my horse for all he had, it was back to the wagon train to relay the changes. These trips back and forth were anywhere from a hundred to a thousand yards, and even Seabiscuit didn't have that much endurance. So each time I went to camera the wranglers would have a fresh horse for my next trip. It was not unusual to use four or five horses a day.

For authenticity, the production company had brought in ten head of oxen from the East Coast, as well as their wrangler. We hooked six oxen to one wagon and four to another. Though I didn't know this at the time, oxen are more sure-footed than horses, they don't panic like horses, and one ox can pull as much as two horses.

Andy McLaglen had chosen some terrain that looked impossible to traverse with a wagon train. One mountain was so steep and rocky we had to hitch twelve horses to a single wagon. We repeated this process until all the wagons, animals, and actors reached the top. We then had to lower all the wagons, horses, and oxen—as well as the actors—over a 450-foot cliff. The special effects man and I had different ideas on how to rig the apparatus to lower everything. He rigged it while I was working on the set. Once we arrived at the cliffside location, I looked at the rigging and questioned its safety. He assured me it was safe and had himself lowered over the cliff to prove his point. But the real question was, would it hold a wagon, a horse, or an ox?

We began by lowering a wagon, then some animals, then the actors. So far, so good. There was a ledge about halfway down the cliff. Andy decided he wanted a camera set up there to get an additional angle. So we put three camera people and a camera in a wagon bed and lowered them down to shoot the wagons, animals, and people as they descended the cliff.

After Andy said he had enough footage, the cameramen and crew were loaded into the wagon to be brought to the top of the cliff. They'd only traveled fifteen feet when the gin pole broke, dropping them back down on the ledge. From the top we couldn't tell how bad things were, and with the gin pole broken, there was no way to get them back up. The only way off the ledge was for them to go down another 250 feet to the canyon floor. One of the crew stranded below radioed that a cameraman had a broken leg and possibly a broken arm. Two other crew were okay except for minor cuts and bruises. (By the way, the very expensive Panavision camera had fallen off the ledge and was now in small pieces.)

This is where my young, multitalented stuntmen became invaluable. Not only could they do Western stunts, some of them were excellent at rappelling. The effects man had 2,000 feet of half-inch rope. We cut the rope into four 500-foot lengths and tied those to trees. Four of us prepared to go over the cliff and down to the ledge to see what could be done. The girlfriend of one of the men trapped below went bananas and said she wanted to go down with us. First of all, it was all show on her part. There weren't enough people in the company to tie her up and throw her over that cliff. Second, we had people who were hurt and needed medical attention. I grabbed her hand, pulled her to the edge of the cliff, and asked her if she still wanted to go. Staring straight down 450 feet, she had second thoughts and went back to join the rest of the company.

The four of us rappelled down to the ledge. The young guy with the broken leg and arm was in bad pain. We gathered tree limbs and lashed them together to make a stretcher. Then we tied the injured man to it and began lowering him. About 50 feet down, the leading end of the stretcher caught on some rocks, which caused the top of the stretcher to tip forward. Our patient was now facedown and looking at a 150-foot drop to the canyon floor. If he was screaming before, there was nothing to match the sounds he was making now.

We carefully pulled him back flat against the cliff and decided that someone would have to climb down from the ledge and free the end of the stretcher from the rocks. That would leave three men to lower him while the fourth guided the stretcher. Since I was the boss, I thought it only right that I volunteer. I went down the rope and worked my way past the guy by holding on to the sides of the stretcher. I freed it from the rocks, and the guys on the ledge slowly lowered us to the canyon floor. The injured guy was loaded into a station wagon and rushed to the hospital. The stuntmen on the ledge tied ropes around the other two stranded cameramen and lowered them, which was pretty simple compared to what we had just gone through. Needless to say, the movie was wrapped for the day.

By the time we got back to the motel, the head cameraman had sent the stuntmen a case of really good scotch. We tried to drink it all that night — and nearly succeeded. The following day we paid the price for our efforts. I've never seen such hangovers, but at least nobody had been killed.

When I was the stunt coordinator on *Shenandoah,* we were shooting in Eugene, Oregon, and I met a young man who impressed me right from the get-go. His name was Stan Barrett, and he was a medical student in need of some cash. Hearing that the movie company was hiring extras, he'd applied and was hired. As we chitchatted on the set, I found out he was a Golden Glove boxer and all-service boxing champion, and he held a black belt in karate. Obviously he was athletic, and he was full of piss and vinegar. From his questions about stunt work, I could tell this was a challenge he couldn't pass up. The three weeks on *Shenandoah* changed both of our lives forever. Stan ended up quitting school and moving to Hollywood to become a stuntman. I was in a position to give him some work, and in a short time his talents and ability were well known.

The fact that Stan had been in medical school would also come in handy when we worked on the TV show *Custer.* I was the stunt coordinator, and one day we did a stunt that didn't turn out exactly as planned. I sprained an ankle, and he sprained a knee.

I knew my injury was pretty serious because at the end of the day I couldn't get my boot on. By the time I got home my ankle was badly swollen. I did my usual thing. With a bucket of ice water and a bucket of hot water with Epsom salts, I soaked my foot first in one, then the other. I did this until midnight with no relief of pain or swelling. Concerned that I wouldn't be able to work the following day, I called Stan and told him my problem. Could I stand on it? he asked. I told him I could, but it was hard on my teeth, the way I gritted them when I tried to stand up. He asked if I thought the ankle was broken. I didn't think so. He said if I could make it to the location, he could fix me up, so I told him I'd try. Bruises and small cuts were not enough reason not to go to work. Broken bones were on the "maybe" list, depending on what bone it was and how much it impeded your movement. Having decided my injury was only a sprain, I would be at work the next day.

When I woke, my ankle was twice its normal size. I slowly got dressed and used a crutch to hobble to my car. Normally when I drive, I brake with my left foot and use my right foot for the gas. This morning would be different. The moment I touched the brake with my left foot I knew my teeth would be ground down to nubs if I continued to do so, so I switched to my right. With my new driving style, I arrived at the location. I called one of the wranglers over and asked him to bring me a horse. The one thing I didn't want to do was let the company know I was hurt. It was bad for a stuntman to have a reputation for being hurt, and worse yet to report it. The wrangler brought me a horse and helped me mount.

I rode over to the stuntmen's dressing room, and the wrangler followed me to help me off the horse and inside. Stan had also arrived early. His knee looked worse than my ankle. I asked how it felt, and he said about the way it looked. He examined my ankle and agreed it probably wasn't broken. Unwrapping a syringe, he said, "Hang on, son, this is going to get your attention." He wasn't lying. In a few minutes, he assured me, I would be able to walk without a limp. He handed me the needle and pointed to the spot in his knee he wanted me to inject. Don't ask me why, but I just couldn't do it. He laughed and injected himself. Right then, he got my vote for being tough.

I started getting dressed, but I had a problem—I couldn't get my foot in my boot. So I sent for Walter Wyatt, a stuntman who was working with us that day. Wyatt was six two, weighed 250, and wore a size 14 boot. When he came into the dressing room, I asked him to give me his left boot. My ankle wasn't swollen *that* badly. I slipped it on, no problem. By now Stan's magic potion was starting to take effect, and I was ready. With a size 8 boot on one foot and a 14 on the other, I thought I would have a lot of explaining to do. Wrong. Not one person noticed. Stan kept the needle handy just in case. We both worked all day, and nobody suspected either of us was hurt. It was one of many adventures I would have with Stan.

Not all my injuries were work related. As a hobby, I raced motor-cycles in the desert with a lot of stuntmen and a few actors like Steve McQueen. McQueen was a fierce competitor, and he loved to race with the stuntmen—so much so that he joined our motor-cycle club, the Viewfinders. To qualify, you had to work in the movie industry. In one race I was flying along when I saw a rider in Viewfinder colors (every club had its own colors) off to the side of the trail. Obviously, he had troubles. As I stopped, I saw it was McQueen. He'd fouled a spark plug. I took tools and a spark plug out of my parts kit. With the new plug, he fired up his bike, and we were back in the race. While I was changing his plug, at least twenty or more riders passed me. So what? Anything for another Viewfinder.

A few races later I was the one with a fouled spark plug who ended up stranded off to the side of the trail. Looking back, I saw a rider with team colors heading toward me. As he got closer, I could see it was McQueen. Help at last—or so I thought. He never cracked the throttle or even waved as he flew past me. Later he apologized, explaining that there were two guys ahead of him that he just *knew* he could pass. So much for team colors.

The start of these races was the biggest land rush you've ever seen. They were a little bit dangerous, too. As many as three thousand motorcycles lined up abreast and at the drop of a flag rode helter-skelter toward a giant smoke bomb a mile or more ahead of them. With no road or trails, you chose any spot of desert that wasn't occupied by another racer and tried to be first to the smoke bomb, which was where a single marked trail indicated the route of the race. The more riders you could beat to that single trail, the fewer you would have to pass to get to the front. Dodging ditches, rocks, cactus, and other riders kept you pretty busy.

In one race another rider and I were headed for the same piece of real estate with a crater on one side and a large cactus on the other. We raced for the narrow ground between them. He beat me to the spot, hitting my front wheel, which sent me and my bike into the crater. My bike hit a boulder and stopped in the bottom of the crater, catapulting me off the seat and onto the desert floor. I landed on my shoulder. I didn't need a doctor to tell me I had broken my collarbone; I heard it break. Word of my accident got back to our pit area. They sent a truck out to pick up me and my bike and take me to the hospital. The doctor told me what I already knew, and then told me a second thing I also knew from experience: there's nothing you can do for a broken collarbone except put a figure-eight bandage around your shoulders to hold the ends of the bones in place while Mother Nature does her thing and sends calcium to the break to heal it. This normally takes two to three weeks.

At home my wife wasn't too pleased to see the bandages. First, she didn't like the idea of me racing motorcycles. Second, she'd warned me I might get hurt and not be able to work. I was supposed to leave the following Tuesday for location on a film called

Posing with my sister Gwen on Kit, the family mule. *(Personal collection)*

Sergeant Needham— 82nd Airborne. *(Personal collection)*

Bulldogging Cliff Rose from an airplane at 58 mph in *You Asked for It*.
(Courtesy of Sandy Frank Entertainment, Inc.)

Bulldogging Cliff Rose from horse to horse (easier without the airplane) in *You Asked for It*. *(Courtesy of Sandy Frank Entertainment, Inc.)*

My first horse fall in front of the camera, doubling Richard Boone in *Have Gun — Will Travel*. *(Courtesy of CBS Entertainment)*

High fall, doubling Richard Boone in *Have Gun — Will Travel*. *(Courtesy of CBS Entertainment)*

Left to right: Ed Sullivan, Richard Boone, stuntman Chuck Couch, and me before the fight on *The Ed Sullivan Show*. *(Courtesy of CBS/Landov)*

Playing Duke's foreman alongside Chill Wills and John Wayne in *McLintock!* *(John Wayne name and likeness used with permission of John Wayne Enterprises, LLC)*

Any time you see me and a runaway buckboard, there's a wreck in my future; here, I'm with stuntwomen Stephanie Epper and Patty Elder in *The Rare Breed*, starring Jimmy Stewart and Maureen O'Hara. *(© 1966 Universal Pictures, courtesy of Universal Studios Licensing LLLP)*

The great stuntman Ronnie Rondell flies through the air and takes me with him in *Kings of the Sun,* starring Yul Brynner. *(© 1963 Metro-Goldwyn-Mayer Studios Inc. All rights reserved. Courtesy of MGM Media Licensing.)*

The "Duke" Wayne and Hal Needham.

John Wayne delivers a round-house to my chin in *Donovan's Reef.* *(© Paramount Pictures. All rights reserved.)*

My fourth high fall before lunch in *The War Wagon,* starring John Wayne and Kirk Douglas. *(© 1967 Universal Pictures, courtesy of Universal Studios Licensing LLLP)*

"For Hal—whose horse supported both of us last year, Charlton Heston."
Chuck rearing my horse Alamo in *Major Dundee*. *(© 1964, renewed 1992*
by Columbia Pictures Industries, Inc. All rights reserved. Courtesy of Columbia Pictures.)

Taking a punch from Kirk Douglas in *In Harm's Way*. *(© Paramount Pic-*
tures. All rights reserved.)

"To Hal—with my thanks and respect, Jimmy Stewart." Stewart "shows me the door" in *The Rare Breed*. *(© 1966 Universal Pictures, courtesy of Universal Studios Licensing LLLP)*

"To Hal—who stays in the background and makes me look good in the foreground! Thanks, Kirk Douglas." Left to right: Kirk Douglas, me, stuntman Jack Coffer, and director Andy McLaglen in *The Way West*. *(© 1967 Metro-Goldwyn-Mayer Studios Inc. All rights reserved. Courtesy of MGM Media Licensing.)*

Presented with my Mach Buster certificate by Colonel Chuck Yeager at Clark Air Base in the Philippines. Left to right: Colonel White, my pilot, me, and Yeager. *(Personal collection)*

Squaring off while doubling Dean Martin in *Bandolero!*

"To Halbert—I Need-him. With love, Raquel Welch." Hal, please look at the camera! From *Bandolero!*

"Sure, we can stampede 2,500 horses, Duke!" Left to right: Duke's stunt double, Chuck Roberson, alongside me, Duke, Rock Hudson, and crew in *The Undefeated.*

Teaching Dustin Hoffman how to fan a six-shooter in *Little Big Man*.
(Courtesy of CBS Entertainment)

Jumping from a runaway stagecoach onto the back of a galloping horse in *Little Big Man*. I hope I put my cup on. *(Courtesy of CBS Entertainment)*

Tobruk, and I really didn't want to stay home for two weeks and listen to her saying "I told you so."

A broken collarbone isn't really painful—unless you lift your arm above your shoulder, which causes the broken bone to move. Now, that smarts. I had an idea. I went to a buddy of mine who ran a saddle repair shop and had him build me a strap to put around my chest with small rings in the front, back, and directly under my armpit. He then made a strap to go around the bicep of my arm and attached three leather strings on the inside of it. Using the strings, I could tie my arm tight against my side with the ring below my armpit, then tie one string to the front and one to the back, and presto, my arm wouldn't move except at the elbow. Plus, I always had a bottle of Percodan to take care of the small stuff. I thought I was ready to go to work; the studio had said I wouldn't be doing any big stunts. It was just soldiers running and getting shot. (We stuntmen call that a high-speed moccasin blowout.) No problem.

On location I found out that I had been lied to. The first stunt was three guys getting shot off a sixty-foot ledge. They knew I did high falls, so I was one of the three picked. I didn't dare tell them I was hurt. So up we went. The cameras rolled, a machine gun fired, and down we came. When you do a high fall, you use your arms to guide your body, somewhat the way a cliff diver does. Well, I must have looked like a wounded duck, with one arm flapping only from the elbow down. I hit the pads, and the only thing that kept me from crying was the crowd of people watching.

The director, Arthur Hiller, came running over and said he had never seen a high fall that looked so out of control. He wanted to do it again with a close-up lens. Are you kidding me? But I couldn't say no. Another Percodan, and I did my wounded duck act again. Do two of those with a broken collarbone and then try to smile. What happened to the high-speed moccasin blowouts? It was only 10 a.m., and it looked like it was going to be a long day for ol' Hal.

I next found myself and another stuntman in a machine-gun nest fifty feet up on top of a slope so steep you couldn't walk up it. In the scene, a tank rounded a curve in the canyon, swung the turret toward our position, and fired. You're probably ahead of me by now and you're probably right. We got blown out of the machine-gun nest and had to tumble to the bottom. The other stuntman was complaining about all the rocks we had to go over, but that was not my major concern. I wanted to know how I could tumble fifty feet without hitting my bad shoulder. I never got that one figured out. It was a wreck all the way to the bottom. That was it for the first day. I was eating Percodans like gumdrops. I even threw in a few scotch and sodas, but the sandman couldn't find my room that night.

The next day I was a German officer riding in a convertible command car that stopped in front of the camera. As I stood up with a pair of field glasses to scan the horizon, the vehicle was hit by an explosion. The director wanted me to fling my body over the door, flip, twist, and land flat on my back while biting a blood capsule so he could zoom in tight on my face and see the blood coming out of my mouth. Landing flat on your back from four feet up will test your ability to try and play dead as the camera zooms in—as well as your ability not to wince from the pain of a broken collarbone. I toughed it out until they finished with the stuntmen and sent us home.

As you know by now, I've done a lot of stunts where I've gotten hurt and had no one to blame but myself. I was never so intimidated by a director that I did something I thought was unsafe. No director ever pushed me off the top of a building; I jumped of my own free will. There was never a scene where a director put me in a car with him remote controlling the throttle. I always chose the speed I thought was necessary to get the stunt done.

6

"Get It Done, Needham"

With hours and hours of practice, routining fight scenes became one of my specialties. We were shooting a fight scene in *The Undefeated,* and John Wayne had to throw a jab and a roundhouse. It wasn't a difficult routine, but Duke kept throwing the wrong punch. The camera operator would say "That's a miss"— meaning that it didn't look as if Duke had hit his opponent. I could see what he was doing wrong, but Andy McLaglen, the director, wouldn't let me show him how to correct it because he was afraid I might embarrass Duke.

The problem was that the camera was positioned directly behind Duke's opponent. Duke was throwing a straight-on jab by the side of the guy's head. You could tell he was missing the guy by a mile. What he needed was to throw a big roundhouse, so his fist would appear to be sweeping across the guy's face. After a few failed attempts, I just thought, here goes nothin', and stepped in. I said, "Duke, you're throwing the wrong punch. Watch this." I threw the correct punch. The camera operator said, "That works." I stepped back. Without saying a word, Duke stepped in and did one rehearsal. The operator said, "Perfect," and they shot the scene. I made myself scarce the rest of the day.

Every Saturday night, Duke had a party for the cast. He loved stuntmen, and because there was nothing to do and no place to go in Durango, Mexico, we were always invited. I arrived at the party and had a drink or two. I could tell Duke had obviously started drinking before I did. He spotted me and walked over. Towering above me, he wrapped one arm around my neck like a vise and then pointed a finger in my face. "I've been doing picture fights for thirty years, you young pipsqueak. Who do you think you are telling me in front of the whole crew how to throw a punch?" he said. I told him I was sorry and would never do it again. A few seconds passed, and I wasn't sure if he was going to release me or tear my head off. Then he said, "If you have a good idea, tell me. If it's a bad idea, keep it to yourself." With my head still locked in his arm, he gave me a friendly Dutch rub and turned me loose, saying, "Get it done, Needham."

I really liked Duke. He was a no-nonsense guy. He worked hard and expected others to do the same. He knew everybody's job on the set. Maybe he didn't know how much powder to put in an explosion, but he could tell you the effect he wanted from that explosion. I was always on the set, at the ready to help in any way I could, regardless of what had to be done. Having come up through the ranks, I also knew what everybody's job was and whether or not they did it well. Duke was aware of my alertness and let me know from time to time when I would jump in and help an electrician or drive a vehicle out of the mud or sand. He would walk by and say, "Attaboy, Needham, get it done."

My greatest challenge on *The Undefeated* was controlling the biggest herd of horses ever filmed—2,500 head that we had to stampede in three different scenes, which meant we had to stampede them numerous times throughout the film to get all the shots. If you lost control of that many horses, it could take days to round them up, and chances were you would never find all of them.

Andy would pick the location where the stampede was to happen, and I would have a corral built five hundred yards away.

Then I would go to the other side of the stampede area and build another corral. I'd have the wranglers put the horses in the first corral with no food or water all day. That evening, they would drive the horses very slowly to the second corral, where there was plenty of both. After doing this for a few days, we would be ready for the stampede, and we wouldn't lose a horse. As far as they were concerned, they were just going to get some food and water.

Creating a stampede is complex and time consuming. Here's the way we did it. With the horses in the corral, we opened the gate and slowly started herding them out at a walk. It was necessary to have all the horses moving in the same direction about thirty or forty abreast, which cowboys call "lined out." Then we began pushing them by hollering. When they reached a trot, it was time to start firing pistols and yelling louder to make them run. Once they started running they gained their own momentum—and we had our stampede. Heaven forbid something should go wrong, because they wouldn't stop until they reached the other corral. If one horse tripped and fell, others would trip over him, and the next thing you'd see is a pile of horses. It wasn't unusual to have four or five piles of horses with ten to thirty in a pile. The wranglers and stuntmen would physically roll them over so they could get up. What's unbelievable is that we didn't hurt one horse on the movie.

When horses are stampeding, you never see a cowboy riding in the middle of the stampede. If his horse trips and goes down, the cowboy is dead. And that's exactly what was written in the script. Impossible to do, unless you have a plan. Which I did. I had read the script a month before we started shooting. Of all the stunts and action sequences, this was going to be my biggest challenge. On location, the stuntmen and wranglers kept asking, "How are you going to pull this one off, Needham?" I told them I had a plan.

The script read something like this: Duke, his men, and the

herd of horses are confronted by a hundred mounted French soldiers. Duke orders his two chuck wagons filled with riflemen to the front of the slow-moving herd. Then Duke gives the command "Turn them loose!" The wagons charge, with the onboard riflemen laying down a deadly field of fire, and the herd is stampeded. The wagons and the stampeding horses blow through the charging French soldiers.

A week before we were scheduled to shoot the scene Andy said, "Okay, so you're not talking. I hope to hell your plan works." I told him, "I was hoping the same thing."

Three days before the shoot I took the construction foreman to the location and told him what I wanted built and where. Four diamond-shaped wooden fences would be used as safety zones. The diamonds would divert the stampeding herd around my stuntmen. Each diamond safety zone would be a hundred feet long. The fence would need to be lower than the height of the backs of the horses — about four feet six inches. The fence would then disappear from camera view as the horses stampeded between the diamonds and the camera. This would make the stuntmen appear as though they were doing battle in the middle of the stampede.

When we shot the scene I positioned one of Duke's men at one end of the diamond and a French soldier at the opposite end. We rolled the cameras, and when the frame was full of stampeding horses, I waved a flag, the cue for the stuntmen to charge each other. When they met in the middle of the diamond, that's where the fit hit the Shan. As my stuntmen battled and fell, they looked as if they were falling into the stampeding herd.

On the first day of shooting *The War Wagon,* which starred Duke and Kirk Douglas, Kirk requested that I double him, as I had done on *The Way West.* Duke and Kirk were waiting for their horses. Kirk was five eleven; Duke was six three. Standing on the boardwalk, Duke looked down on Kirk. But Kirk mounted on my horse Pie—fifteen three hands high, a blazed face, three socks, and looking wonderful—towered over Duke, who was mounted on a small, squatty palomino. "Who picked this damn horse for me?" Duke wanted to know. The wrangler told him it was his stunt double, Chuck Roberson's, horse. "Let's all have a laugh and start shooting this movie," Duke said. I was shocked that Duke rode that little palomino all through the movie. If after the first day's dailies (film footage shot the previous day) he was unhappy, he could've added a scene to kill off the horse. But he didn't.

In another scene on *War Wagon*, Duke was confronted by five guys that he had to take out in a short fight. Not being the stunt coordinator, I wasn't involved in setting up the scene. Duke was supposed to take the bad guys out in a flash. They rehearsed it four times with various stuntmen suggesting different ways to do it, but nothing worked. Duke got mad and walked away. As he departed, he told them, "When you figure it out, let me know. I'll be over here playing chess. And try to choreograph something quick and smooth like a hero would do."

Okay, Needham, put on your thinking cap. I went behind the barn and devised a routine I thought would work. It was quick and got the job done. I went back to camera and said, "At the risk of being embarrassed and possibly sent home, I have an idea of how to do the fight." Duke sauntered over. "Okay, let's see how Mr. Needham would do it," he said. I stepped forward and showed him my routine. Duke said, "Okay, do it once more." I did. Then he stepped forward, rehearsed it, and said, "Let's do it."

They shot the scene, and it was over in a second. Duke looked at me. "Needham, if I'm ever in a fight, I want you on my side," he said. He gave me an attaboy wink and went back to his chess game.

In the movie Kirk played a fancy-dressed gunfighter. He wanted to look good as he rode in on Pie, so he told me to stand by camera and make sure he looked his best. I explained that if I stepped in after a scene was over and told the director to do it again, I would be on the first flight out, regardless where it was going. Kirk agreed with me and came up with a plan. He told me to wait until the scene was over. Then he would look at me, and if I shook my head no, he would find a reason to do the scene again. If I shook my head yes, everything was okay. We did this throughout the shoot. I always found an inconspicuous spot so nobody could see what I was doing. It was a good job, and I didn't want to be sent home. There were a lot of stunts yet to do.

We had a big fight scene to do in a bar. As usual, Duke's stunt coordinator was Cliff Lyons. He saw that Duke liked me, and since the upcoming fight wasn't his cup of tea, he pulled me aside and told me to help Duke and the director, Burt Kennedy, set it up. Of course you remember Cliff...the stunt coordinator who wouldn't hire me on *The Alamo*. Here's the capper. Eight of Duke's old stunt buddies were on the set, and Cliff was asking *me* to set up the fight.

I approached the director and Duke, and told them what Cliff had said. Duke's head whipped around to find Cliff in the corner of the room nodding yes. Duke turned to me and said, "Mr. Needham"—it was Mr. Needham when he wanted to put pressure on me in front of the crew; otherwise it was Hal—"what do you suggest?"

"First of all, this bar is too big to stage a fight with nine stuntmen," I said, referring to the total number of stuntmen we had on the movie. "I think we should call Hollywood and bring down a dozen more men." Duke said that sounded reasonable. He turned to the assistant director, Murphy, and told him to get twelve more stuntmen for the fight. I asked if I could choose them. "Hold it, Murphy," said Duke, "Mr. Needham will give you a list of who he wants."

I had a group of Needham-trained young stuntmen who could do it all. I gave Murphy the list, and they flew in the next day. The morning of the fight Duke looked at the new stuntmen and didn't know a single one of them. To start the fight, a man was to run at Duke, who was standing at the bar. Duke would then grab him and throw him over the bar into the back bar filled with bottles and glasses. The fight would be on. Duke wanted to use one of the old regulars for this. I took him aside and told him the guy couldn't do it. Duke countered that he had worked with this man for years and trusted him to say he couldn't do it if he wasn't capable.

We went back and got ready to shoot. The director called "Action." The guy charged, and Duke tried to help him through the air to the back bar, but he barely cleared the bar and fell to the floor. We set up and tried it again. No luck. And again, no good. Duke turned to me and said, "Damn it, Needham, why don't you use one of your young Supermen to do this? We've been around too long to do this kind of stuff."

"You're right. My fault," I said so everyone could hear.

I called for Gary McClarty, who was one of the best all-around stuntmen I ever worked with and a hell of a heavy-equipment driver. I took Gary aside and told him if he didn't hit halfway up on the back bar, we'd all be on our way home. He said, "No problem." The director called "Action." McClarty really did look like Superman as he hit the top of the back bar and destroyed every bottle and glass on it. Duke looked at me and winked. My stuntmen were still on the job.

We spent half a day destroying that bar. Bodies were flying through the air and through windows, tables were smashed, chairs broken over men's heads. It was some kind of a wreck!

With the fight done my men were scheduled to go home the next day. However, when the studio looked at some film we had shot earlier of an Indian battle, there were scratches on the negative, so the scenes would have to be reshot. The studio also wanted more action. Duke wanted to know if my men could cowboy up. "They're great athletes, but how will they do tomorrow?" he asked, referring to their ability to do horse falls, saddle falls, and bulldogs. I told him not to worry, just take a seat and watch. I knew what they could do on a horse. Not only had we practiced every horse stunt known to man, I had used them numerous times on Westerns.

The next day Duke watched to see if they had the right stuff—horsebacking stuff. Sure enough, they showed that they did. They performed every stunt with flair. It was obvious which men were mine, even from a distance.

While shooting *The War Wagon* in Durango, five of us stuntmen lived in a house we'd rented instead of staying at the motel where the crew was quartered. One Sunday we all went dove hunting. Nobody knew what the limit was, but I'm sure we went over it. While cleaning the birds, Jerry Gatlin, one of the stuntmen, had an idea. He would stay home on Monday and cook a big dove dinner with all the trimmings. The company was shooting dialogue scenes, and nobody would miss him. Gatlin was some kind of cowboy cook. It was decided that we should invite Duke and the director over. After all, a home-cooked dinner was hard to come by in Durango. It was a good thing we'd bagged a lot of birds. Duke chowed down big-time, as did the director.

During dinner Duke said he didn't understand a bunch of young hot-blooded guys hanging around Durango, where nothing was going on, when Mazatlán had all the sandy beaches and pretty ladies. Besides, his boat—and I don't mean a yacht, I mean a navy ship named *The Wild Goose*—was anchored in Mazatlán and we could stay aboard it for the night. We told him the problem was that Mazatlán was a four-hour drive over the mountains, which would leave us little time to enjoy ourselves. He told us to pack our bags; the following weekend would be on him. He knew a local rancher with a plane who owed him a favor. The following weekend we flew to Mazatlán, stayed on *The Wild Goose,* and had a blast—all because of a bird hunt and a home-cooked meal. It was like a luxury hotel with first-class accommodations. There was 24/7 food service, and a drink wasn't hard to find.

Now, I know you're thinking hot-blooded young studs, John Wayne's boat, lots of bodied-up beautiful girls. And it did cross our minds to party all weekend on *The Wild Goose*—but only for a second. Truth is, we were scared of what Duke might think, so we found other ways to entertain ourselves.

There was also the fact that even though I had a good relationship with Duke, one of my falling horses, Hondo, had almost gotten me fired from *War Wagon.* I would cue Hondo to fall by grabbing the right rein and pulling it back. The way you train a horse is pressure and reward. Most people who own horses think reward means to feed them a carrot, but that's not what I am talking about. When I grabbed the rein and pulled, it put pressure on the horse's mouth. To prevent that, he would fall to the ground as fast as he could. If I had to do a horse fall, I would normally rehearse one time to get his mind on the job at hand. That way, as soon as he saw my right hand move, he would be on his way down.

Duke had a scene that called for him simply to ride into town. No particular horse had been chosen yet. I was mounted on Hondo, just giving the horse some exercise. As I rode by Duke he said, "How's about I ride Hondo in this scene?" Sure thing.

I stepped off and handed him the reins. He mounted, and I adjusted the stirrups, because his legs were longer than mine. Duke was riding around getting a feel for Hondo when his wife appeared on the set. Duke made a move with his right hand to wave at his wife. A split second later he and Hondo were on the ground. Luckily, Duke wasn't hurt, but he changed his mind about riding Hondo. He whispered, "That horse is a danger to mankind."

With filming on *War Wagon* completed in Durango, the company moved to Mexico City to shoot interior scenes on a soundstage. Between shots Duke pulled me aside and told me his next film would be *The Green Berets*. He said that Cliff Lyons, his longtime stunt coordinator, was retiring, and he wanted me to coordinate the show and bring all my young Supermen with me. Flabbergasted, I asked when it would start. He told me that as soon as he got back to Los Angeles, they would begin preproduction. I should come over to his office at Paramount Pictures and see him. I told him wild horses couldn't keep me away. This was what I'd been waiting for.

Back in Hollywood, I had my antenna up, listening for word that *The Green Berets* was prepping. Sure enough, the static cleared and I heard Duke was hiring. I showed up at the Paramount lot and told Duke's secretary I was there to see him about a job we had discussed. She rang through and told me to wait just a bit. After a few minutes I was told to go in. I was feeling really good. Duke told me what a fine job my men had done in Mexico. We talked for a while, but he didn't say anything about *The Green Berets*. So I cut right to the chase and asked when I would start prepping. He paused, and I knew there was a problem. Then he explained that Cliff hadn't retired, and out of loyalty he had to let him run the show. But he said he wanted me and my men to be part of the movie, adding that he would depend on me to help him out.

My mind shorted out. What to do? Then I made a split-second decision that I knew would cost me a lot of money. I told him I had waited a long time for an opportunity like this and had prepared myself as best I could, but for me to work on the movie and contribute all my ideas while Cliff took the credit just didn't make sense. I would have to pass.

Duke replied that he would take me on two contracts (which was unheard of), as an actor and as a stuntman, plus give me stunt adjustments every time I hit the ground. What about that? I asked about the movie's credits. The answer was clear: you couldn't have two coordinators. I told Duke I was flattered by the offer but couldn't accept. He said he understood but asked if I would do him a big favor.

"Name it," I said.

"Give me a list of all your young stuntmen and point out the one I should go to for help," he said. I promised he would have the list the following day. The meeting was over.

I was in the dumps for a long time. But every name I put on that list worked on *The Green Berets,* and Duke would later tell me what a great job they'd done. When Cliff Lyons finally did retire, I became the stunt coordinator on Duke's movie *Hellfighters,* which was directed by Andy McLaglen. The movie told the true story of Red Adair and his two right-hand men, Boots and Coots, who put out wild oil-well fires all over the world.

For the opening scene I had five stuntmen with me. While working at the base of the oil rig, one of them is supposed to turn and hit a lightbulb with his steel helmet, breaking the bulb and causing a spark. The well explodes, and all five men come running out engulfed in flames. Red, Boots, and Coots were on the movie set. They said that if we planned any more of those kinds of scenes, to warn them so they could leave, because that was their worst nightmare.

One day on *Hellfighters,* I was told by the production manager that he was sending all the stuntmen home except for Duke's and Jim Hutton's doubles, since they were the only two who had to work during the next couple of weeks. I reminded him that we were doing the big fire scene the next day and I would like to have some safety people, just in case. He said they were going in the morning and that the special effects crew could act as the safety. The next day the stunt doubles for Duke and Hutton are in these cumbersome fire suits in the middle of the oil fires, working on a control valve. I see Duke's double, Chuck Roberson, turn, slip, and fall down, landing on his back in this big suit. He can't get up. I'm the only one who realizes Roberson is in trouble. I run into the flames, push him over on his stomach with my foot, and run back out. Roberson got back on his feet and they completed the scene.

When I ran into the fire I had used my hands to protect my face, and now half the skin on the back of my hands was curled up and blistered. My hair was singed, and I was lucky my clothing wasn't in flames. When I ran out of the fire, my clothes were smoking and burning my skin. There were two special effects men holding foam fire extinguishers. I ran to them and fell flat on my stomach. They hit my back with foam. It felt so good I rolled over onto my back and they gave my front side a blast.

Duke walked up and said, "Okay, you're a hero, but where the hell are all your stuntmen, who are supposed to be working safety?"

I said, "Ask your production manager. He's the one who sent them home this morning."

Duke was in shock. He turned and bellowed the production manager's name. The guy came running out of his trailer and proceeded to get a tongue-lashing, along with orders to catch the stuntmen as they got off the plane and get them on the next flight back to Houston.

Duke was one of my heroes. I believe what cemented my relationship with him and impressed him the most was that I would not sell myself out on *The Green Berets*. I worked on ten movies with Duke, and he liked my just-get-it-done attitude. He also knew that for me, it wasn't all about the money—it was about self-respect.

7

Movies of War and Real War

When my director pal Andy was hired to direct *The Devil's Brigade,* as usual I was there to help set up the action and hire the stuntmen. We were going to shoot the major part of the movie, the story of a special fighting unit in World War II, in Salt Lake City and then move to Italy for the balance of filming. Before we started, Andy and his key crew, which included me, went to Salt Lake City to look at all the locations and prep for the shoot.

On arrival we checked into our rooms. Mine was so small I had to go out in the hall to change my mind. I was budgeted to bring fourteen stuntmen. At that time stuntmen were kept incognito, treated like second cousins or a redheaded stepchild, which didn't set too good with me. I decided to act.

I stayed in my tiny room until the morning the other stuntmen were due to arrive. That day I went scouting for a motel to put my troops in and found one that was satisfactory. I reserved eight rooms. In those days stuntmen had to share, so there was a room for every two stuntmen and one for me, the boss.

When the bus left to pick up the actors and stuntmen at the airport, I was onboard with my stuff. The bus arrived at the baggage claim, and everybody loaded up their luggage. The bus then made its way to the official hotel. When it stopped out front, I told the stuntmen to stay seated because we weren't staying there.

After the actors and crew got off, I told the driver where I wanted to go. He protested that nobody had told him about a second drop-off. I responded, "Now they have. Let's go." At the new motel I gave the clerk the address and phone number of the production company and said it would pay the bill.

Ten minutes after I hung up my clothes, the phone rang. It was the production manager, whose job was to get the movie made for as little money as possible. He asked what was I trying to pull and told me to bring my troops back over to the hotel and stop my bullshit. I had been in his room at the hotel, a suite no less, so I informed him that unless my men got decent rooms, similar to his, we were staying put. He said, "We'll see about that" and hung up.

I had just played my trump card. After all, I was Andy's fair-haired boy. Would they force me to move my troops back to the hotel and risk making Andy mad? No. We stayed put for the duration. I won that battle, not only for me but also for the other stuntmen. Use whatever means necessary to get your point across.

Later in the shoot, we had an enormous fight scene scheduled that would take two days to film. I would bring up fifteen more men (the motel loved me). We started shooting early and were moving along at warp speed. About four in the afternoon, Andy told me what else he needed and wanted to know if I thought we could finish by working a couple of hours overtime. I assured him we could, and we did.

Don't ask me why, but most of the time you negotiate the money for hazardous pay over and above your contract after the stunt is over. The coordinator's job is to talk to the men and reach an agreement about how much they want, and then tell the company. The troops asked for a little more than I expected, but I reasoned that we were doing two days' work in one. That's a bunch of money saved. The extra stuntmen I'd brought up would go off salary a day earlier; more money saved. Overall, I thought the company got a bargain, so I put in the agreed amount for hazardous pay and assumed everybody would be happy with the savings.

The next morning the production manager and the producer, David Wolper, cornered me and demanded to know why the stuntmen were asking for so much money and why I'd agreed with them. We happened to be standing by an eighteen-wheeler. The trailer was dusty enough that by using my finger as a pencil I could get my point across.

I wrote a series of numbers down one side. The production manager then took his turn. We went down that side of the truck, across the back, and started on the other side. Finally he got fed up.

"Okay, pay them and send them home. You can get some other stuntmen," he said. "When you say pay *them,* are you including the original fourteen I hired?" I asked. "Yes, he answered."

It was time to play trump card number two. "No," I said, "I won't get any others. You'll have to get them. I'm going home with my men."

Wolper quickly spoke up. "All in all, we're ahead of the game. We saved a day on our shooting schedule. Pay them."

Not once did I get fired for standing up for the rights of my stuntmen.

Back in Hollywood a few months later, I had a call from Wolper, whom I'd gotten to know pretty well on *The Devil's Brigade.* He told me he was planning a World War II movie in Czechoslova-kia called *The Bridge at Remagen,* and he wanted me to coordi-nate the action. I asked if he had a dusty truck so we could agree on who'd get paid what. He said it wouldn't be a problem because he wanted to use Czech stuntmen, who would work cheap.

"Hold on, David," I said. "You want to do a war film and you want me to coordinate with men I don't know and whose language I can't speak?" He assured me they had some great stuntmen in Czechoslovakia and that I would have my own interpreter. Like a fool, I said okay.

I landed in Prague at 4:30 in the morning. It was foggy, damp, and dreary. This was 1968, and even though it was a Communist country, the person who came to meet me walked me right through customs. In the car he told me the director, John Guillermin, wanted me to come directly to the location. When I arrived, Guillermin outlined the action scene he wanted to shoot two days from then. It didn't sound that complicated, so I told him it shouldn't be a problem. I was then introduced to a pretty, twenty-five-year-old interpreter named Suzanne, who would introduce me to the stuntmen.

We drove to the little town of Dovey, which had the bridge we'd be using for filming. Standing on a corner waiting for us were twenty men of all shapes and sizes. I can more or less look at a person and tell if he can walk and chew gum, and I prayed that my eyes were lying to me. The guys were all friendly enough, but when I asked what movies they had worked on, they seemed stuck for an answer. After a lot of language I had never heard, Suzanne told me that none of them had worked on a movie before, and their understanding was that I would train them. One was a boxer, one a gymnast, another a race driver, but there was not a stuntman among them. Sure, they have stuntmen in Czechoslovakia. Thanks, David.

On the set I went to work, showing each man where to fall and how to fall. I would give Suzanne something simple to interpret, like "Come out of the door four or five steps, pretend to get shot, and fall down." She and the stuntmen would talk for three or four minutes, and then I would ask them to show me what they were going to do. I called, "Action!" and they came out of the door, ran twenty yards, and fell—nowhere near the zip code where they were supposed to fall. This was going to be a job to remember.

When the director showed up, I explained my problems. I told him what I was trying to set up. He called a rehearsal. The "stuntmen" took their positions. He called "Action!" Men ran everywhere. Some fell, while others ran right up to the director and stopped. Guillermin looked at me. I explained that they were worse on the first rehearsal. He didn't see the humor. He turned around and walked off the set. I thought to myself, I can't wait for tonight: Wolper's coming in.

David Wolper's penthouse in Prague was beautiful and quiet, and I, on the flip side, was loud. "You promised they had good stuntmen here, that they had made a lot of action movies," I began. "Bullshit! There's not one so-called stuntman here that's ever been on a movie set, and if you think I'm stretching my story, ask the director. We did one little action scene and I had to play every German that got killed, at least in the foreground."

I went on to tell David there were a couple of sequences where I'd have to have some help. David said that it wasn't in the budget to fly over a bunch of stuntmen. I told him I could name two or three shots where multiple vehicles had to wreck at the same time. How the hell do I do that?

David finally said, "You can bring over one man. I've watched you work; you'll figure it out."

"Okay," I said. "But remember, you told me in Hollywood that I didn't have to do any stunts, just set them up for the Czechs. So from now on, every time I put my body in harm's way, get out your checkbook."

Back in my room, I tried to place a call to the States, but the language barrier proved too hard. I finally had to get my interpreter to do it for me. An answering service called Teddy O'Toole's handled all the stuntmen. When I finally got through,

I told Teddy to stay on the line until I found someone to agree to come help me.

My first call was to Gary McClarty, one of my protégés, a friend, and a helluva stuntman. He was versatile, and heaven knows I needed versatility. I explained the situation and told him it was going to be a tough job but one that would increase our bank accounts substantially. He said that although he was fearless, the way I was talking scared him to death. Still, he agreed to come. I told him the production company would call him later that night with his travel schedule.

After the fiasco in which the Czech stuntmen ran up to the director and stopped cold, I became every German who got killed or anything else that had to be done on a precise cue. In the end, the stunts were my responsibility.

The next day Guillermin set a camera in a high position looking over the top of a tank. He wanted a soldier to run across in front of the tank and, once he had cleared its cannon, the cannon would fire. That soldier would be me. No big deal. I told Suzanne to make sure the "soldier" inside the tank waited until I was clear before he fired. We rehearsed it a couple of times. I would run in front of the tank, and as I cleared the cannon, I would raise my hand to signal to the guy inside where I had to be before he fired.

Everything was ready. Guillermin called "Action," and I started my run. As I reached the point in front of the cannon, about twenty feet from the tank, I was hit by the muzzle blast, which ripped off my helmet and sent me sprawling. I rolled over to see people running toward me. I could see their mouths moving, but no sound reached my eardrums. All I heard was rumbling. As they tried to communicate with me, they began to realize I couldn't hear them. A car was brought in, and as they were loading me into it, someone put a note in front of me with one word on it: "Hospital." Suzanne got in the car with me, and we were on our way.

As we drove I began hearing the car engine and Suzanne's voice very faintly, which gave me hope that my hearing was coming back. A half hour later we arrived at the hospital. I could see Suzanne trying to tell them what had happened, but nobody seemed overly concerned. Eventually we saw a doctor. He and Suzanne talked for a couple of minutes and then she wrote me a note: "Who will pay?" I took out my wallet and handed a hundred-dollar bill to her. That got the doctor's attention. Hard currency was in great demand with the Czechs, and a hundred dollars probably represented a month's salary. At least it got him to start the examination. With his little light, the doctor looked in both ears. He then talked to Suzanne, who wrote me another note that said, "Time will heal." The doc made a fast hundred, and I didn't know any more than I had when I entered his office.

But I can tell you he was wrong. The following day my hearing was coming back a bit. At least I could communicate with people if they talked *loud*. But when I returned to the United States, I went to a hearing specialist who told me my hearing would never be the same. He was right. From that day forward I have had to wear hearing aids.

Two days later Gary McClarty arrived with a big smile on his face. It disappeared when I told him one of the stunts I had planned. "As the American forces are making a run for the bridge at Remagen, to capture it before the Germans can blow it, they come under artillery fire," I explained. "The director wants to wreck as many trucks as I have drivers. Well, that's two—you and me. But the director wants more than two wrecks. The producer threw the ball my way and said to make it happen, so here's my plan: ten trucks nose to tail, coming down the highway all hooked together. You in the first truck, me in the second, with nobody in the other trucks."

Gary was known in the industry for his ability to drive heavy equipment. He knew what he was doing. "You and I will need a mile, towing all those other trucks, to get up to speed," he said.

I continued, "Ten trucks cabled together nose to tail…with a bomb in each truck. The trucks will be rigged so I can release them one at a time. As each one is released, a bomb will explode to make it look as if an artillery shell hit the truck. If everything goes right, we'll have wrecked, burning trucks scattered for a quarter of a mile. Then I'll release my truck from yours so we can do our wrecks in front of separate cameras."

McClarty looked at me as if I were out of my mind. He then voiced his opinion: the trucks wouldn't track that far or that fast. I told him he was probably right, and if things started to look out of control, I would release all the trucks at one time, which would create one hell of a wreck and explosion. He and I would then continue on to our designated cameras and do our thing. The company would have to settle for whatever happened; after all, we were two men trying to do the work of ten.

The day arrived, the trucks were rigged, and Gary and I were behind the wheels of our respective trucks waiting for them to radio us. The radio barked "Needham, are you ready?" Trying to sound calm, I said, "As ready as I'll ever be." "Come on" was the response.

They wouldn't roll cameras until we reached a certain spot, giving us the time to get up to the necessary speed. In a low, low gear, Gary and I moved out slowly. We started gathering momentum. I glanced in my side mirror and saw what looked like a giant snake behind me, with those trucks weaving all over the road. Gary stuck his hand out the window and waggled it, knowing I would understand his signal—we were in trouble. But Gary had never been fainthearted, and I heard him shift to a higher gear. So did I. As we gained speed the trucks started to settle down and not swerve back and forth. Again Gary stuck his hand out and gave me the double-time signal. Faster was better.

I called camera on the radio and told them to have their hand on the switch, because there was a wreck headed their way. They called back and said, "Bring it on." The cameras were rolling. As we reached the spot where I would release the truck at the back of the convoy, I hit the button, then looked in my side mirror to see it cut abruptly to the left, explode in a fireball, and disappear over the embankment. Next were two trucks: one turned left, one right, and both exploded. I couldn't believe it. I thought, Needham, if you pull this off you'll be a hero.

McClarty stuck his hand out of the window and gave me the okay signal. The more trucks we released, the faster we went. I cut more trucks loose — *crash! boom! pow!* Then I hit the button to release Gary. He went for one camera position, I turned for the second. We hit our ramps and the trucks went over right on the money.

They pulled us out of our trucks as the crew and spectators applauded for five minutes. David Wolper walked over with a smile on his face and said, "See? Nothing to it, Needham."

The crew was staying in Prague, a forty-five-minute drive from the set, but Gary and I stayed in a cabin, which was only a block from the set. We had to do our own washing and cooking. Wait a minute...I don't cook, and neither does Gary. There was one small neighborhood restaurant in town, so we decided to try it. As we entered, everyone looked at us, knowing were not from the 'hood. A waitress approached, and I held up two fingers. She showed us to a table and left us menus. I glanced around the room. All eyes were on these two English-speaking Americans.

I ignored them and looked at the menu. Of course, it was in Czech. Now what? I told Gary when the waitress returned to just follow my lead. She came back, talking a mile a minute. I held up my hands for her to stop. Then in English I told her to follow me, and I moved to a nearby table of four and looked at their food for a beat or two. They all looked at their own food as if it had worms in it. Finally, I made up my mind and pointed at one of their plates and then pointed to myself. The waitress and the table caught on. They thought it was humorous. I asked Gary which plate he liked. He turned up his nose and moved to another table. The customers laughed even louder. Gary found something to his liking and used the same gesture to order. By now, the whole restaurant was smiling and laughing.

From that day forward, the minute we walked through the door for dinner everybody in the place would start jabbering and motioning for us to look at what they were having for dinner. They would use facial expressions to tell us how good it was. Sometimes Gary and I would hold our nose and turn away, and the whole place would break up. When we finally chose our dinner, they would applaud. I must say the Czechs were really nice to us.

Our little cabin had kerosene lamps, which were nothing new to me. I felt like I was back in Arkansas, with a well just outside the back door, a woodstove for cooking and heating, and no shower or bathtub. Clearly, we had to do something about the shower. Behind the cabin were four small trees forming a square that looked about the size of a shower. We thought that if the trees were covered, people in the other cabins wouldn't be able to see us. The next day we stole a tarp from the movie company that was four feet wide and twenty feet long. We wrapped it around the trees and nailed it in place. Okay, so the cabin people could see our head and legs. Big deal.

Next we took a five-gallon bucket and hung it in one of the trees. We punched nail holes in the bottom of a one-gallon bucket and hung it about two feet below the big bucket. We took a piece of inch-and-a-half-round rubber hose and stuck one end in the big bucket of water and let the other end hang down into the small bucket with the nail holes in it. The water would siphon down, and we would have a shower. To control the flow, we ran a string over a limb higher than the big bucket and tied it to the lower end of the hose. When we wanted water, all we had to do was just untie the string and lower the hose into the small bucket—and presto, running water. To turn the water off, we'd just pull the string until the end of the hose that went into the little bucket was higher than the water in the big bucket. Pretty simple.

We filled four or five big buckets each morning so the sun would heat the water. On days when the sun didn't shine—and there were lots of those—the water was cold, and we took the fastest showers in history.

Not only did we shower, but we were supplying entertainment for our neighbors. God only knows what they did to stay clean. A shower is called a *spreka* in Czech. Our neighbors would point at us and say, *"Spreka! Spreka!"* and then laugh. I wondered if they had some kind of mirror system set up and possibly saw more than our heads and feet.

Gary and I had a lot of free time while the company shot dialogue scenes. One day we took a ride with our driver, Eugene, to the top of a hill that overlooked the bridge at our main shooting location. We could easily see the movie company below. The top of the hill had mounds and ditches, and was big enough to lay out a motorcycle racetrack. We thought that would be a good way to kill time, if we could get a couple of bikes. Suzanne told us that if we exchanged our dollars on the black market and paid for them with Czech money, the bikes would cost only about three hundred dollars. We told her we had been warned that if we sold dollars on the black market, we could go to jail. She said she could arrange the exchange without a problem. We thought about it for five seconds and said, "Do it!"

Two days later, Suzanne took us to an office where she used to work and had a lot of friends. As we entered, she invited us to have a seat and said that she would handle everything. She walked over to the receptionist and spoke to her in Czech. She then went into one of the offices. Killing time, Gary and I exchanged a few choice comments about the very attractive receptionist...like she could slide her shoes under our bed anytime. We then began discussing whether Czechs had breast implants and wondered if hers were real.

Suzanne returned all smiles, and then introduced us to her friend the receptionist, who in perfect English said it was a pleasure to meet us and yes, in fact, her breasts were real. She then spoke to Suzanne in Czech, and the two broke up laughing.

A couple of minutes later, a man walked in and introduced himself to Suzanne, who directed him to one of the offices. Completely in charge, she looked over at us, smiled, and nodded for us to follow her. Now we were all in the office together. She told us he wanted to buy fifty dollars. The exchange was made, and we headed back out to the reception area. Soon another person came in. Same routine. After three or four buyers had come and gone, Suzanne excused herself, saying that she was going to the ladies' room. Just as she left, a policeman entered. Gary and I looked at each other, thinking we might be in trouble. I told Gary I wasn't going to jail. I reminded him that we were on the second floor, and if this guy tried to take us, I was exiting through the window. Gary shot back, "Don't get in my way!"

Suzanne returned and began talking to the police officer. Then she pointed him toward the office and nodded her head for us to follow. He wanted a hundred American dollars, in small bills if possible. Two customers later, we were off to the motorcycle dealer. With our new CZ dirt bikes, Gary and I designed a racecourse on top of the hill. We stationed Suzanne in a specific spot on the bridge and gave her a flag. If the company wanted us, she should wave the flag.

Gary and I soon found a new way to entertain ourselves with

our motorcycles. The streets and sidewalks were cobblestone, which meant the curbs were smooth and rounded off, not like the concrete curbs in the States, with their sharp edges. One day as Gary was riding in the gutter next to the sidewalk, he hit the gas, causing the front wheel to lift and come down on top of the sidewalk. He gave it more gas with the intention of getting the rear wheel up there too, but as the wheel came into contact with the smooth cobblestone curb, it failed to get enough traction to jump it. Gary gave it even more gas; still no traction. With the front wheel on the sidewalk and the rear wheel spinning against the curb, he rode thirty or forty yards before he fell. Not to be outdone, I gave it a try. After a short distance I fell too.

A new game had been invented: curb riding. Who could ride farthest? Foot traffic on the sidewalks was negligible, but after a couple of days we had an audience of mostly young people. They would applaud if Gary or I made a long run and laugh when we fell on our butts. We became the evening's entertainment, but each town had a Communist leader, and I guess this one didn't want anyone to have that much fun. Eventually he told Suzanne to tell us we were setting a bad precedent for the kids and would have to stop playing our little game. For sure he didn't make any brownie points with the local folks.

Now, with our own wheels, Gary and I had freedom. We also became friends with the family in the cabin next to ours: a man and wife, two daughters about twelve and fifteen years old, and a son who looked about eight. Trying to communicate with our English-Czech dictionaries became a game. One night the family invited us over for dinner. On the menu was chicken and dumplings...I know, because they gave me the chicken's head. I could tell by the expression on their faces that it was an honor, but I knew I would gag if I tried to eat it. I turned to their son and pointed to the head, rubbed my stomach, and smacked my lips. He got the message that I thought it was delicious, and smiled. I immediately speared the head onto his plate. He wasted no time doing what I couldn't—devouring it.

The next day we asked Suzanne to tell the family that we would take them to dinner at our favorite—and the only—restaurant in town. We saw them heading out the door that evening to walk to the restaurant; cars were a luxury, and they didn't own one. We mounted our bikes and caught up. Using hand signals, I seated the mother on my gas tank and the father on the back, while Gary seated the boy on his handlebars, one girl on the tank, and the other on the back. Off we went, as the family talked and giggled all the way. At the restaurant they told all the diners about their ride over. As Gary and I made our way to the table, the entire restaurant applauded. To show our appreciation we bought wine for everyone. We had a great evening, and it wouldn't be the last.

Things were moving along on the film, and we were about two weeks away from finishing. Gary and I thought it would be a good idea to ask our wives to come over and then all go home together. Each time I went on location, Arlene would come visit me and bring one of the kids. This time it was Danny's turn. She made arrangements, and they arrived on a Friday morning. One look at the cabin and Arlene was ready to go back to the States. I promised we would move to the hotel with the rest of the cast and crew, but tonight I had reservations at one of the finest restaurants in Prague, with a wonderful view of the city. It was a lovely dinner, and I was happy to see Arlene.

I woke up the next morning ready to go to work. As I walked outside, one of the neighbors came running over screaming a lot of things. The only word I thought I understood sounded a lot like "Russkies." She kept repeating "Russkies," so I got out my Czech–English dictionary and handed it to her. She found a page and pointed to the word "invaded." Pointing frantically at "invaded," she kept saying, "Russkies, Russkies." I tried to assure her every-thing was okay.

Gary and I walked the block to the set, but nobody was there. Gary said, "You don't think she was right, do you?" "I don't know," I answered, "but something is happening, and I don't like it."

About that time my driver came barreling up with Suzanne in the car. She laid it out for us. The Russians had invaded Czecho-slovakia overnight. Everyone was at the hotel, and nobody could leave. There were Russian tanks and soldiers all over Prague. I asked how she'd gotten out. She pointed to Eugene, my driver, and said he'd done it. She advised us to go to the hotel where all the other Americans were staying. When I asked if Eugene could get us there, she smiled, winked, and gave a thumbs-up. We had a small problem, though: there was Gary, his wife, me, my wife and son, Suzanne, Eugene, and lots of luggage. We decided to put our wives, my son, and the luggage in the car. Gary and I would ride our bikes, and Suzanne would ride with me. Suzanne said there was another female interpreter who needed to go with us. Okay; she could ride behind Gary.

I went into the cabin, explaining the situation and telling our wives we needed to pack and leave as quickly as possible. A new world record was set for two ladies packing, and we were off to Prague.

We rode along for fifteen or twenty miles and saw nothing unusual until we turned a corner and came face to face with two Russian tanks forming a roadblock with half a dozen well-armed foot soldiers patrolling. The soldiers stopped us, and Suzanne started talking to them (she spoke eight languages). I could tell by her tone that she wasn't happy. Finally she said, "They won't let us through." She told them we were Americans working on a film, but the guard still refused to let us pass. She turned back to the guard and said something in anger. His weapon was cradled in his arm, and he swung it so the muzzle was pointed at us. I told Suzanne to knock it off; we'd go back the way we came.

I leaned the bike to turn, and at that moment she spit on the guard. I almost had a heart attack. I could nearly feel the bullets tearing through me. What was she doing? I asked. "I hate them," she said. I explained the English expression for what she was doing: going to a gunfight with a knife. The odds were not on our side.

Eugene took a lot of back roads and alleys to get us to the International Hotel in downtown Prague. There were two tanks and two trucks loaded with troops parked in the front of the hotel. As we stopped, Suzanne got off and ran inside. Moments later she was standing on a balcony where flags from all the Communist countries were flying. Calling, "Hal, watch this!" she removed the Soviet flag from its holder and threw it to the ground. I expected to see her shot on the spot, but the soldiers paid no attention. She was fiery, brave, and crazy.

Later that day the company held a meeting. *What to do?* The meeting included all the cast and crew and the stars, George Segal, Robert Vaughn, Ben Gazzara, E. G. Marshall, and director John Guillermin. No planes, trains, or buses were leaving Prague. The only way out was by car, but the company had zip for cars. Some fool suggested we continue shooting our movie as though the Russians weren't there. I told them I wanted no part of being in an American uniform or around a tank firing blanks with all those Russians nearby loaded to the hilt with the real stuff.

Someone asked if we had talked to the American Embassy. The answer was no, because we couldn't get through by phone and weren't allowed to leave the hotel. Gary and I had a powwow and decided that with our super driver and Suzanne, we could get there. Everyone wished us the best of luck, and off we went. Troops and tanks were everywhere. When we approached a tank or a roadblock, Eugene would turn into an alley, dart across a vacant lot, or duck into someone's driveway. If you had seen all the cars that had been flattened or pushed up on the sidewalk by the tanks, you would know why he didn't challenge them.

We made it to the embassy. Gary and I went inside. Holy mackerel! A lot of Americans were looking to get out of Prague. We waited our turn to talk to a lady who was being bombarded with questions and told her our story. We needed to get seventy people out. She told us the embassy couldn't help with any kind of transportation; we would need our own cars. I replied that a car without gas wouldn't get the job done. She said that the embassy had plenty of gas; all we had to do was drive over and pick it up. We thanked her and proceeded to run the gauntlet back to the hotel.

On the way, Gary and I formulated a course of action. We would tell the company that he and I would go to the studio. They had trucks, and surely we could find gas barrels and a hand pump; I had seen the crew use them on the set. The company hired local taxis to transport the cast and crew to and from the locations, so if we could convince those drivers to take us to Austria, we could get the gas for the taxis at the embassy. One tank of gas wouldn't be enough to get the taxis there and back, so we'd have to take an extra truckload of gas and leave it at a midway point. That way the taxis could refuel and make it back to Prague.

Some of the company thought our plan was good—provided we could pull it off. Others said it sounded real risky. One man said that we should let everyone go it alone. Fine by Gary and me. We had already thought about that; after all, we had two motorcycles. I would put the kid on the gas tank and Arlene on the back. Gary would carry his wife, and we'd be off. We were both desert motorcycle racers, so we figured that by taking back roads and open fields, with a pair of wire cutters for cutting fences, we could make it.

After lengthy discussion and a vote, our plan to gas up the taxis and go as a group won out. The production manager would gather the taxi drivers and wait for our return. Gary and I were given the blessing and prayers of the crew and off we went. On the way to the studio Eugene was his cunning self, so we didn't see any Russians. We arrived, but there was nobody in sight. The gate was chained and locked. Eugene to the rescue. In his toolbox in the trunk, he kept a handy-dandy hacksaw. A couple of minutes later we were through the gate and headed for the motor pool.

We found lots of trucks — all without keys — and picked out the two we wanted to use. Gary and I probably should have been in jail as youths, because hot-wiring those trucks was a snap. We found barrels for the gas and loaded ten empties on each truck. We also found a hand pump. Since Gary could drive anything, he showed me the gear pattern, and with Eugene in the lead we headed back to the embassy. There we found the same lady and told her we had come to get gas. She assigned a Czech man to escort us to the pumps. When he saw all the barrels, he asked in pretty good English how much we needed. I told him this load and one more. He looked astonished, but we filled the barrels.

On the way back to the hotel I was carefully looking out for moving tanks. If one of them ran into us, there would be one hell of an explosion. Worried that time might be running out, Eugene led us directly through the heart of Prague and the Russian troops. Had we been stopped, we might have ended up in Siberia. At the hotel the taxis were lined up on a side street, out of view of the Russians. We went from one to another until every gas tank had been filled. For Gary and me, it was once more into the breach, running the gauntlet to the embassy for another load of gas that would refuel the taxis for their return trip.

Again we made it back to the hotel, where the taxis were now being loaded with luggage and people. The Czech driver-captain was barking orders at all the drivers. After he finished, Eugene brought Suzanne over to me to explain the situation. She told me the Russians had closed the route the driver-captain wanted to take, and there was only one way out. I went to the production manager and told him what Eugene had said and let him know that the rest of the company could go where they wished, but I was going with Eugene. Pretty soon there was a screaming match among the drivers. I took Suzanne and the production manager and got right in the middle of them and screamed "Stop!" Then I asked Suzanne to tell them that they were going to follow Eugene, so they needed to get in their cars because we were leaving. I turned to the production manager and asked if that was okay with him. He said, "Lead the way, Needham." On the way to the car, one of the young waitresses from the hotel asked if she could go with us. I looked at my wife and Gary, and we all agreed. Why not?

With Eugene at the head of the convoy and the two gas trucks following, we moved out. We took back streets and roads around Prague and then hit the highway. It was uneventful, except that somehow the locals found out we were coming their way. Even thirty miles out of town, they gathered by the roadside and waved. Many of them had small American flags. How they knew we were coming and where they got those flags, I don't know.

It was getting dark when we turned off the main highway onto a two-lane gravel road and traveled ten miles or more. I asked Eugene, through Suzanne, how he knew about this road. It turned out that the town we were headed for was where he and his family spent their holidays. Earlier in the shoot Gary and I each had given Eugene two hundred dollars so his family didn't have to sleep in their car or tents while they were on holiday. That turned out to have been money well spent.

The night was pitch black. Up ahead I could see a bare light-bulb burning. As we drove closer, I made out a small guard shack. As we approached two guards stepped out. We were at the

Austrian border. Eugene and Suzanne spoke to them briefly; she told me they were Czechs. Here were two kids out in the middle of nowhere, looking over our convoy. One of them approached us and the other went to the car directly behind. They didn't know what to say, so we handed them our papers. Of course, the waitress traveling with us had no papers. I asked my wife to hand me my movie contract, which she was carrying along with our passports. I handed the guard the passports and pointed at my wife, my son, and myself. Then I showed him the movie contract, pointed at the waitress, and told her to smile.

The guard said he would let us pass, but not the vehicles. Eugene pulled the car to the side, and we began to gather our belongings. I told Eugene he could have Gary's motorcycle and gave Suzanne mine. Gary and I shook Eugene's hand and embraced him. No words were necessary. I kissed Suzanne and told her how important she had been in making this whole thing happen. We all had tears in our eyes.

From the guard shack, we looked across five hundred yards of a bushy wash to the town of Gmund. The crew gathered their things and prepared to walk to freedom. It was the longest walk I'd ever made — and I've been down the aisle three times.

Lights were on all over this small town, but not too many people were out. There were two small hotels with a total of eight vacancies. Crew members who had families and small children with them got first choice. For everyone else, it was catch as catch can. The people at both hotels were unbelievably nice. They let us sleep on the couches in the lobby, in chairs, or on the floor, anywhere we wanted to lie or sit down. Gary and I went to the end of a long hallway. In front of someone's door, we very quietly laid out purses and luggage and coats for pillows and covers. Just as I was dozing off, something woke me, and I looked up to see a lady in evening dress picking her way over and through us. She took her key out and quietly entered her room without saying a word. Moments later she returned with pillows, blankets, and a big smile as she handed them out. You know, there are good people all over the world.

We spent a couple of days in Gmund while diplomats worked out the details, and then were on our way to the good old U.S.A. David Wolper never called me again, and I'm glad he didn't. Just kidding. Thanks, David. It was one unbelievable experience.

8

A Horse Named Pie...and Horses I've Known and Horses I've Owned

I owned 250 head of horses with two partners, and a stable from which we rented horses to the studios. Not only did we have riding horses, we had mules, burros, workhorses, trick horses, falling horses, jumping horses, and any other kind you can think of, as well as stagecoaches, buggies, wagons, surreys, and ox carts. Just name what you needed, we had it.

The most famous horse in our stables was Pie, ridden by Jimmy Stewart for years. Pie was one of a kind. He was a star and he knew it. When he heard "Roll the camera," you could see he had an attitude. He would point his ears forward. (This is the only way to photograph a horse. When you're ready to take a picture of a horse, have someone behind the camera snap their fingers or call the horse's name, and he will automatically throw his ears forward.) Pie had a smooth gait at any speed; anybody could look good on him. When you rode him into a mark by the camera, you could drop the reins on his neck and not worry about him moving. He had been around so many explosions and so much gunfire that nothing spooked him. He was the perfect cast horse, and he knew it.

Stewart wouldn't do a Western without Pie. I was to be the

stunt coordinator on Stewart's next movie, *Bandolero!*, starring Dean Martin, whom I would also double, and Raquel Welch, whom I would not double — wrong plumbing. At a production meeting the director — my pal Andy McLaglen — the producer, the production manager, and I were going over details of what was needed for the movie. One detail that came up was my salary. I thought the offer was low and stated what I wanted. They told me this was their final offer, and I could take it or leave it. Sure, I wanted to do the movie, but by then I could pick and choose jobs, so I said I would pass and headed for the door. As I left, I turned around and asked who was going to tell Stewart he couldn't ride Pie in the movie, then closed the door behind me. I had only gone a few feet when the door opened and a voice said, "Come on back." Sometimes when you're trying to make a deal, it's good to have a secret weapon: a director, an actor, or a horse named Pie.

I looked for a number of things when we chose a horse to be used as a cast horse. First, it was looks, like Jimmy Stewart's horse, Pie. He was tall, well put together, with a blazed face and two white socks. Being docile and a little bit on the lazy side didn't hurt either. You didn't want a spirited horse or a horse that spooked at his own shadow, because a lot of actors weren't the best horsebackers in the world. If an old horse spooked and jumped to the side, the actor might wind up on the ground and possibly hurt. Also, when the director is shooting a close-up of an actor on a horse, it's important that the horse stand still, otherwise the cameraman has a tough time following the actor. If two or more actors are in the same shot, the camera operator can't keep them all in the frame if one or more of the horses are stepping forward, backward, or turning.

By the way, there's another reason for a director having to do a retake on a shot with a horse, and that's if he decides to take a crap during the scene (the horse, that is). Did you ever notice, in a Western movie or TV series, that there's no manure on the streets? Every time a horse takes a dump, a craft service person comes running out with a shovel and a broom and cleans it up before you're ready to continue shooting. Can you imagine what a Western street must really have looked like around the hitching rail in front of the local saloon? During the day movie companies always have a table set up with sandwiches, fruit, candy, snacks, and drinks for the cast and crew. It may sound great, but guess whose job it is to keep the table supplied? You're right: the same craft service person who cleans up the manure.

When we found a horse that looked and acted the way we thought a cast horse should, we would send him out on a movie where they needed twenty or thirty background horses. We wanted to see how he would act around the crew, cameras, lights, and in the overall atmosphere of a movie set. We would have one of the good cowboys ride him and put him through as many tests as he could during the day—circulating him among the crew, wedging him between two arc lights, putting him close to a wagon and team racing by.

Here's a short story. A guy was selling a horse to a cowboy. The cowboy asked whether he could fire a gun while riding it. Sure you can, said the seller. The cowboy bought the horse. A few days later he brought the horse back, and he had a broken arm. He explained that the horse bucked him off at the first shot he fired. The seller said, "I didn't say how many times you could shoot, just that you could at least once."

Why that story? The good guy is going to fire his gun sometime during the movie, so we had to make sure he could fire more than once and not be thrown off. We tested each horse to make sure it was safe. We would start by firing a few blanks some distance from the horse and gradually move closer. The final test required firing while riding the horse. If you are on a horse and you fire a gun, most always you are firing forward with your arm stretched out. Add six inches for the gun barrel, and that puts the muzzle almost over the horse's head. It's going to make his ears ring, so to help the old horse out, we'd pack his ears with cotton whenever the actor had to shoot, and we'd also use light loads of powder just to produce muzzle flash. The shot could be made louder in the editing room.

Now let's talk about doubles. We had a double for every cast horse. Sometimes we had to paint a blaze on him or a white sock, or even paint over a white sock. It didn't take a Picasso to do the painting, because if the horse got close enough to the camera for you to see a badly painted blaze, you were also sure to see the stuntman doubling the actor. Double horses are used for all the chase scenes. You don't want a docile horse for chase scenes; you want hot blood and speed. A hot-blooded horse will always try to outrun the rest of the herd, which can create a problem if you're a posse member riding in the back of the bunch and your horse wants to go to the front and pass the double for the lead actor. That's sure to anger the director, and you can bet you'll have to do the shot over. That costs time and money—not a good way to get on the list to work another day.

Just when you think you know horses, you learn another lesson. If a horse is going to try to buck you off, he'll probably do it first thing in the morning. If the weather is brisk, chances are better that he'll give it a go. But that's not a guarantee it will be the only time you'll end up on the ground. Almost anything can spook a horse if it surprises him—a jerky movement from someone close by, a rabbit jumping out of the bushes, a gunshot, or an encounter with an animal he's never seen before, such as a camel. I don't know why and have never talked to a cowboy who did know. Is it the camel's smell? They do have bad BO. Is it the shape? Or does a horse instinctively know he should stay away to keep from being spit on by the camel?

On *Beau Geste,* Universal Studios built a fort in sand dunes that were supposed to be the Arabian Desert. The French Foreign Legion was to do battle there with hundreds of Arabs. The first day of shooting was a brisk morning, and my stuntmen selected the horses they would ride that day. They were outside the fort by the horse trucks. The first shot was of them riding into the fort in a column of twos. The scene also called for some camels to be tied up inside the fort walls. In rehearsal the stuntmen came galloping through, and as they rounded a corner close to the camels, a couple of the camels snorted and kicked at the horses. The rodeo was on—horses bucking, stuntmen flying through the air. It was a wreck. When the dust settled only four men had not been thrown off. Catching loose bucking horses is no easy task. Crew members were scrambling for safety while wranglers and stuntmen tried to catch and calm the crazed horses. It took some time to get the horses to accept the camels so we could shoot the scene. Don't ask me why horses don't like camels.

There's a saying that a cowboy only has one good horse in his life, but I must have gotten in line twice. I had two of the best stunt horses, and both at the same time: Alamo and Hondo. In most cases a falling horse is used only to fall, and the same goes for a rearing and jumping horse. But not Alamo and Hondo. They did all three, and much more.

One of the most dangerous Western stunts is a stirrup drag. The stuntman gets shot off his horse and falls, but his foot is attached to the stirrup by a cable. He is then dragged by the horse, who is running free. Usually you drag fifty or sixty yards— or as far as the director wants. But first things first. You clear your drag path of rocks, limbs, or anything that could cut a gash on your back or head, or knock you unconscious. Next you pad up with a thick leather vest, elbow and knee pads, baseball catchers' shin guards—all worn under your costume—and add to this a pair of heavy leather gloves. Problem: once you hit the ground the horse has a tendency to swing you under his back legs, which means his rear hooves and your head are in the same area. You have to use your free foot to push against the horse's belly to keep that from happening—at least you hope.

It takes a while to get a horse used to dragging a man beside him. But if all goes well and you reach the spot where you're supposed to come loose, all you do is pull a short rope attached to a quick release that separates you from the horse—if you didn't get knocked out when you hit the ground, or if the horse didn't kick you or step on you along the way. If that plan goes awry, a few feet past where you were supposed to release is a second quick release attached to a small cable that will free both you and the saddle from the horse. Should that fail, you have two friends (you hope). These guys are usually wranglers mounted on the best and fastest horses money can buy, riding ahead of you. Their job is to move in on both sides of the horse, grab the reins, and stop him. I've only seen one case where the wranglers had to catch a runaway horse, and it worked out fine. I say fine because it wasn't me being dragged.

Alamo and Hondo were great for drags. Of course, we always used the safety precautions, but you could be absolutely sure they would go dead straight and you wouldn't need a release or wranglers to help you. The reason you didn't need too many safety devices with Hondo and Alamo was that they were buddies. I kept them together in a small corral, with no other horses around them. When I wanted one of them to take a straight line to a certain point, I would put them together at the start of the stunt. Then, just before the director called "Action," someone would ride away on the one not being used to where we wanted the other one to go. It didn't matter what else was happening: the one doing the stunt never took his eyes off the one that had been ridden away from him. So if the stunt called for a stirrup drag, Alamo or Hondo would make a beeline for his buddy, and you knew when he reached him, he'd stop.

I had a stuntman named Dick Bullock do that exact shot in *The Undefeated;* however, it took place inside a circle of wagons, and I wanted Hondo to jump a breakaway wagon tongue while dragging Dick, whose body would strike the tongue and break it. For Hondo and Alamo, that was no problem. We got the shot on the first take.

A good stunt horse can make you a lot of money for the stunts you do with them. They are on rental to the studio and you are paid a premium every time they perform. I trained both horses, first to rear, then to jump, and finally to fall. It took me eight months until I felt they would perform when it counted, in front of the camera. On one show the script called for a bunch of soldiers behind a log to be firing rifles while an opponent charges them on horseback, jumping the log and falling the horse. The wranglers predicted that Hondo wouldn't run into all that muzzle blast, that, instead, he would stop short and you could forget about falling him. But I knew Hondo would try to do anything I asked. He charged into the rifle fire, jumped the log, and fell right on the designated spot. Hondo made believers of them, and he also got us a lot of jobs as word spread about how spectacular he was.

I knew my horses so well that I could tell right away when they were ailing. An old wrangler had given me some wisdom. He told me that if a horse has a stomachache, he will look at his stomach. The horse will look at whatever part of his body is hurting. If he breaks into a sweat standing in his stall, call a vet. If he's accustomed to having a stablemate and the stablemate isn't around, the horse will nervously move about the stall. If one of my horses was sick or alone, I would go to the stall, make a bed out of hay, cover it with a tarp, and lie down. I never worried about him stepping on me. Eventually he would come over and smell me, and even take a few bites of the bedding. One thing was for sure: he would calm down.

While I was training Alamo to fall, Arlene was watching. I charged to my fall area and cued him. Down he went. I made a couple of rolls and sat up on my butt. Alamo came up behind me and leaned his head on my shoulder. I scratched him affectionately under the chin. Arlene walked over and said if I treated her that well, maybe we'd have a better relationship. I didn't listen, and a short time later we split.

One of the most dangerous stunts I ever did involved horses. I was working on the film *Little Big Man,* the story of Custer's Last Stand, starring Dustin Hoffman and directed by Arthur Penn. I had gotten the job through Bob Rosen, who was the second assistant director on *Have Gun — Will Travel.* Second AD is the bottom rung on the ladder in that category, but Bob was sharp and ambitious. When *Have Gun* ended its run, Bob moved on and up, working on various TV series and features. The next thing I knew, CBS had gotten into the feature film business, and Bob Rosen was in charge of production. That gave him lots of power to hire and fire. One of the first films CBS did was *Little Big Man,* and Bob asked me to come aboard as the stunt coordinator.

There were loads of stunts, not only in the battle scenes but all the way through the script. I would also be the second unit director, which means I would direct all the action scenes where the stars were not involved. When the stars were involved, I would be there to help the director set up the action and make sure the actors were safe while in the middle of a battle scene. And believe me, they were in the middle. With 1,000 mounted Indians and 250 mounted cavalry troops doing battle, everyone was in the middle.

Last but not least, Bob also wanted me to supply the cast

horses and stunt horses, about forty-five in all, and the trucks to move them from California to Billings, Montana, then to Calgary, Alberta, and back to California. It turned out we had to do more moving than that. We went to Alberta for the snow scenes, but a week into shooting, Calgary was hit with a chinook, a warm wind that melted every flake of snow for miles. This forced the company to move back to Hollywood and shoot until it snowed again, adding three thousand miles of travel for the horses and trucks.

While we were waiting for snow, we shot a sequence in California with the most physically demanding stunt I ever did in my career. My buddy Alan Gibbs, who by the way was Needham trained, was small in stature but got things done big-time. He also had to perform the same stunt. Here was the scene: Dusty (Hoffman) and his new bride are in a stagecoach pulled by a six-up (six horses) that is being attacked by Indians. The shotgun guard gets hit and falls off. The stagecoach driver, who's a wimp, cowers and drops the reins. We now have a runaway coach with attacking Indians. Gibbs (doubling Dusty) climbs out of the coach and up onto the driver's seat. Then he jumps to one of the nearest horses pulling the coach. At that moment an Indian (me) rides up and transfers from his horse to the coach horse next to Gibbs. No big deal. But the next move we had to make could be a killer.

First, Gibbs stands on the back of his horse and leaps to the next horse in front of him. I follow. Standing on the back of my horse, I jump to the next horse in front of me. Now, *that's* a big deal: a standing broad jump of fourteen feet, from the back of one galloping horse onto the back of another galloping horse.

When Penn did my close-up, he told me to act as if I was having fun. It was anything but. We repeated the jumps until we reached the lead team of horses, which meant one more Superman leap. Depending on where we were in the stunt, if we missed we would have two, four, or even six horses and a 4,500-pound stagecoach run over us.

Penn shot the sequence first from the driver's point of view, meaning that the camera was mounted on the driver's seat of the coach. Another angle was looking back at the stagecoach and horses, which were following the camera car and us two nuts trying to commit suicide. The final shot had the camera car tracking the stagecoach and action from the side.

Gibbs and I did this stunt thirteen times. It took two days to shoot the sequence, but it took Gibbs and me three months to train the horses. Most of my workhorses had never been ridden, so first we had to train them to ride. None of them had ever had a 180-pound man land on his back at full gallop while pulling a stagecoach. With blinders on, the horses couldn't see us about to land on their backs. That kind of surprise could cause them to go into a bucking fit, fall down, and wreck the whole outfit, coach and all.

To train the horses Gibbs and I would stand on the tongue between them as Billy Burton drove the coach. Billy was the best cowboy in the business. He drove that stagecoach and six horses with ease. At first we would just slap the horses' backs with our hands. Then we would sit on them, easy at first, and then land progressively harder and harder until they got used to it. We pulled it off, but there was never a guarantee that a wreck wouldn't happen. Horses have minds of their own.

Speaking of wrecks, there was a bad one in the last scene of the stagecoach sequence. The coach was going too fast around a corner, and it accidentally turned over. A stuntman Indian was standing on the coach step with his head and shoulder sticking inside the coach window. He felt the coach turning over, pulled his head out of the window, and bailed off. The coach missed him only by inches. Four stunt people were inside; they suffered some bruises but were basically okay. Penn thought the wreck was so spectacular he kept it in the movie.

One other reason it took three months is we had to train eighteen horses. After we made a run, the Society for the Prevention of Cruelty to Animals would make us wait for the horses to rest. Rather than lose that shooting time, we would switch to fresh horses and keep going. By the time we had used the last six, the first six were rested and ready to go.

To give you a little extra bang for your buck, let me tell you about the Battle of the Little Bighorn sequence. Try to imagine what had to be done to get 1,000 mounted Indians and 250 mounted soldiers to do what I had planned for the scene.

The script read that as Custer is being annihilated, his troops split into small groups and make a run for safety. So I split the cavalry into small groups and told them where I wanted them to ride. I wanted groups of Indians to follow each group of cavalry. I explained the scene and rolled the camera. A stuntman named Roy Clark was doubling Custer, and it seemed as if every Indian wanted a piece of him. Most of the cavalry troops were riding away without a single Indian chasing them, while Custer's group had a thousand Indians chasing them and trying to do them bodily harm.

When we cut, Roy told me that those Indians were beating him with tomahawks, coup sticks, and anything else they could get their hands on, and he had been fighting for his life. He was pretty well bruised up, and we couldn't use the shot anyway, so I turned to plan B. (By the way, these were real Native Americans. I guess they just wanted to get even for what Custer did.)

Plan B, I dressed ten of my stuntmen as Indians. I put one of them forty yards away from everybody else, and then I took about a hundred Indians, put them with him, and told them no matter what, just to follow him. Of course he knew where to go and what to do. I did the same with the remainder of the Indians and stuntmen, which really made Roy happy, because now he only had to fight a hundred of them. It worked. Penn was happy, I was happy, and Roy was delighted.

In another scene the Indians had to cross a river at full speed while chasing Custer's men. The river was a foot deep, which would hardly slow the Indians' horses. However, in the middle of the river, in an area about thirty feet wide and eighty feet long, the river became five feet deep. For sure if the horses ran into that deep hole they would go end over end. I gathered the Indians who'd be riding through that part of the river and told them to avoid the deep spot because their horses would probably fall. My warning was met with dismissals and boos as they let me know what great horsemen they were.

I figured if there was going to be a wreck, I might as well photograph it. I had four cameras: two placed to get wide shots of the river crossing, and two strategically placed with close-up lenses focused on the deep water. With the Indians lined up four deep and ready to charge, I called "Action." As they approached the deep part of the river, not one of them tried to avoid it. When the first line of horses hit the drop-off, they went head over heels, throwing the riders off. The next three lines never even attempted to slow their horses and rode head-on into the deep water as floundering Indians and horses tried to escape to safety.

I would never have set up a stunt like that if I thought someone might get seriously hurt. But those Indians must have done a safety dance the night before, because other than a few minor cuts and bruises, everyone was fine. After the scene was over, they laughed and celebrated for half an hour. It was one hell of a shot.

When we did a battle scene I would tell the Indians not to shoot at anyone's head; even though they had rubber tips, the arrows could still do damage, and there were so many arrows flying through the air, the camera couldn't tell the difference. My words fell on deaf ears. Every time I called "Action," they went crazy shooting at each other's horses, trying to get someone bucked off. If that got boring, they would shoot each other and then laugh like hell after we cut the cameras.

Unfortunately, they didn't listen to me. After one shot I called "Cut." All of my stuntmen were riding in the direction of a man lying on the ground. After a few seconds they radioed in and I learned that one of my great stuntmen, Gary Combs, had been shot in the eye with an arrow. Our ambulance picked him up and raced him to the hospital, where he learned that he would be permanently blind in that eye.

Each morning the Indians would report to makeup to have their war paint applied before riding their horses about a mile to our location. On the way they passed the Little Bighorn Battlefield Museum, where visitors standing on the balcony overlooking the battlefield could see the grave markers of Custer's troops. As the thirty or so visitors took in the view, the thousand Indians came riding by. The tourists couldn't believe such a show could be performed daily and marveled at how realistically the Indians were dressed. The stuntmen never said a word. We just left the visitors to believe this happened every day.

Little Big Man was among the top movies with the most mounted troops ever filmed, until digital technology came along and a computer could make a hundred men look like five thousand.

Hard luck struck again on *Little Big Man*. Arthur Penn wanted a shot of me riding Hondo prior to the stagecoach transfer. I was to charge from the top of a hill toward camera. I came as fast as Hondo could run, and in the blink of an eye I was sailing through the air. I hit the ground, sliding and rolling. I looked back to see Hondo rolling down the hill. He had stepped in a gopher hole. I jumped up and ran back to him. He was trying to stand up, but it was obvious he had a broken leg. I held him down and tried to keep him quiet.

As the wranglers and stuntmen gathered around, they told me

to try to keep him quiet until a vet could be called to put him down. They said that if a vet didn't put him down and verify he had a broken leg before he died, I couldn't collect the insurance on him. I knew that would take an hour, and I couldn't let Hondo suffer. I turned to the prop man and asked whether he had a gun and live ammo. He said no. Billy Burton told me that he did. I asked him to get it. When he returned, he handed it to me. Regardless of how much pain Hondo was in, I couldn't bring myself to pull the trigger. I just couldn't. I handed the gun back to Burton and asked if he would do it. I turned and walked away. In a few seconds I heard the gunshot and stopped dead in my tracks. I was devastated and started to cry in front of the whole crew. Don't tell me grown men don't cry.

Alamo later retired to a ranch where he died of old age. I was lucky. I had two: Alamo and Hondo. The stuntmen who made a lot of money doing stunts with Hondo gave me a bronze engraved with the tribute "One of a kind. Hondo."

9

Just Tell Me What You Want, Not How to Do It

I've been known to challenge directors when they came up with harebrained stunt ideas, especially if they could be done better another way and I wouldn't get hurt. When we were at Universal shooting a World War II scene for a TV show, I was playing a German soldier who had to be blown up by a tank shell. Effects rigged the explosion to go off as I hit a mark about five feet from it; I would try to fling my body through the air to simulate the impact. This was before the invention of the air ram, a great device that makes flying through the air a snap.

They rolled the camera, and I took off. I hit my mark, and the explosion went off. It got real hot, real quick. I went to the effects man and said, "Son, I think you overloaded that a little." He replied that the director had told him to make it big. "Okay, but next time give me a mark farther away from the explosion," I said, showing him that my hair was singed and pointing out that my eyebrows had disappeared.

About that time the director came over to say we had to do it again. He wanted an explosion three times as big, and he wanted me to be on top of it as it went off, so it would lift me in the air and fling my body the way a *real* explosion would. I took off my helmet and put it on the director's head.

"You do the stunt, and I'll sit in your chair and holler 'Action,'" I said.

The crew laughed. He was embarrassed. "Okay, know-it-all, how do I get the shot I want?" he asked.

"Simple," I said. "Bury a spot tramp [a small trampoline, about three feet across and fifteen inches high] on the opposite side of the explosion. When the stuntman hits the tramp, set off the charge. The explosion will hide him for a split second, and when you next see him he'll be upside down, flying through the air."

The director asked why I kept saying "stuntman" rather than referring to myself. I told him it was because I couldn't do this nearly as well as my pal Ronnie Rondell. Ronnie was some kind of gymnast, and he could do this stunt blindfolded. With no other choice, the director told me to rig that stunt so he could get the shot. The effects man really loaded the charge, but it didn't matter, because Ronnie would be far enough away to be safe.

When the director called "Action," Ronnie came running in, and as he hit the tramp, effects hit the explosion. He disappeared behind the blast for a heartbeat, then reappeared upside down, landing with a thud. To the camera, it looked like the explosion had lifted him and flung his body through the air. After they cut the cameras, the director asked Ronnie if he was okay and told him the shot was perfect. At least he knew what he wanted when he saw it.

Once, we were doing a car chase for a TV show—the usual good guy chasing the bad guy routine. When a movie company does a chase scene, all the cars in the shots are driven by extras and stuntmen. You rehearse every shot until everyone knows exactly what they have to do. This time, the director came up with a bad idea and wanted me to do it on the QT. Normally we used off-duty police to block traffic so we had full control of the street. That works, but this director wanted to put a camera in the bad guy's car and have me drive like a madman through regular, uncontrolled traffic, at night! He thought it would be different and exciting, with me weaving in and out of the shadows. The only real difference I saw was that I could wind up in jail if anything went wrong. Speeding in L.A. was nothing new for me, and I had the tickets to prove it, but this was crazy. Not to mention that the studio would have a fit if they knew about his plan.

The director had used me on all his jobs, which added quite a bit to my annual income, so I decided to go for it. But I had another plan. With the camera mounted in the car, I asked him to go for a ride with me so I could show him the route I'd chosen. Once on the street, I turned on the camera and mashed the gas. Over curbs, down alleys, and broadsliding around corners I went. He was screaming, "Look out! Stop! We've got enough!"

I knew better than to stop. Half a dozen patrol cars would be out looking for someone driving like a madman. I stayed on the gas until I reached the studio lot, where I pulled in and parked.

"Needham," the director said, "you're crazy, you know that?"

"I know that," I said. "And you win the prize for the dumbest shot I was ever asked to do, with a chance of me going to jail, people getting hurt, and the studio getting sued big-time, along with putting both our reputations on the line."

After he'd thought about what we'd done, he was afraid to show the footage to the studio. He knew both of us would be looking for new jobs. He made me swear never to tell a soul. Me tell? Never.

I was doubling my old friend Richard Boone on *The War Lord*, which starred Charlton Heston. Boone was on top of a castle wall and had to slide down a rope about fifty feet and land in a water-filled moat. I asked the director, Franklin J. Schaffner, how fast he wanted me to go, and he said as fast as I could. I told him I could go really fast, maybe too fast. "The faster the better," he said. So I got ready. I put on a Swiss seat, a nylon webbed harness worn under my clothes. I attached a rappelling hook to it, which came out through the fly in the pants. I took the necessary wraps of the rope around the rappelling hook and announced that I was ready.

When the director called "Action," I bailed off headfirst and hardly took the slack out of the rope until I was ten feet above the moat, when I applied the brakes that righted me so I would enter the water feet first. Most of the crew and the director thought the rope had broken; some of the ladies even screamed. I wasn't in the air more than three or four seconds.

The director wanted to know what the hell *that* was. I said that was as fast as I could go. The camera operator said it was no good. I'd gone so fast, he missed the shot. The director said he had no idea I could go so fast. I reminded him that I tried to tell him I might go too fast.

The director told me to go much, much slower and not to flip upside down. This time I did it the way he wanted, but I had proved a point: tell me what you want the shot to look like, not how to do the stunt.

That one rappel got me a lot of jobs. No one had ever seen a man free-fall headfirst and stop so close to the ground. It didn't take long for all the stuntmen to hone their rappelling techniques. Throughout the filming of *The War Lord*, every time I did a stunt, even ones that didn't involve speed, Schaffner would ask me how fast I was going to do the stunt. And I would ask, "How fast do you want it?"

My old friend Bob Rosen called to tell me he was going to produce *French Connection II* and wanted me to be the stunt coordinator and second unit director. John Frankenheimer, who had done *The Manchurian Candidate,* was directing, and there were a lot of stunts and second unit to be shot. I said to count me in. I arrived in Marseilles, France, ready to do battle — though I didn't know it would be against the director and the French crew.

During the shoot I rode to and from the set in various cars with various people and couldn't understand a word they were saying. Most of the crew could speak English but seldom did, so my conversation on those rides was nil. One morning I was given the address of a theater where dailies would be shown that night at 7 p.m. I was in the lobby of my hotel at 6:15 waiting for a car to pick me up. Seven o'clock rolled around and no car. At 7:15 I got a phone call at the front desk. The voice on the phone wanted to know why the hell I wasn't at the theater to see the dailies. I told the person that I'd been waiting in the lobby for an hour, but nobody had come to pick me up. I was told to stay put and a car would be there soon, which it was.

At the theater everybody was waiting for me. Frankenheimer was mad as hell: he wanted to know why I didn't catch a cab. I told him there were two reasons. One, most companies send a car to pick up key people, and two, if I, not speaking French, took a cab, I probably would have wound up in Paris. He huffed off to his seat, and we watched the dailies.

The next day I suggested to Bob that I should have an interpreter and my own car to solve the problem. He agreed, and I was assigned a lady about thirty years old to ride with me in my car to and from the set and the dailies. It took only one day to see that she didn't like me, and given her attitude, the feeling was mutual. I asked her what her problem was. She answered with a question: why did I have my own car, when the best cameraman in France had to share his ride with two other people? I decided to have a little fun with her. First of all, I said, my job was more important (which of course it wasn't). That upset her. Second, I must have a better agent. She didn't say another word all the way to the location.

On the set she started talking to the cameraman in French. I asked that she speak English so I'd know what was going on. She grew really angry, and I knew why. She was telling the cameraman that I thought my job was more important than his. Now he was upset. How dare I? Word must have spread pretty fast, because soon none of the crew would talk to me unless it concerned the shoot.

One Saturday I had to do a pretty scary stunt. I was doubling the bad guy, who was going to escape from a warehouse in a speeding van. As the two giant sliding warehouse doors closed, they would catch the van, bringing it to a sudden stop. I would be thrown through the windshield and land on the cobblestone street. The French didn't have the kind of breakaway glass we used in the States; they had a very thin glass called surgeon's glass that instead of shattering broke into long, sharp shards. Also, the camera would see any pads we placed for me to land on, so I would have to hit the cobblestone street. We were all set to shoot when the crew called a meeting and I was informed that we were wrapping. The shot would be done on Monday. Why? I asked. I was told that it was a union rule to wrap at noon on Saturdays. The only way you can shoot past twelve is if the entire crew votes to continue. It was their revenge; make me sweat it out until Monday. Chalk up one for the French. Now *I* was upset.

That night the cameraman had a cocktail party for the cast and key crew. He must have made a mistake, because I was invited. After a couple of drinks I told him I thought it was a crazy rule to quit when everyone, especially me, was ready to shoot, and that it would never happen in the States. "You Americans are too money hungry," he said. Then he swept his arm around the vista that was his living room and asked, "What more could one ask for?"

That was easy. "Screens on the windows to help keep the bugs out." Then I opened my jacket to show a shirt wet with perspiration and added, "An air conditioner wouldn't hurt." I also mentioned that I'd used the bathroom earlier, and it was tiny. I told him it would be nice if the toilet were big enough that you didn't have to go outside to zip your pants. The only person who laughed was a German actor—I think he also made it onto their don't-talk-to list.

On Monday morning I did the car stunt. It was pretty spectacular, but there was no applause.

Later that week we were shooting at night on the street. I didn't have anything to do, but I knew that sure as hell, if I left the set the French would think of something to ask me, which would make the director aware that I wasn't around. There was a bar a couple of doors down, so I asked my interpreter if she would like a drink. To my surprise, she accepted. After three or four she was getting loose, so I figured now was the time to ask whether she disliked all Americans or just me. Wow. Did that push a button!

"First," she told me, "Americans are obnoxious and egotistical. They think they're better than everyone else and that the world owes them." I agreed with the last part. I thought a lot of the world owed America, especially the French. After all, we had saved them twice in fifty years, and as the saying goes, "If it wasn't for America, the French would be speaking German."

She asked, "If the United States had so much, why did it take so long for you to get here to help the French in World War II?"

I shot back, "Not help, *save* the French. First of all, we had to gear up our defense plants, draft and train our troops, fight the Japanese, and cross the biggest body of water in the world to get here. It would've happened faster if the Vichy had been on our side."

I really enjoy a drink—but not when I'm wearing it. She stormed out and requested to work with the special effects crew.

Good. I wouldn't have to put up with her French attitude anymore. She never spoke to me again.

If you've ever been to France or seen movies made there, you know you have to walk in the street most of the time, because sidewalks are used for cafés. In the script, there was a scene where Gene Hackman had to chase the bad guy on foot. I looked at one block of the Marseilles sidewalk at lunchtime with all those people eating and came up with a great idea for the chase. I'd put the bad guy just ahead of me and chase him with a helmet camera. With one guy chasing the other, I anticipated that jumping tables and knocking waiters and people on their butts might make things exciting. Of course, we would do the shot without permission from the restaurants, patrons, or the police.

I conferred with Frankenheimer, and all was ready to go. We would arrive in a van so as not to draw attention to ourselves. Then we'd jump out, make the shot, and meet the van at the other end of the block for our escape. In dailies the shot looked great. A genius idea. The best actors in the world couldn't have reacted to what was happening as well as the real people we captured on film. But Frankenheimer saw it differently. He pulled me aside and told me I was fired as the second unit director. Good, I thought. I'll go home. However, Rosen wanted me to stay on to coordinate the action. I agreed, but only because of our friendship.

You guessed it; I didn't have a good time in France. One day on the set, Hackman and Frankenheimer had a difference of opinion. It got pretty hot. Hackman said something that really upset Frankenheimer, who came to me and asked what I would do if someone talked to me like that. He must have forgotten he'd fired me days earlier, but I hadn't. This might be my chance to get even. Knowing Hackman could flatten him with one punch, I told him to go knock Gene on his butt. My scheme didn't work, but I can't say I blame Frankenheimer for not taking my advice. I don't think I would have wanted to duke it out with Gene, either.

I have never been one to accept *this is the way we've always done it*. I was working on the TV series *Wagon Train* and we had a jousting scene. The loser of the joust (me) had to be knocked off his horse. Here's the way *they* always did it: Special effects and wardrobe helped me put on a heavy leather vest with a cable attachment in the middle of the back. The other end of the cable was attached to a tree. In full knight's armor, I charged my opponent. About thirty yards later I hit the end of the cable, which is a pretty sudden stop, considering the horse was running full speed. I hit the ground flat on my back, and the noise inside that armor sounded like someone shaking a rock in a tin can. The impact twisted my headgear completely around and broke my nose. I couldn't see with the helmet backward, but I could feel the hot blood running from my nose. When they pried the helmet off my head, I told them that if this is the way they always did it, please don't call me next time.

There were two problems with their way. One, they always hooked the cable at ground level to a tree, a large rock, a truck, or anything that wouldn't budge, so when you hit the end of it, the snap would jerk you off the horse backward. Your feet would fly up in the air, and you'd land on the back of your head and shoulders. The other problem was that the cable had no elasticity to it.

I looked as if I'd gone a few rounds with Mike Tyson, with a broken nose and two black eyes. I had time to think while I healed. I devised an apparatus that would take a lot of the hurt off the stuntman when he had to be snatched off of a galloping horse or a speeding motorcycle, or anytime he had to come to an abrupt stop and be knocked off a moving object. It consisted of a tube with four strands of bungee cord attached to the end of the cable. When you came to the end the cable, the bungee would stretch four feet. You would hardly feel it. The final part of my idea was to mount the apparatus fifteen or twenty feet high so it picked you up and out of the saddle, landing you more on your butt than your head. Within a month every stuntman owned what they called the Needham Ratchet. It's not the way they'd always done it, but it's the way they still do it today.

I've had the air knocked out of me more times than I can count doing high falls into cardboard boxes and pads—because that's the way they always did it. But there always had to be a better way. One afternoon Alan Gibbs and I were at a sports equipment show, just looking around. When we got to the pole-vaulting area, they were giving a demonstration of a new catch pad for the vaulter to land in after he cleared the high bar. Instead of foam-rubber pads, they used an air bag. The vaulter would land and disappear into the fabric, then he'd pop out and the bag would reinflate.

Wow. I wondered from what height you could fall into this thing. I approached the manufacturer and asked that question. At least twenty-five feet, he said. I asked, "Could you fall fifty feet into it?" He asked if I could pole vault that high. I explained what we did for a living and said that we were tired of landing on what they presently used and not being able to breathe for five minutes. I then asked if he could build a bigger air bag. Why not? But he didn't know if it would work the same as the ones the vaulters used. I agreed not to hold him responsible and ordered one to be built thirty by forty feet. I told him we would test it and let him know the results.

A couple of weeks later, the air bag arrived. Eight or ten of us wasted no time setting it up and inflating it. Fully inflated, it was about five feet high. I asked who wanted to go first. No one volunteered, so we decided to drop some things into it to see what it looked like. First we dropped a bag of cement. It looked good.

Next we dropped a two-hundred-pound bale of hay from twenty-five feet. It looked good, too. With the bag inflated, you could crawl inside and see how close the hay bale came to hitting the ground. After we dropped it several times, someone felt brave enough to give the jump a shot, so we went inside the bag to see how far the stuntman would sink. He perched himself in the hay-loft of the barn about twenty feet high and jumped off. From inside the bag, we estimated he missed the ground by about a foot and a half—meaning that from forty or fifty feet, he'd hit the ground.

We were beginning to think the air bag was a waste of time. The stuntman said he would go up another five feet and try it again. He hit the bag, and those of us inside determined that he hadn't come any closer to the ground than he had the time before. We couldn't figure out why. He went another five feet higher, with the same result. It worked that way until everybody was jumping from fifty feet into the bag. No one was quite sure why a higher jump didn't put the jumper closer to the ground; all we knew was that the airbag compacted to form an air mattress under our bodies. But by the time we got to sixty feet, the impact was getting harder.

I called the manufacturer, and he tried to explain the theory of how it worked—to no avail. However, he did tell me that if we wanted to go higher, we would have to get a bigger bag. So I ordered a fifty by fifty bag that would inflate to seven feet high. When the new bag arrived, we found a building with an old-style fire escape on the exterior. This would allow us to gradually increase our height to ninety feet. It worked beautifully, and we didn't get the air knocked out of us. That's the way they do it today.

Later, younger and braver stuntmen than me wanted to go higher, so they ordered bigger bags, perfected their high falls, and took it to another level. When I directed *Hooper,* I had a stuntman fall 250 feet from a helicopter into an air bag, a world record high fall. I was glad to be the director. That high fall might have been — no, it definitely was — a little much for ol' Hal.

Most people are afraid of heights, so if I was going to do a high fall off a building or a rock, I would always try to get the assistant director in the position where I would fall from because he was the person who negotiated the fee. I would walk him to the edge and ask if he wanted me to fall backward or forward, demonstrating the move of getting hit by gunfire. I could tell by how close he got to the edge how much heights affected him.

It always looks higher from the top looking down than from the bottom looking up. Let's say you're six feet tall, looking up. You've already subtracted six feet from the top. Looking down, you're adding six feet. There was a big difference with him on top looking down, and it was the perfect time to negotiate my fee for the stunt. The farther from the edge he stood, showing his fear of heights, the more you could ask for.

Remember I mentioned the air ram? In days past, if you wanted to blow a man up on a battlefield, you'd plant an explosion in the ground. When the stuntman got close to it, you'd trigger the charge and he would fling his body through the air as best he could to indicate the impact of the explosion. That's the way they always did it, but I had another idea. I went to engineer Bill Fredrick. Bill was self-taught and became my go-to guy when I came up with ideas to build new equipment. I asked for his input in creating a mechanical way to throw a man into the air and make it look like an explosion had caused it. The gadget, a square metal frame only four inches high, became known as the air ram. Easy to hide from the camera, it had a flat metal plate on top hinged on one side. On top of the plate was a contact trigger, so when you stepped on it, it would set off the explosion and activate an air valve that kicked the plate up and threw the stuntman through the air. The more air pressure you used, the higher and farther it would fling you.

If you want to hit a man with a car, it's easy. You just put the air ram on the pavement and let man and car come together. Just before the car hits the man, he steps on the air ram and goes over the hood or completely over the car. It really looks as if the car has hit him.

I don't know if I was smart or just trying to take the hurt out of stunts. Probably the latter. During my stunt career I broke fifty-six bones; I broke my back twice; I punctured a lung; I knocked out a few teeth; not to mention bruises, cuts, and multiple sprains. I was always looking for a better and safer way to do stunts and to make them more visually dramatic. And that's how they do it today.

I was always on the lookout for better equipment to get the job done. Another area where I realized there was a need for improvement was the camera car, the vehicle used to shoot exterior footage when doing chase scenes, be it cars, motorcycles, horses, or anything else that moves, even a person running.

A camera car in those days was a pickup truck with the bed removed and the frame covered with flat diamond-plate metal with pipe railings to mount the lights. It had a small, noisy generator to power the lights, but the noise from the generator prevented the soundman from recording anything. They were Stone Age design, but if you wanted to do a chase, it was all the industry had.

The second piece of equipment used for exterior shots was a crane, a vehicle with a large arm on which the camera was mounted, to allow the director to start the camera at ground level and rise about forty feet for a vista shot. The arm would swing about 350 degrees, but not completely around.

The third piece of exterior equipment needed was the truck-mounted generator. Its electric cables had to be unhooked, wrapped, and stowed each time you moved to a different location. The generator also had to be far enough away from camera that the noise wouldn't interfere with the sound recording, and that meant laying out lots of cable. This took time, but again, it was all the industry had.

In all, exterior shooting required renting three vehicles and paying a driver for each. Wouldn't it be nicer, easier, and cheaper to put all those units into one? Thus the Shotmaker was born.

The Shotmaker was a vehicle with an arm designed to fold up and disappear when not in use. It could be rotated continuously, giving the director more creativity to move the camera. Cameras could be mounted anywhere on the vehicle. The camera platform on the front of the Shotmaker started at ground level and rose to thirteen feet, a function it could perform during a chase scene. The Shotmaker had a generator that could be used when noise wasn't a factor, or it could be used to charge the gigantic electric battery pack that powered the lights noise free, so there was no problem recording sound. Other cranes had to have heavy board tracks laid down to keep the camera from vibrating during moving shots. They could only travel at walking speed and about a hundred feet at a time. The Shotmaker had so many sensors that all vibrations were eliminated, and it had no limitations on distance or speed.

The Shotmaker was in a class by itself. It was so state of the art, we were awarded an Emmy as well as an Academy Award.

10

Busier Than a One-legged Man in an Ass-kicking Contest

People outside the movie business began to hear about my reputation as a stuntman, and that paved the way for some interesting opportunities. One day while I was in a production meeting at Paramount, my answering service put through a call from the Allstate Insurance Company. The man on the phone told me the Eaton Corporation had developed an air-bag safety device for cars, and Allstate was pushing to make the air bags mandatory. They had done numerous tests with dummies but felt that one with a live passenger would be more impressive. Basically, they wanted someone to drive a car 25 mph into a concrete barrier, which is equivalent to a 50-mph head-on collision into a parked car.

The man asked me what I thought about doing the air-bag test. I told him my only concern, if the air bag didn't work, was finding a doctor who could remove a steering wheel from my mouth. He didn't think that was funny, so I got down to business. I asked what they were willing to pay for a breathing dummy; he said he was open to suggestions. I told him I'd get back to him in a few minutes; I needed to think it over.

After I hung up, I took a survey of the room. There were some negative thoughts, but one guy who was thinking positively said I should do it and charge them a hunk of money. I asked what he thought a hunk was. He said, "Ask for twenty-five thousand." Without hesitation I said, "If I can get that much, I'll do it." I called the Allstate man back and quoted him my price. He said he'd get back to me. I finished my meeting, went home, and told my girlfriend, Lada Edmund, the story. I added that she shouldn't worry that I'd asked for so much money, because I was sure they'd get some other dummy to do it for less. Lada was an actress and a professional dancer, and she was in some kind of shape. She was always bugging me to let her do stunts, but I kept putting her off. After all, you can get hurt doing stunts.

At work the next day, my answering service called with All-state on the line. They had decided to move forward with the project for twenty-five grand. He wanted to know whether next week would be okay, and he had another question. They wanted a second man weighing about 110 pounds to ride in the passenger seat. Did I know anyone they could contact? I was thinking, okay, Lada wants to do stunts. This is dangerous, but the payoff is so good that I think it's worth the risk. I said, "You don't want a small man, you want a lady." He agreed that was better. I asked the same price for her, and we had a deal. I told him to book the second plane ticket in the name of Lada Edmund and that we would see him next week.

At the testing grounds in Detroit, Lada and I were shown films of dummies being thrown into air bags at various speeds. If they were trying to build up our confidence in the air bag, they weren't succeeding. All I wanted to know was how far it was to the nearest hospital or at least the nearest chiropractor. Because they wanted us to hit the wall at exactly 25 miles per hour, they made the speedometer extra large and mounted it on top of the dashboard so I could read it easily. Then they showed us the con-crete barrier. It was big; for sure it wasn't going to budge. That night Lada and I had a couple of drinks and dinner and waited for tomorrow.

Tomorrow came, and so did snow. When we arrived, things were ready. They must have had fifteen cameras. Clearly, they didn't want to miss anything. After a few minutes they asked whether we were ready. I looked at Lada, and she said, "Let's go." We put on our safety belts. The engineer checked them and signaled okay. We heard someone holler, "Roll the cameras." I looked at Lada, who took her glasses off. I told her that wasn't fair; without her glasses she couldn't see the wall coming at us. Someone yelled "Action." She said, "Okay, chauffeur, drive."

As I hit the gas, the wheels started to spin on the ice and snow. I got concerned. The speedometer needle was jumping from 10 miles per hour to 50 and back again. I was trying to make it reach 25 and settle, but it wasn't working. I nursed the car along, trying to gain as much speed as possible. I sure didn't want it to be under 25, because then I'd have to do it again. Finally I said, "Here goes" and mashed the pedal to the floor.

Here came the barrier. *Crash!* It was over in a heartbeat.

Later, when we looked at it in slow motion, all kinds of things had happened. From a side angle, you could see both of our bodies thrust forward, then the air bags deployed and our faces were buried in them. Our combined weight rebounding off the air bags caused us to break the front seat mountings, which forced both of us to disappear behind the back window frame. When we reappeared, you could see Lada brushing her hair back with both hands. Talk about vanity. The impact shortened the car by two feet and drove the engine back so far it was almost between us. But most important, the air bags had worked. No hospital or chiropractor was needed, and $25,000 apiece later, we were on our way home.

My stunt ability also paved the way for work in a number of commercials. In one of my first jobs, I was cast as a cat burglar for

Allstate homeowner's insurance. The director apparently thought I looked like a thief. We were shooting on a high-rise balcony, fifteen floors up, with the camera looking out over Los Angeles. The director had me stand out of frame, and when he called "Action," I would jump into frame, look around, and then enter the apartment through sliding doors. I suggested to the director that it would be more exciting if I swung into frame from the floor above. It would also be much more believable that I was a cat burglar. He was excited by the idea but concerned about my safety. I told him if they could get permission from the people above, I would do a demonstration for him.

Permission was granted. I took a three-foot length of rope upstairs, tied the rope to the bottom of the railing, and climbed over. I jumped away from the balcony holding on to the rope, which swung me back toward the building and right onto the balcony where the crew was standing. The director went crazy and set up the camera for the shoot. I did it two more times, and that was a wrap.

The company that shot the spot produced all kinds of commercials. They even hired me for some funny situations that weren't stunt oriented. One time I was picking up a grandma at a country railroad station in a buckboard pulled by a team of horses. As I put her belongings in the buckboard, a roll of toilet tissue fell out, and she did a pitch about how good the toilet paper was. Another time I was the Pillsbury Doughboy, cutting wheat with a hand scythe. I also did a Spam commercial in a canoe with a kid who was supposed to be my son. That one ran for five years. I did six commercials promoting car air bags. At one point, I had ten class-A (prime-time) commercials on the air.

Once I went on an interview for a Kellogg's cereal commercial. The requirements were this: in a cornfield, ride up on a galloping horse while popping a sixteen-foot target whip overhead, come to a complete stop, rear the horse, and with whip in hand slice through an ear of corn positioned twelve feet in front of the horse. I looked around the room at my competition and knew there wasn't a cowboy in the bunch. I waited my turn and then went in for the interview.

"Can you ride a horse?"

"Yes."

"Can you rear a horse?"

"Yes."

"Can you use a sixteen-foot whip?"

"Yes."

"Thank you, Mr. Needham. We'll get back to you tomorrow."

As I was dismissed, I asked whether they believed I could do everything required. "Why wouldn't we?" they replied. I responded, "Because after looking around this office, not one of you, or anyone I've seen come in here so far, can do any of those three things."

I didn't stop there. "I'm going to save you a lot of time and money," I continued. "I own two hundred fifty head of horses, including two of the best rearing horses in the movie industry, so here's what I'll do. When you've narrowed down your talent choices, bring your top five out to my barn, and we'll see what they can do."

The next day the executives and the talent arrived in two vans. The horses were ready, along with two sixteen-foot target whips, which I supplied. Using whips takes a *lot* of practice. The lead exec said, "Okay, show us what you can do." I said, "No. I'm last." So they chose one of the "cowboys," and I handed him the horse's reins and a whip. The executives asked him to come riding straight toward them, popping the whip above his head. When they told him to "Come on," he screamed "Yahoo!" to the horse — which instantly broke into a runaway gallop. He dropped the whip and grabbed the saddle horn, but as the horse made a sharp left turn into the barn, he still fell off. Each cowboy was worse than the last, and none of them even wanted to try to rear the horse.

Finally it was my turn. I rode away from the executives to my starting point at a slow gallop, popping the whip above my head. As I turned for my run, I reared the horse and popped the whip, and then charged full bore. I slid the horse to a stop and reared again, this time popping the whip a foot from the executives. I stepped off the horse and said, "Let me know."

Needless to say, I got the job. The day of the shoot, dressed in a black Zorro-style costume with a cape and mask, I hit my mark, sliced the ear of corn in half, and got it on the first take. It was so good, not only did Alamo and I appear in the commercial, they also put our picture on the Kellogg's Corn Flakes box.

The Vietnam War was in full swing, and Uncle Sam needed me again—this time for my stuntman skills. The air force was looking for someone to make an escape and evasion film, which would show pilots what to do in the event they were shot down. I thought I'd be a good candidate and went to the USAF office in a building on Lookout Mountain, near Universal. I was hired on the spot, partly because it was a very physical job, and also because the director thought I looked like a colonel.

I was flown to Clark Air Base in the Philippines. In the film I would play a colonel who was shot down, captured, and interrogated. While being transferred by the enemy guards to a POW compound, the guards and I would come under attack by U.S. fighter planes, which gave me a chance to escape and be rescued. Colonel Sloan, the officer in charge of the shoot, drove me to and from the location every day in a military jeep. I sat in the back, Sloan drove, and the director rode shotgun.

On location I met a tribe of Negritos. There are hundreds of stories of how they harassed the Japanese during World War II. One legend claimed they could sneak up on a Japanese soldier on guard duty and mark the heel of his boot without the guard knowing anyone was nearby. Another said they could slip into Japanese barracks and slit the throat of every other man as they slept without being caught. I guess you could say they were pretty stealthy.

The air force hired the Negritos to train the U.S. pilots how to avoid being captured. Here's how it worked. The air force would gather all the Negrito men in the village so they couldn't see where in the jungle the pilots were being dropped off. They had to evade capture by the Negritos all night and radio to a pick-up chopper the next morning to complete their training. The air force believed that if the pilots could evade the Negritos, they could evade anyone, as 70 percent of the pilots were caught, sometimes more than once. The pilots claimed they would be camouflaged, sitting by a tree, when a hand tapped them on the shoulder and a voice would say "Chit." A chit was a token issued to pilots, who in turn gave them to the Negrito that found them in the jungle. It was their pay, redeemable at the base PX.

Being a country boy, I had my doubts that these superstealthy people could catch me. I told the sergeant in charge my thinking, and he said try it, you'll see. I told Colonel Sloan I wanted one night to join the pilots evading the Negritos. I was wearing a flight suit and carrying the radio I used in the movie, and I knew the call sign for the choppers, so why not? He told me to forget it. So I did—but only until the next night the pilots were scheduled to evade.

I had a plan. On the way back to the base I knew we had to cross some creeks. I would jump from the jeep into the water, leaving no tracks, and hope that Sloan and the director wouldn't see or hear me as I jumped. It worked, and I was evading with the big boys.

I waded up a creek about a quarter of a mile and I spotted a big tree within a few feet of the water. It had a big multilimb crotch about ten feet off the ground, which I figured would make a good spot to spend the night. I climbed up to my new home and settled in for the night. I'd been careful not to use aftershave, perfumed soap, or anything else that might give away my position. And hard as it was, I wouldn't smoke a cigarette. I also made sure I didn't go to sleep, as I have a tendency to snore. It was a long night. I tried to move as little as possible, and when I did, I changed position slowly and quietly.

The Negritos might have raised hell with the Japanese guards, but they didn't find me. Twice during the night I heard them moving through the jungle below me. My heart was pounding so hard I thought they might hear it. I'm sure they never caught a pilot up in a tree. The only way they could have found me was to climb the tree. The crotch was so big I could lie down, making it impossible for them to see me from the ground. It was a game to me, but I played it like everything else I did in life: *to win.*

I was sure glad to see daybreak. When the chatter started on the radio, I joined in and called in a chopper to pick me up. They lowered a jungle penetrating seat. I got on and told them to take me up. When I entered the chopper, the doorman asked my name so he could mark it off the manifest of the pilots that were to be extracted. I told him I was Hal Needham. He smiled and over his headset told the pilot to call Colonel Sloan and tell him they had his man. Word came back to return to the base immediately.

When we landed, Sloan was waiting for me. As I approached he said, "I hope you had a good night's sleep." We got in the jeep and headed for the film location. Not only did I have a long night, I also had a very long day, but I never said anything about being tired. The sergeant in charge of the Negritos came up to me, shook my hand, and announced, "By God, you did it." Colonel Sloan didn't say anything to me all day.

When I was hired for the job, I had to obtain top security clearance. Once I was working, the military cut orders on me as if I were one of their own. I could eat and drink in the officers' club, which I did. One day at lunch I noticed a colonel talking to the sergeant who ran the club. The sergeant headed for my table. I knew what was coming; believe me, I didn't look like an officer or a gentleman. I had five days' growth of beard, my uniform was filthy, and my hair was long. As the sergeant approached, I handed him my orders and told him to tell the colonel I was an actor doing a film for the air force. Back he went with my orders in hand. After a brief conversation, he returned with an invitation from the colonel to join him. We introduced ourselves. His name was Colonel White, and he was the base commander. How bad can this be? I'll bet the sergeant won't question my eligibility to visit the officers' club now. Remember, I had only been a sergeant in my military career, and no colonel ever invited me to have lunch with him.

After lunch Colonel White told me he was having dinner at seven that night and said that if I didn't have other plans, he would like me to join him. I accepted, and it became a daily routine: lunch at twelve, cocktails and dinner at seven. On the third night White said he was having a little party at his house. Would I like to join in? You bet. We jumped in his car, he flipped on the red light, and we blew across the base to his house. Inside there was enough brass to sink a battleship. Some of that brass was being worn by Colonel Chuck Yeager, wing commander for the fighter wing stationed at the base and the first man to break the sound barrier. I was impressed.

As the night wore on and the drinks flowed, I caught White and Yeager together and asked if there was enough brass in the room to give authorization for me to take a ride in a jet. White smiled, turned to Yeager, and asked what flights were on the schedule that could take a hitchhiker along. Yeager said he had two planes flying to Taiwan at eight in the morning.

"There you go," White said. "Was that quick enough?"

"Sure, but there's a problem," I said. "I have to work tomorrow. Sloan is already upset about the night-evading thing, and this might push him over the edge if I don't show up." Colonel White said he would take care of Sloan and told me to check in to be fitted for a G suit at 7 a.m. sharp.

The next morning on the flight line, fitted with a G-suit, I met the young captain who would fly me. After takeoff in his F-100F fighter jet, the captain asked if I would like to take the controls. You bet I would. After a few minutes of my flying, our wingman begged the captain to take the controls away from me, as he couldn't follow all the moves I was doing. Flying a fighter jet is not simple.

As we approached Taiwan, the wingman said to enjoy the sights and left our formation. We flew to the ocean, made a right turn, and headed up the coast, dropping down to 1,000 feet. After ten minutes, my pilot told me the joyride was over and radioed for permission to land. The landing strip lay just ahead of us. We touched down, and I could immediately feel the pilot was really on the binders. Antiaircraft batteries were positioned on both sides of us. He deployed our drag chute. I thought for sure we were going to crash.

We finally stopped less than fifty yards short of the barrier. I thought, "Damn! This is more dangerous than doing stunts. These pilots have to be really good." He said, "Holy shit! I landed at the wrong airbase! This is the Chinese airstrip. Ours is ten miles farther down the island, straight ahead." "What now?" I asked.

A voice came over the radio: "Yankee jet fighter, you have landed at the wrong airstrip." My pilot responded, "I would like permission for an immediate takeoff." The tower radioed, "Permission granted." The pilot cocked the plane sideways, released the chute, and revved the jet to blow it off the runway. As we taxied for takeoff, he said, "Hang tough with me. This airstrip wasn't built for our jets — too short to land and take off from. But we're light on fuel, so I believe we'll be okay."

As he turned for takeoff, he held the brakes and firewalled the throttle. That jet was vibrating like a Harley rider. When he released the brakes, we shot forward. As we gained speed, the end of the runway was approaching fast. He pulled the nose up and we cleared the security fence by forty feet. That's when I took my first breath.

Once airborne he asked, "Hal, please don't make mention of this when we land." I agreed not to say a word. As he called for permission to land at the American air base in Taiwan, the radio reply was, "Clear to land. By the way...will this be a no-chute landing?" They had had us on radar. As we taxied over to the hangar, there must have been fifteen pilots there to greet him, and each one commented on his navigation and flying skills.

After lunch it was back to Clark. As we approached, our wing-man broke away and said, "Ring him out." Colonel White had told my pilot to show me how well the jet could climb, dive, execute high-speed turns, fly upside down, and break the sound barrier. We did all these, and I'm sure White was thinking I would get sick and everybody would have a good laugh. But I was having too much fun to get sick. When we landed, White and Yeager greeted me, along with the air force band, to present me with a Mach Busters certificate. I was really enjoying myself, until Sloan told me it was time to go back to work.

In the movie, I called in a rescue chopper, which lowered a jungle penetration seat to pick me up. As the seat reached me, I climbed on and told them to take me up. About fifteen feet off the ground, I was no longer going straight up but moving forward very fast, with tree limbs thrashing me worse than Mom ever did. I decided something was wrong and it was time to save myself and let the chopper fend for itself. I grabbed a big limb and turned loose of the seat. Now I was fifty feet up in the trees and knew the shot was no good, so we'd have to do it again. What happened? Once on the ground, I found out. The mountain altitude was so high and the weather so hot that the chopper couldn't hold its hover long enough to clear me from the trees. The only way to keep from crashing was to drop the nose and get some forward speed.

We set up to try again. The second time it worked. As I cleared the trees, the chopper started moving forward with me dangling a hundred feet below. They winched me up and in, where the doorman told me there was a very happy pilot flying the chopper. On the first attempt, when he had to nose-down to reach flying speed, he had a pretty good idea what was happening to me. He asked the doorman if I was still in my seat as it cleared the trees. Hearing "No," he thought he might have killed me. When he heard from the ground that I was okay, he'd had second thoughts about doing it again, but my willingness to give it a try convinced him to go for it.

That night the pilot and the doorman took me out on the town. The pilot said I'd saved his career when I grabbed that limb. I guess I had saved mine, too.

Back in Hollywood, I got a call from a company looking to make a film to show in General Motors car dealership showrooms, to keep customers entertained while their trade-ins were appraised and they filled out paperwork. Did I have anything in mind that could work? They wanted about fifteen minutes of film. To keep things interesting, I would need to start a big stunt, then stop before the climax, go back and show all the preparation that went into the stunt, and then come back and show the finish.

After some serious thinking, I proposed putting a 15,000-pound thrust rocket in a pickup truck to blow it across a 140-foot canal. I'd be at the wheel, and I told them it would be spectacular. They would have all the footage of the prep of building the launch and catch ramps and a talk about the fundamentals of the hydrogen peroxide rocket. They liked it.

Bill Fredrick designed the rocket-powered truck, and we started building the ramps and installing the rocket engine. Would this work? Who knew? It had never been done before. All I knew was I'd be doing about 90 mph, and if I didn't clear the other side, it'd be a wrap for Hal.

The day arrived, and word had spread through the stunt community about the rocket truck. Thirty or more stuntmen came to watch, as did three news crews. They rolled the cameras, and I approached the ramp at 55 mph. As the front wheels touched the ramp, I hit the rocket. That thing got some gone quick. The nose of the truck kept rising, and I couldn't see the ramp or the ground on the other side of the canal, just blue sky through the windshield. But no one had to tell me that I had landed. The truck hit back-end first, causing a whipping effect on the front end. It bent the truck almost in half and blew out the windshield and back window.

I was hauled away in an ambulance. It turned out I had a broken back and a compression fracture. We had telemetry on the truck, and it showed that I pulled 29 Gs when I landed. That meant I weighed more than 5,000 pounds. No wonder I had a compression fracture!

The jump made national news, and executives at Marvin Glass and Associates in Chicago saw it on TV and contacted me about making a Hal Needham Stunt Doll. What a shock it would be to people I grew up with back in the hills of Arkansas to see a Hal Needham doll. The toy company had just dumped Evel Knievel, and it wanted me to stage a spectacular PR stunt to make my name better known among young boys to launch the doll. That was all I needed to hear. Boys like macho, and they like speed.

Bill Fredrick was building a car to break the sound barrier with a land vehicle. All he needed was a little cash to finish the car. I talked to him, and he agreed I could drive the car if the toy company would supply the money to finish the car and fund the necessary runs. A deal was struck with CBS to cover the run on *CBS Sports Spectacular.* Big publicity if I broke the sound barrier. I told the toy company the plan, and they bought in.

A few months later we were at Mud Lake in Tonopah, Nevada, ready to break the sound barrier—more than 700 miles per hour. We would make a few slow runs to check out the car and, not incidentally, me. On the line for the first run, I listened as the countdown went from ten to one. I hit the throttle. Wow! What a kick this thing has. It was a hydrogen peroxide rocket that developed full power in five milliseconds. Thank God we only had the pressure up about 20 percent, because the car still hit the speed traps at over 250 mph. It scared me just a tad.

By 10 a.m. the car was back on the line, refueled and ready for run number two—at a higher pressure to feed more fuel into the catalyst, which would mean more speed. This time I was better prepared for the jolt of energy leaving the start line. I hit the pedal and was launched across the lake. Things zipped by pretty fast, and at the end of the run I was told I had been clocked at 357 mph.

I thought we were going in leaps and bounds toward our objective of 700 mph. CBS, on the other hand, was worried that it was going to take too long and announced that they wanted more speed faster or they would have to pull up stakes and leave. The toy company wasn't going to like this: no TV show, no PR. We had to do something. I walked over to Bill and told him we had to go for it. "Boost the pressure," I said. "Let's show them some real speed!"

He did and I did—to the tune of 620 mph. But I had a slight problem with the three braking parachutes onboard. One was small, to be deployed at 600 mph or faster, the second to be deployed at 400 mph, and the last at 150. I hit the switch to deploy the 600-mph chute and waited for it to open. Nothing. I then hit the 400-mph switch and waited. Nothing. I hit the 150 switch and waited. Nothing. I was closing in on the end of the dry lake much too fast.

I slammed on the foot brake, which really didn't do much good. The back wheels were only two inches wide and made of metal. The wheels were sliding, but I couldn't feel the car slowing down. I could see the greasewood and small ravines at the end of the dry lake approaching much quicker than I liked.

I ran out of dry lake traveling 350 mph and was heading cross-country through the brush and ditches. The car was extremely tough. It stayed upright and in one piece, but took out a path of greasewood 300 yards long before it stopped.

The crew saw my problem and started after me in a chase car, but I was seven miles downrange and locked inside. While I waited for my rescuers, I took inventory of my body parts and determined that I was in one piece.

Why didn't my chutes open? I later found out that someone who shall remain nameless poured battery acid on them and was trying to kill me. There was a race on for who would break the sound barrier on land first, and that person didn't want it to be me. I knew who did it, but for lack of evidence couldn't get the prosecutor to file charges. As I think about it now, it's just as well, because I might have done him some bodily harm and wound up in jail.

That was my last run at the sound barrier. The car had to be taken home and Magnafluxed for cracks or breaks. I had reached a speed of 620 mph, making me the second fastest driver in the world; the record stood at 622. I was close to the record, but so what? Close only counts in horseshoes, hand grenades, and dancing.

I didn't break the sound barrier, but it was pretty exciting footage, so CBS ran the show. The toy company made the doll and packaged it with all the necessary accessories. In the box was a Western saloon breakaway set complete with camera and lights, an air ram, and a launcher cable. The Hal Needham Stuntman Action Doll: "Tumbling, rolling, leaping, flying, the action figure that really reacts."

I always considered Universal my home studio. They probably didn't, but I did. As a young stuntman, because of my friendship with Ronnie Rondell and the fact that his father was a bigwig at Universal, I had worked on every TV series they made — at that time, I guess there were about twenty-five — plus I'd worked on a number of feature films on their lot. I had met Burt Reynolds there on *Riverboat* and later worked as stunt coordinator for Andy McLaglen on many Universal films including *The Rare Breed, One More Train to Rob,* and *Shenandoah.* The head of the studio, as well as the labor on every set, knew who I was. So I thought it was great when the studio called me for my expertise to create a live Western stunt show for the Universal Studios Hollywood theme park.

This job required some thought. You couldn't do big, spectacular stunts because you would run out of stuntmen, as they would have to perform in seven or eight shows a day. I suggested they put in a lot of comedy and some big special effects. The first idea I had was for a visual stunt: having a wall fall on a man (but not hit him). The wall was operated hydraulically, for absolute control. As it started to fall, it looked like the cowboy would be crushed to the ground, but as it landed, the wall missed him and the audience saw him standing in the open second-story window that had provided his escape. Nonchalantly, he would then walk away as though nothing had happened. It went over big with the audience.

I also built what looked like a small stage with bunting around it. Actually it was a catcher for a stuntman doing a high fall. With foot-thick pads on top of ten one-by-twelves sitting on top of sawhorses, it made a perfect catcher and at the same time offered shock and wonderment to the audience. As the stuntman hit the one-by-twelves, his weight would break four or five of them while cushioning his landing. The noise of all the boards breaking at once created the illusion that the fall had killed him and left the audience wondering how a person could walk away. Throw in a couple of guys getting shot off their horses, some funny trick riding, and clever dialogue, and the show was a hit. It's still playing today.

The Universal theme park executives liked what I did for the Western show, so they asked me to go to their Florida venue and put together a show to be performed on one of the lakes inside the park. They wanted me to create boat chases, crashes, explosions, gunfire, and any other exciting stunt I could think of— and they didn't want me to put any limit on my imagination. So I headed for Florida. I followed their instructions and let my imagination run wild. Feds chasing rumrunners during Prohibition would be a good scenario for boat chases, with lots of gunfire and explosions. To take it a step further, I added a couple of airplanes to bomb a boat, causing it to sink. This would have to be mechanically rigged to resurface for the next show, but with Universal's know-how and loads of money, that shouldn't be a problem. Besides, what a spectacular show it would be. I knew they'd think I was a genius and realize that nobody else could've come up with such a great idea.

Back in Hollywood, I sat with the head honchos and laid out the show as I envisioned it. No one said a word as I talked them through the sequences. As a matter of fact, no one said a word for five minutes after I finished. They all looked at me as if I were from outer space. I had the feeling something was wrong. Their responses started very slowly and built to a crescendo, with all ultimately agreeing that the show would bankrupt Universal. There was also a suggestion that I be committed. As you might guess, that show never came to fruition, and they never asked me to create another show. What a shame; all those creative ideas just tossed away.

11

A Few Good Men

A few good men were exactly what I was looking for when Ronnie Rondell, Glenn Wilder, and I quit the Stuntmen's Association, the only stunt organization in the movie industry, and in 1970 formed Stunts Unlimited.

About fifteen stunt coordinators had a stranglehold on the stunt business. They ran most of the features and a major portion of the TV shows being shot. They would hire each other first, and then if there were any crumbs left over, they would dole them out to their closest friends. The only way to get work was to have a talent nobody else had—or to suck up to them and politick your ass off.

Ronnie, Glenn, and I had a little meeting about this issue. We felt that between the three of us we could keep fifteen or so stuntmen working pretty good. Ronnie was coordinating three or four TV series. Glenn bounced back and forth between features and TV. I was mostly coordinating features, thanks to Andy McLaglen, who was directing one action feature after another, and working with Burt Reynolds, who was on his way to becoming the number-one box office star in the world. We decided that we would resign and let everyone know that we were going to form our own association.

At the next Stuntmen's Association meeting, Ronnie stood up

and announced, "Wilder, Needham, and I are resigning. We're going to start our own organization."

That put a hush over the floor. I stood up. "If the guys in here who've worked for me want to come along, follow us out the door," I said. With that, Ronnie, Glenn, and I walked out. Fifteen guys followed us, and Stunts Unlimited was born.

To say we created a ripple in the stunt world would be putting it mildly; we created a tsunami. Longtime friends hardly spoke to each other. Stuntmen's Association members would not hire Stunts Unlimited members, and vice versa. The Association thought—and hoped—Unlimited would fail. They could not have been more wrong.

Before Stunts Unlimited was formed, I had always been on the lookout for talent, which is one of the reasons Stunts Unlimited ultimately became successful. When Duke wanted me to coordinate *The Green Berets,* he said I want you and all your young stuntmen. He didn't know the names of any of them. Many times, when I went in to talk to producers or directors, they would tell me to bring all my regular guys, knowing that I would hire the best for the job to be done.

On *Devil's Brigade,* in addition to the usual stunts you'd expect in a war film—explosions, high falls, wrecking vehicles—I needed some specialists. The film was a true story about a special-forces unit made up of Americans and Canadians in World War II, and I had to stage a complicated sequence in a rugged mountain range near Salt Lake City. The American soldiers' mission was to wipe out a German stronghold on top of a mountain—but the tough part was that the Germans had a perfect view of the only road through the mountains that the Americans had to use. The Germans would pour artillery fire down on the American troops to stop their advance, and the Americans couldn't make a frontal infantry attack on the mountain, because the Germans had such an advantage and the terrain was too rugged. The allied unit's commanding officer thought his troops could climb a five-hundred-foot sheer cliff with full equipment and attack the Germans from the rear. For sure the Germans would not be expecting it. My job was to make it happen in a way that could be photographed. I hired stuntman Jerry Gatlin, who had been trained in the military and was an expert mountain climber. He would be the instructor for the others. Remember, he was teaching stuntmen who weren't afraid of heights and understood the basics of what he was talking about.

In real life, because of the noise factor, the soldiers couldn't drive pitons into the rock to hook their safety ropes, as any sane climber would, because the Germans would hear them—so we had to scale it as best we could, without any safety lines.

I was the boss and chose to lead the first four stuntmen up. There was an overhang five feet from the top—no way around or over it—but the overhang had a crack three inches wide. I stuck my hand into it, turned it as far as I could, and made a fist. With my fist locked in, and alternating my hands one above the other, I could reach the top. There was no room for error. I told the other stuntmen that, if and when I reached the top, I would tie off a rope for them to climb. Once up there, I saw nothing close by to tie the rope to. So I took two wraps around my body, sat down, braced my feet against two small, partially buried rocks, and signaled for the next man to come on. Gatlin, the first stuntman over the top, almost had a heart attack when he saw I was supporting all three men. He ran fifty yards, tied his rope to a tree, threw it over the edge, and told the other guys it would be safer to climb that one.

The next group up carried long ropes that they tied off and dropped down for the other troops to ascend with all their equipment. We had hired some expert local climbers as part of the cast. They thought the first guys up the mountain without safety ropes were crazy. It was straight up and dangerous.

Prior to filming the climb, the stuntmen, wearing safety lines, scoured every inch of the cliff looking for the best routes and dislodging any loose rocks that might fall and hit a climber or one of the film crew below. We had one accident while filming. A climber dropped his rifle, which hit another climber below, causing him to fall. Thank God, he wasn't too high off the ground. He was in the hospital for a few days but recovered.

All that prep paid off. The sequence enhanced the movie, which is worth a look. Surround yourself with talented people: they'll make you look good.

Talent comes in many forms. Ability is the most important element, but there are other things to look for: someone who doesn't panic in a dangerous situation, especially if you are doing a stunt with him where your life is in his hands. If a stunt goes a little off course, a person who can compensate and move it back on course can be a shot saver or a lifesaver. "Heart" in stuntman jargon means not afraid to go for it with gusto.

The stuntman term "bulldog" comes from the rodeo circuit. A cowboy jumps from a galloping horse, grabs a steer by the horns, and throws it to the ground. In stuntman jargon, a bulldog refers to any time one man leaps from a balcony, a rock, a horse, or an airplane—and hits another man. You have the jumper and the catcher, and there are two ways to do it: their way or the Needham way. Their way: the jumper goes down feet first, hits the catcher on his shoulders, and they both go to the ground. On my set, that's the wrong way. The Needham way is for the jumper to dive *head*first, hitting the catcher's shoulders to stop his upper body and allowing his feet to hit the ground first. It's spectacular; it makes the hero look superhuman, which the actors like, and it draws oohs and aaahs from the audience.

Here's where heart comes in. Say the jumper is in midair, diving headfirst, and the catcher sees the jumper's shadow coming at him. His natural instinct is to duck. This could be disastrous for the jumper, who'll end up landing headfirst. The catcher has to have heart and not flinch, even though he knows he's about to take a big hit. Ideally, the jumper should be small and the catcher big. The bigger and stronger the catcher is, the better.

There was one stuntman, Walter Wyatt, who fit the need as a catcher. He was six feet three, 250 pounds, strong as an ox, with a heart as big as a bucket. He never saw a shadow or flinched, and he made a lot of money as a catcher. You knew you could trust him when you were the jumper. I made Walter my main target whenever possible. One time we staged a brawl in a bar in the movie *The Great Race.* My job was to dive over a balcony banister and land right in the middle of the fight. When I cleared the banister, I would be sixteen to eighteen feet up. I wasn't coordinating the show, so I had no say as to which stuntmen were hired. The coordinator chose ten stuntmen as catchers. I knew all of them, but only trusted four to save my butt. So Walter was my primary target, and the other three were secondary targets.

When I sailed over the banister, Walter took most of my impact but all ten of them went to the floor as if they'd been knocked down by the force of my fall. The reason they all fell was when it came time to negotiate hazardous pay for the day's work, everybody who was in the group got paid the same. That's not fair, but a lot of so-called stuntmen made a pretty good living because they had a friend who would hire them. These guys knew all along that they'd never be put in a spot where they would really be in harm's way, but they'd be close enough to the action to collect hazardous pay. Of course, they didn't work for me, *ever.*

When you do a horse-to-horse bulldog, you have one horseman chasing another. When the jumper catches up to the bad guy, he jumps from his horse, grabs the other rider by the shoulders, and both go to the ground. To do it properly and safely, the jumper should land feetfirst while holding on to the other man's shoulders, to keep his head from hitting the ground. If the jumper is only concerned for his own safety, sometimes that isn't what happens. Once I got a call on a TV Western to do the stunt I just explained, only this time I was doubling the bad guy. I knew the stuntman doubling the star and had some concerns for my health, but I figured, how bad could it be? Well, I found out.

We did the stunt, and the guy grabbed me around the neck, drove me headfirst into the ground, and landed on top of me. I was out cold. As the world came back into focus, I saw his face looking down at me. He said, "Man, I'm sorry. Are you okay?" Without answering, I got up and found a chair and the nurse on the set to see if she had anything to stop the thumping in my head. Later, he came up with the excuse that his horse had ducked off as he jumped, and therefore he couldn't stop. I accepted his excuse until I saw the show. When it aired I saw clearly that his horse had never ducked off. He was worried about only one thing: his own skin. He had literally landed on my head. I never put him on my to-hire list.

Car stunts can go bad quickly, too, either for lack of speed or too much speed. In one instance, it was the former. I was to turn a car over at 60 mph. I had told the director it would roll over three or four times. Another stuntman was going to drive a car across in front of me just before I hit the turnover ramp. He and I rehearsed our speed a couple of times. I told him it was better if he was a little early rather than late; that way he wouldn't interfere with the speed I needed to be going when I hit the ramp. He agreed.

The director called "Action," and I accelerated to sixty. I looked to my left and knew right away he was late. I backed off, but I could see that he was still late. I backed off a little more and timed it so I missed the rear end of his car by only four, maybe five feet, and then I floored the gas. I knew this wasn't going to be a spectacular stunt—and it wasn't. The car tipped up on its right side and slid to a stop. I got out and walked over to the director, who asked if I was okay. I responded: "No, I'm embarrassed. I want to do it again. I'll do it for nothing, but please take the other car out of the shot." Luckily, we were shooting the left side of the car, which wasn't damaged, because only the right side was scraped from sliding on the pavement.

With no one to blame, I knew my reputation was on the line. This time had to be great. Up by camera, I saw the green flag waving to cue me. I held the pedal to the metal until the speedometer read seventy. I hit the ramp and instantly knew my reputation was going to be okay. I couldn't count how many times the car rolled, but the crew told me it was seven. The director said he was glad we did it a second time; it was worth the wait. The other driver never made Hal Needham's A-List.

Cowboys and stuntmen have a good sense of humor and hate a braggadocio's big mouth. On a job at Disney, about thirty of us were dressed as Mexican soldiers working on the TV series *Zorro*, and we had one in our group. He was new in the business and didn't hesitate to talk about what a good cowboy he was and how he could ride anything with four legs. We were going to be chasing Zorro all day long. Each man had two or three horses so he could change mounts and not have to wait for the one he'd just used to get rested. When the director set up for the first shot, in which Zorro's double would be trying to escape, with the Mexican Army giving chase some 150 yards behind, we had one guy doubling a lieutenant and another doubling a sergeant. Of course, the doubles were out front leading the chase.

We listened to Bigmouth on the bus on the way to location, and now we had to listen to him while waiting for the word to go. Finally the walkie-talkie blared out "We're rolling." Those old horses had heard that before, and they knew the race was about to happen. Horses were rearing up, spinning around, and just raising hell. Knowing the next word on the walkie-talkie would be "Action," one of the cowboys reached over and took the bridle off the horse Bigmouth was riding and said, "Let's see you ride this one." Action was called. Zorro's double led the way. A few beats later, we gave chase. We damn near had two or three wrecks, because Bigmouth had no control of his horse, which was racing to the front and jousting horses and riders on his way through. It didn't take long for him to pass the doubles for the lieutenant and sergeant; if we'd had another fifty yards, I think he'd have caught Zorro. He was hollering "Whoa!" to the horse and screaming "Coming through!" to the crew.

You're talking about one mad director. The first thing he said was to send that damn son of a bitch home. Then he asked for volunteers to step forward if they couldn't ride, promising not to fire them. Of course, nobody stepped forward. Bigmouth went home. His days in the business were numbered. He just couldn't keep his mouth shut. To tell the truth, he was a pretty good cowboy, but he had a big mouth.

Stuntman humor is different than a guy cracking a joke or dropping a one-liner, and it usually involves a little bit of payback, like the time I was driving back from motorcycle racing in the desert with Alan Gibbs, and he asked to use my lighter. I handed him my one-dollar Zippo. He tried it a few times but it wouldn't light, so he rolled down the window and threw it away. I didn't say a word. A few miles later he asked me to stop at a gas station. He went inside, got a handful of matchbooks, threw them in the glove box, and said they'd get us through the weekend. Some months later I asked if I could borrow his lighter. He handed me his solid gold, hundred-dollar Dunhill. You guessed it. The lighter didn't work, so I threw it out the window. A few beats later he said, "I'll stop at the next gas station so you can get us some matches."

Here's another example. Fifteen stuntmen and I—one being

Billy Burton—were in Tucson shooting *Dirty Dingus Magee,* starring Frank Sinatra. Burton was full of mischief. The stunt-men were practicing their driving skills on a big parking lot when I realized I'd left my wallet in the hotel. I asked Billy if I could use his car to go get it. He flipped me his keys, and I was gone. Wallet retrieved, I return to the parking lot. Did I park and give Billy his keys? Oh, no. I did 180-degree turns and spun donuts until I blew out one of the rear tires. I drove over to the group with the flat, threw Billy his keys, and thanked him for the use of his car. "Anytime," he said, and everybody went back to practicing.

When we finished, Billy went to his car and started to change the flat tire. I asked if he needed help and he said no, he could handle it.

After *Dingus Magee* wrapped, we were back home at my stables, training falling horses in a sandy riverbed. Burton asked if he could use my car to go to the barn and get a different bridle. I tossed him my keys. While they were in midair, I hoped he wouldn't remember Tucson. When he returned from the barn, he began to do circles, burnouts, and things I didn't know he—or the car—could do. You absolutely could not see the car for the dust. Billy kept blowing the horn so everybody would stay out of his way. I knew he couldn't blow out a tire on the dirt, but I was beginning to worry about the engine. You could tell he was in low gear and the pedal was on the floor. Finally he stopped and let the dust settle so he could see us. Then he pulled up, got out, and thanked me, saying the keys were in it.

Gary McClarty also had a good sense of humor. While shooting *Beau Geste,* I was getting ready to do a stunt so I handed my camera to McClarty, asking him to take a picture of me doing it. After the stunt was over, I asked if he'd gotten a good shot. Gary assured me I would love it. When I had the film developed, the first shot was of McClarty's face; he had held the camera at arm's length and hit the button. For the next shots, he had someone hold a horse's tail up while he snapped a long shot, a medium one, and a close-up. He had taken various shots of other interesting things, but not one of the stunt. When I asked why he hadn't shot the stunt, he told me he'd run out of film.

We were shooting *Little Big Man,* and Roy Clark was doubling Richard Mulligan playing Custer. Clark never bought a pack of cigarettes or a candy bar. If some guys were talking, Roy would walk up, reach into one of their shirt pockets, help himself to a cigarette, put the pack back, and join in the conversation as though that were the norm. If you were eating a candy bar, he'd reach over and break off a chunk for himself as if that's what anybody would do. One day the guys decided to get even. When they saw him coming, one unwrapped a chocolate bar. Without breaking stride, Roy broke off a big chunk and continued on his way. He made a big mistake. He didn't look at the wrapper; it was Ex-Lax. He paaaiiiiddd the price.

Boys will be boys, men will be boys, and stuntmen are no different. There were twelve of us dressed as Indians, complete with bows and arrows, working on a Western on the back lot at Universal Studios. The lot consisted of four or five Western streets, one European town, a few city streets from various eras, a giant lake with a riverboat, and hills, mountains, and country roads. After filming in the hills, the company was setting up to shoot some dialogue scenes. They told the stuntmen to get lost for a couple of hours, so we wandered over to one of the Western streets. This street had a bar, hotel, dry goods store, jail, and hardware store. It was a typical Western town. A conversation started about the best way to sneak up on a man and ambush him, and this led to a game. Call it hide and seek — or better yet, seek and shoot.

We divided up into two six-man teams. Team One, my team, disappeared two streets over and promised not to peek for ten minutes as Team Two hid. On our return, we'd seek out our opponents and shoot at each other with bows and arrows. The bows were very weak and would only shoot an arrow about twenty yards, and the arrows had rubber tips for safety. Robin Hood couldn't hit a man at twenty yards with this equipment, and if he did, it wouldn't hurt. What we hadn't thought about was getting shot at close range. Team Two had a distinct advantage; they could hide and wait. Team One had to search them out, and it was tough to be stealthy. Every time you took a step, the old floors would squeak. A little oil on the door hinges also would've helped.

I was the first to get shot. I stepped through a door of the hotel and moved toward the middle of the room. I heard a "Pssst." I turned around and saw nothing, but then a voice said, "Up here, Hal." As I looked up to the rafters, I saw an arrow on its way. I turned, took it on the back, and let out a scream of pain. The shooter was only five feet away and laughing his ass off.

Team One lost the battle 6 to 0. Each loser had a story of being ambushed and shot at close range, with a welt to prove it. But no matter—a new game was born. Thereafter it wasn't unusual to see stuntmen sneaking around the Western set or through the woods with bow and arrow in hand. There was never a doubt when someone got shot. While you might hear them beg for mercy, for sure you would hear them yelp as the arrow found its mark.

The mention of my name could start a fight among stuntmen. Once, on a TV series, I was doubling for a guest star and another stuntman was doubling the star. We were chasing a runaway stagecoach. The star's double was to transfer from his horse to the coach and start climbing up to the driver's seat, and then I would do the same. He rode as close to the side of the coach as possible, reached out and grabbed the railing on top, and pulled himself onto the coach. Then he started climbing into the driver's seat. My turn. I rode up even with the coach, but I was four to five feet away. I jumped from my horse and laid out flat in the air, barely able to reach the top railing. My feet came down in the coach window. A moment later I was sitting in the driver's seat with the other double. We turned the coach around and went back to camera.

The star was upset. His double had made him look clumsy and scared, whereas I had made my actor look agile and brave. Two days later I got a call for the same show, this time to double the star. They just wanted a shot of him doing his transfer, because they planned to use the shot I had done doubling the other actor days earlier.

You have to make the star look good, or he'll get some guy who just likes climbing trees, like me on *Have Gun—Will Travel*. By the way, the other coach-jumping stuntman didn't make my A, B, or C list for future hiring. He would never be one of "Hal's Guys."

Besides heart and talent, practice helps. You can't practice being a stuntman in front of the camera. If I've been working on a movie doing car stunts for a month and am called to do a horse fall the next day, even though I've done hundreds of horse falls, I'll select the horse I'm going to use and head for the sandy riverbed to practice. Let's say the horse hasn't worked for three months. He also needs to get his mind on the job at hand. Almost every time, guaranteed, the first fall won't be perfect. Sometimes it's my fault, and sometimes the horse isn't performing up to par. I always wanted to be perfect on the first attempt every time I was in front of the camera.

Even after I became a stunt coordinator and second-unit director, my normal days consisted of working on several movies as well as TV shows. I had more jobs than I could handle.

Stuntman Buzz Henry and I once worked five days and five nights without going home. At night we were on the Universal back lot doing a movie called *Four for Texas,* starring Frank Sinatra and Charles Bronson. I doubled Bronson; Buzz doubled Sinatra. The company shot until the sun came up. Then Buzz and I jumped in the car and headed for MGM. I drove and Buzz slept. At MGM we were working on the Glenn Ford comedy Western *Advance to the Rear,* Buzz doubled Ford, and I was a utility stuntman. As the sun set, we headed back to Universal. This time Buzz drove and I slept. Anytime the company called lunch, Buzz and I would find a place to sleep and have one of the stuntmen bring us a sandwich. We did this for a week. Boy, did my bed feel good when I finally got home.

Because of my versatility, I became the highest-paid stuntman in the world. My reputation grew to the point that when a studio called, they knew that no matter what the stunt was—cars, horses, high falls, fire, and more—*I never turned down a stunt.* The jobs I couldn't fit into my schedule I gave to the young stuntmen I had trained.

But the thing that really pushed me over the top was that I got the job done on the first attempt. Let's say you're the production manager, and you need a stuntman to roll a car. You call three or four stuntmen and get a quote from each one. Let's say the first three ask for $3,000 to do the stunt. Now the production manager calls me, and I ask for $5,000. You would think the production manager would take the low bid, but consider this: The car might cost $25,000. If the low bidder doesn't get the stunt done the first time and wrecks the car—not to mention the time it will take to set the shot up for take two—this could be far more expensive. The production manager's decision on whom to hire becomes even easier because he knows I have a reputation for getting the shot on the first attempt.

Stunts Unlimited looked for new talent and trained them. Within two years it had a roster of twenty-five members, and every one of them was working on movies and TV shows. The animosity between the Stuntmen's Association and Stunts Unlimited was fierce during the early years. Jerry Gatlin was one stuntman I admired who didn't come with us. I had used him all the time and we had been good friends, but he and I never talked after the split. We were the first stunt group to break away, and the first to include women and minorities as members. Now there are a number of stunt organizations for both men and women, and no one has the hammer as to who works and who doesn't.

Throughout my career I trained hard and worked to build a reputation as a great stunt coordinator, but to be truthful, it was the men I hired who made my reputation. Most coordinators wouldn't hire a stuntman who was more talented than they were because they feared comparison. I, on the other hand, wanted to surround myself with the best talent I could hire. It always worked in my favor.

The stuntmen I have trained have all moved up the ladder to become great stuntmen, stunt coordinators, second-unit directors, and even directors. I believe I had the ability to get more out of a stuntman than anyone in the business — not because I would challenge them, but because they knew I wouldn't settle for second best.

12

The *McQ* Cannon

One thing you shouldn't do if you don't know explosives is try to rig your own. We were in Seattle shooting *McQ*, starring John Wayne. Ronnie Rondell was the coordinator, and I was working as one of the stunt guys. He was talking to us about an upcoming stunt, and he didn't know exactly how to do it. Duke was in a car, being chased down the beach by heavies. As they exchange gunfire, Duke's MAC-10 submachine gun bullets riddle the heavies' car and driver, causing the car to turn over. Problem: how do you flip a car on a flat beach? Normally you'd use a ramp to drive one side of the car up, cut the wheels sharply, and presto, over goes the car. But you need bushes, another car, or something else to hide the ramp. We had nothing but a flat, sandy beach. Rondell told us to think about it.

A couple of days later I explained my plan to Rondell. He listened and said it sounded pretty complicated. We didn't know if it would work or not. He thought it was too risky to try for the first time on the set, so I decided to call home and have McClarty and some of the guys rig it for me. I gave McClarty the following instructions: Pick up an old wreck of a car; it didn't have to run, just steer, because we could push it up to speed with another car. Build a small cannon, and make sure the cannon walls were at least an inch thick, so it wouldn't become shrapnel when I set off the explosion. Cut a hole in the back floorboard of the car, put the cannon in the hole with the muzzle pointed down, three inches from the ground, and weld it to the frame. Make sure it's welded good. Find three pieces of telephone pole three feet long that will fit inside the cannon. Bring some baling wire, a battery, a push button to fire the bomb, and five four-ounce black-powder bombs.

The following Saturday afternoon, I flew home and called McClarty. Everything was A-OK for a test the next morning. On Sunday five of us, with the test vehicle in tow, made our way to a dry lake outside L.A. There, we discussed how many bombs it might take to turn the car over. I told them that first of all, we should put in one bomb and see what happens.

So we put one bomb in the cannon, slid a phone pole up against it, and then put a piece of baling wire under the pole to hold it in place. We used a long extension cord for the push button to fire the bomb, stood back a long way, and hit it. To everybody's surprise, the car lifted only about six inches off the ground. Now we really had a problem. One bomb damn sure wasn't enough. If we used two and it didn't work, then we'd only have two left. There were five of us with maybe a total of ten years' education among us, but we came to a decision: put all four bombs in. Little did we know that powder squares itself.

In went the four bombs, a phone pole, and a hunk of wire to hold it in place. One more thing you should know. When you blow the bomb that forces the phone pole down, it only travels three inches to the ground—and then the car becomes the projectile.

I strapped myself in the beat-up car with a rotten lap belt. There was no roll cage in the car. I told the boys to push me 55 mph, blow the horn, and back off. Then I would cut the wheels sharply, throwing the car into a broadside, and hit the button. McClarty was driving the push car. I signaled to go, and we

The view through my car windshield as I evade a Russian tank during the invasion of Prague. Real war, not movie war. During the filming of *The Bridge at Remagen*. *(Personal collection)*

Doubling Burt Reynolds and doing a car jump to a moving barge...barely. In *White Lightning*. *(Personal collection)*

High fall from a crow's nest to the boat deck in *Lucky Lady*. No landing
pads.

This one almost cost me my life. Doubling Burt Reynolds in *Gator*.

A world-record boat
jump. Doubling Burt
Reynolds in *Gator*.

A record-setting rocket-truck jump over a canal for a GM commercial. My first broken back. *(Personal collection)*

The front of the toy's box—"Hal Needham the Stuntman" action doll.

(Personal collection)

Mike Henry and I enjoy a moment with "The Great One" Jackie Gleason in *Smokey and the Bandit.* *(© 1977 Universal City Studios, Inc., courtesy of Universal Studios Licensing LLLP)*

Left to right: Burt Reynolds, Jerry Reed, and "Fred" the dog, who saw no humor in the joke, in *Smokey and the Bandit.* *(© 1977 Universal City Studios, Inc., courtesy of Universal Studios Licensing LLLP)*

Love at first sight. Burt Reynolds and Sally Field in *Smokey and the Bandit.* *(© 1977 Universal City Studios, Inc., courtesy of Universal Studios Licensing LLLP)*

"Hal, you said it would be fun, but it was great!" Burt and I have a good laugh on the set of *Smokey and the Bandit II*. *(© 1980 Universal Studios, courtesy of Universal Studios Licensing LLLP)*

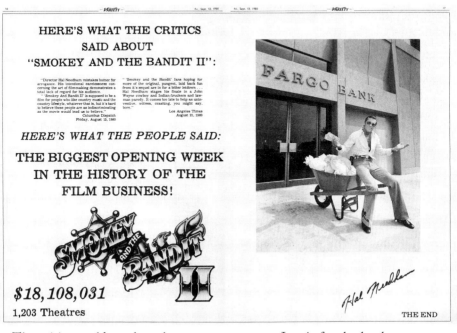

The critics could not have been more wrong as I wait for the bank to open. From *Daily Variety*. *(Copyright © 1980 Reed Business Information, a division of Reed Elsevier Inc.)*

A Happy and Prosperous New Year

Left to right: Kirk Douglas, Ann-Margret, and future governor of California Arnold Schwarzenegger in *The Villain.*

Relaxing with the Chairman of the Board, Frank Sinatra. *(Personal collection)*

I cast myself in the movie because I have a great eye for talent! Posing with Dom DeLuise and Burt Reynolds in *The Cannonball Run.*

"What's your agent's number?" On the set with Sammy Davis, Jr., in *The Cannonball Run*. *(© 1993 STAR TV Filmed Entertainment [HK] Limited & STAR TV Filmed Entertainment Limited. All rights reserved.)*

"I'm telling you, the cops will never believe you two are priests!" Left to right: Burt Reynolds, Dean Martin, and Sammy Davis, Jr., in *The Cannonball Run*. *(© 1993 STAR TV Filmed Entertainment [HK] Limited & STAR TV Filmed Entertainment Limited. All rights reserved.)*

Donating the Budweiser Rocket Car to the Smithsonian's National Air and Space Museum in Washington, D.C. *(Personal collection)*

Celebrating with driver Harry Gant after one of our many NASCAR Skoal-Bandit team wins. *(Photo by David Chobat. Courtesy of Historical Racing Moments LLC.)*

The famous "33" Skoal-Bandit race car. *(Photo by David Chobat. Courtesy of Historical Racing Moments LLC.)*

The Shotmaker, the Academy Award–winning camera car. *(Personal collection)*

started picking up speed. Soon I felt McClarty back off. The horn blew. I cut the car to the left and it went into a broadslide. I hit the button.

The explosion blew the car thirty feet into the air. When I opened my eyes in midflight, I was upside down and going backward. I knew this wasn't going as planned, and at any moment there was going to be one helluva wreck. The car landed on its roof, which caved in, jamming the doors. But the big problem was that I wasn't breathing. I saw that the back window had blown out from the impact, so I made my way to it. Gasping for air, I crawled out from under the trunk of the pancaked car. At that moment the boys working with me on the stunt came skidding to a stop. I heard one say, "Holy shit, he's alive!"

They rushed to me and laid me down flat. Still not breathing, I pointed to my mouth, and McClarty gave me mouth-to-mouth. With his help and my gasping, I was slowly sucking air into my lungs. Someone pulled up in his pickup and said, "Put him in here and I'll take him to the hospital." Another stuntman got in to hold me.

We made it in record time. Every white line on the highway felt as if we were running over a curb. McClarty went into the hospital and came out with a gurney and an attendant. We bypassed the emergency room and went straight to X-ray. I bet the technician didn't weigh ninety pounds, but she rolled me around like a sack of potatoes. I thought she was trying to finish the job of killing me. I told her to stop. "Don't move me again," I said. "If you need me moved, go out and get those stuntmen and let them do it." She said that wasn't allowed. I said, "Get the gurney and bring the ambulance back. I'm going to another hospital."

She followed my first request and brought in the stuntmen to help her move me. I didn't know at the time that my back as well as six ribs were broken, and they were stabbing my insides. I just knew I was hurting.

In my hospital room the doc told me I had a cracked vertebra, six broken ribs, and a punctured lung. I counted the missing teeth myself: three. He added that of course, I would be their guest for a while. He slipped out. John Wayne would have to finish the movie without me.

The guys in the push vehicle said I'd gone so high they'd almost lost sight of me through the windshield. McClarty said I was a bad kisser, and to never ask him to do that again. I told them the next one who made me laugh would be out of work for a long time. It hurts to laugh with broken ribs.

I asked McClarty how scary it looked. Without hesitation, he said it was a 10. I asked if it were a 5, would he do it? He said that if he had a car with a roll cage and he was wearing a five-point safety harness and a helmet, he would give it a shot. I said, "Good. Now get your butt on a plane to Seattle and tell Rondell you're my replacement." I suggested he use a lot less powder than I had. Here was the result. They used eight ounces of black powder. When McClarty rolled the car on the beach, he was doing 55 mph, and he flipped the car twelve times. He was unhurt; it just rang his bell for a few minutes. It's worth renting *McQ* to judge for yourself.

In the hospital the next morning, I was so damn sore I could hardly breathe, but Mother Nature was calling. So I rang my nurse call button and in walked a twenty-five-year-old beauty. She asked what the problem was, and I explained that nature was calling. She asked, "One or two?" I replied, "Two." She said she would get a pan. I said, "No chance with the pan thing; just help me get to the bathroom." She shook her head no. We were at a stalemate. As she walked to the door, she turned and over her shoulder said, "When you're ready for the pan, just ring."

An hour passed and things were getting serious. Then the doc walked in to discuss my physical situation. My vertebra was cracked, but he thought it would heal. Ribs can't be set or helped;

I'd just have to tough it out. "Now, your punctured lung is full of blood and fluid, and has to be drained, otherwise you might get pneumonia, and that could be very serious," he informed me.

I told him with all those broken ribs I could hardly breathe. If I started coughing, I wasn't sure I could stand the pain. He said, "Exactly." So I said, "Let's get to it and drain the lung." He warned me what was going to happen. "I am going to give you enough morphine that you'll think you can fly," he said. "At that point, we're going to stand you against the wall so all the fluid will drain to the bottom of your lung. That's the only way we can do it."

"Doc, you got a deal," I said. While I'm up, I thought, I'll go to the bathroom. No way some pretty nurse is going to be cleaning me after I'd used a pan; I'd show her.

The doc loaded me up with morphine, and I did think that maybe I could fly. At least I wasn't hurting. I thought, now's the time, and I hit the call button. The doc, the pretty nurse, and another nurse entered. The second nurse was going to help me sit up on the side of the bed. She put her arm under my back and between us, we were making progress until her foot slipped and she dropped me. My necessity to go *to* the bathroom ended at that moment.

Embarrassed, I got up on my own. The nurse and doctor stood me against the wall; and the doc stuck a needle between my ribs into my lung. You talk about pain! Not even morphine could kill this pain. The needle was hooked to a vacuum bottle, and in a short time it was over. Now the nurse started cleaning me up. I don't know if it was embarrassment or the morphine, but I looked down at the pretty nurse and said, "I suppose when this is all over, a date would be out of the question." She laughed, but no date. I was a bachelor at this time, so I had no use for all the flowers sent to me and gave them to the nurses. Duke sent a stagecoach and six horses with a flower arrangement. You know who got that one: the pretty nurse.

After I had been in the hospital for eleven days, I was able to walk the halls, but I must admit that I was moving very slowly. I was all humped over like the Hunchback of Notre Dame, because my ribs had not quite found their connecting points, and they let me know when I tried to stand up straight. So rather than arguing the point, I just walked around all humped over. I had to push one of those three-wheeled poles that are used to hold intravenous bottles. Nobody knew it, but I was sneaking out to have a smoke.

In the middle of all this my answering service called and said that Bob Rosen, my old pal from *Have Gun — Will Travel* and *Little Big Man,* was on the line. I thought, how nice, Bob's going to tell me how sorry he is that I'm hurt and wish me well. I said, "Hello, Bob. What's happening, son?" He answered that he was down in Texas producing a movie called *Together Brothers* and had a fight scene to do with a group of kids. He really needed me to come down and show them how to throw punches and set up the fight. "Are you busy?" he added. I told him I was just lying around, resting up. I knew he had no idea I was in the hospital. I asked him to tell me again what I would have to do and when he needed me. He repeated his story and said that he would like me to come in on Sunday. I thought, today is Thursday. I'll tell the doctor I'm checking out on Saturday and leave Sunday. So I told Bob he had a deal.

On Friday I told the doctor I was checking out on Saturday and asked him to get my bill together. He was shocked and came up with a whole bunch of reasons why I shouldn't do that. I told him he was probably right, but I had promised a friend I would see him Sunday in Texas. He said he might have to drain my lung again. I said in that case, he'd better do it Saturday morning, because I was leaving town Sunday. The doctor told me the studio's insurance company would pay the bill, and he gave me the name of a hospital and a doctor in Texas that I should check in with as soon as possible.

I called my ex, Arlene, and asked her to pick me up. Saturday afternoon she dropped me off at Burt Reynolds's house, where I was living. As I walked in all humped over, I saw that Burt was having a business meeting. I excused myself, saying I wanted to lie down for a while. Burt, who never misses a chance to throw in a funny line, told me if I ever intended to amount to anything, I'd have to straighten up. Even knowing how much those broken ribs were going to hurt, I couldn't keep from laughing. I thanked him with a middle-finger salute and went upstairs.

I had a 7:30 flight the next morning, and knew the day would be tough. I decided to pack that night and call a cab to pick me up at 5:30. I had a fold-over bag that I packed and rolled to the top of the stairs. I was pretty sure I wouldn't have a problem waking up. Most likely I wouldn't get much sleep, but I set an alarm clock and called my service and left word for a wake-up call, just to be sure.

I was right on both counts. I didn't sleep but a couple of hours, and was awake long before the alarm was set to go off. I turned it off and called my service to say I was up. I didn't want them to call the house and wake Burt. Taking a shower and shaving were no easy tasks.

When I was ready to leave, I looked at the bag sitting at the top of the stairs and realized there was no way I could carry it down. I took care of that problem by kicking it and watching it tumble down, hoping my can of shaving soap wouldn't spray all over my clothes. My shaving lotion was in a glass bottle—good chance it would break. Do what you have to do. When the taxi arrived, I asked the driver to carry the bag to the cab.

I checked in at the airport only to find out the electric carts weren't running yet. I knew it was a long way to the gate. With no other choice, I started walking very slowly. I stopped about every fifty yards, leaned against the wall, and mustered up enough energy and determination to continue. At one stop a young soldier who just happened to be a paratrooper from my old outfit asked if I was okay. I told him my problem, and he insisted on helping me. He put one of my arms over his shoulder, grabbed my belt in the back, and said, let's go. He practically carried me to the gate. There, they offered me a wheelchair to board the plane. I told them they were a little late and that I could make it on my own. Four hours sitting up straight didn't make for the best flight I ever had, so I asked the flight attendant to have a wheelchair available when we landed.

At the baggage claim, I saw my name held up by the driver sent to meet me. We worked out a plan: my bag and I would wait in front of the terminal while he pulled the car around. Obviously, Rosen had told this guy I was a stunt driver, so he wanted to prove to me that Mario Andretti had nothing on him. He zipped around a couple of corners, throwing me like a rag doll. As soon as I caught my breath and could talk, I told him to pull over and stop. I then informed him that if he didn't slow this thing down, I would get out and catch a cab. He apologized, saying he didn't know I was hurt that bad. I said, "You think I walk all humped over like this all the time?"

At the hotel check-in desk, I was met by a young production assistant. I asked where I could find Rosen; she told me that he and the director were looking at dailies, and led the way to the projection room. As I entered, I stopped to let my eyes adjust to the darkness, then found a seat.

When the lights came on, Rosen turned to see who had come in. I stood up—well, up as far as I could—and Rosen asked what was wrong with me. I told him I'd had a little accident that had broken my back and six ribs and punctured my lung. Then I opened my mouth to show him the vacancy of a couple of teeth.

He didn't quite know what to say. "You don't look like you're ready to do any stunts." "I'm not here to do any stunts," I said. "I'm here to teach and coordinate, remember?" He laughed and said it would help if I could walk.

I told him the first thing I had to do was check in at the hospital. He was concerned that the insurance company would balk knowing someone hurt was employed as a stuntman or anything else. I told him this one was on me. I hadn't come down as an employee; I'd come down to help a friend in need.

At the hospital, as the doctor looked at the X-rays I'd brought, I commented that they looked like the cloverleaf of the 101 freeway in downtown L.A. Of course, he wanted his own X-rays, which he ordered up. He told me my lungs hadn't filled with fluid, but he wanted me to check in every three or four days so he could look at them. He then said that the more I sweated, the less likely it would be that my lungs would collect fluid. Believe me, sweating in Galveston, Texas, in the summer wasn't a problem. The humidity must average 98 percent.

I went to the set every morning and worked with the kids. At first, I tried to *tell* them how to throw punches, but that didn't pan out. So I decided I needed to demonstrate the moves. Each time I threw a punch, it felt like someone was stabbing me with an ice pick. After I spent four hours on the set in the morning, Rosen would insist that I go back to the hotel and rest. Then I'd return to the set in the afternoon. In a week I was operating at about 50 percent. The kids were looking pretty good, and the doctor couldn't believe how fast I was healing.

The night the big fight was scheduled to shoot, I went to the set early. They were shooting a scene on the docks. A police car with red lights flashing was to skid to a stop, and then the actors would step out and deliver a couple of lines of dialogue. They had a real policeman driving the car and a real captain and sergeant doing the dialogue. I watched as the police car drove into the shot at 20 mph. The captain and the sergeant got out and did their lines. I was unimpressed. It didn't have any urgency to it. So I went to Rosen and suggested that I drive the car and come in with a little speed, to jazz things up. He reminded me I wasn't an employee. I told him to just get me a police shirt and hat. I didn't need any pants; the camera couldn't see my legs. Without waiting for his approval, I got in the police car and drove to a place where the company couldn't see me practice. The dock was wooden and wet, and I wanted to see how the car handled. After a couple of practice runs I returned to the set, put on the wardrobe, and was ready to shoot.

I went to my starting spot about three hundred yards down the dock and waited for the director to call "Action." I hit the gas and was approaching camera at 65 mph. I could see the captain tensing up and holding on to the door and dashboard. About a hundred feet from the camera, I threw the car into a broadside skid. The captain hollered to watch out for the camera. The sergeant braced himself as we stopped ten feet from it. All the captain and sergeant had to do was get out, and they'd be on their marks. It took them a few seconds to comprehend that everything was okay before they opened the door. Their next problem was they forgot their lines, so back we went for take two. This time they said some stuff that wasn't even close to what had been written. Take three was perfect, said the director; I thought their voices were up about three octaves. I had stopped the car all three times within six inches of my mark. Rosen pulled me aside and said I should be ashamed of myself for scaring them that way.

The captain saw no humor in the affair and had nothing to say to me. The sergeant said he had never seen anyone do anything like that with as much control as I had and wanted to know how I'd learned to drive like that. I told him, "Practice, son, practice."

Later that night we shot the fight scene, and the kids performed like pros. They were all smiles as I praised them. My job was finished. Rosen told me I was a little crazy, but that's what made me who I was. On the flight home I thought, am I crazy or dedicated? One thing for sure, I never called in sick because I had a headache.

13

Jumping Cars and Flying Boats

In the 1970s Burt Reynolds worked his way up to become the number one box office star in the world. As Burt's double, stunt coordinator, and second-unit director, I had plenty of opportunities to push the edge of the envelope.

Burt played a moonshiner in two "good ol' boy" movies, *White Lightning* and its sequel, *Gator*, which meant that he was constantly being chased by the law. *White Lightning* was a stunt coordinator's dream, because there were car chases on every other page of the script. Normally, I would ask for and get cars with big powerful engines that were especially set up for doing chase scenes. Not true on *White Lightning*. We got two cars that had just been used on a Steve McQueen movie. When I say they were used, I should really say "used up." Their suspensions were trashed. The engines were so down on horsepower you could hardly spin the tires. If I wanted to burn out from a zero stop, I had to spray the tires with WD-40.

Ask a race car driver to tell you the fastest way around a curve or corner, and he'll tell you he doesn't want the rear tires spinning and smoking. That indicates a lack of traction. But for a movie, the more spinning, smoking, and out of shape you are, the more spectacular it looks on film. On *White Lightning,* the only way I could break the back tires loose going around a curve or corner was to back up far enough and come in really fast, throw the car sideways, and stand on the gas. Then I had to try to control it with a combination of gas and steering. If you watch dirt race cars, you'll see what I was trying to do—but I was on pavement. I had four other stuntmen with me on the movie. Their cars weren't any better than mine, but personally I think we did some spectacular stunts, all things considered.

What most people don't know is that in the movies we rig cars for stunts. The rigging changes, depending on the stunt or what you need to get the job done. If you're going to roll a car or do an end-over-end, you definitely need a roll cage, which has to be built in such a way as to conceal it from the camera. If you have a lot of fast driving, spinning, and sliding, the right springs and shocks are a must, and so is air pressure in your tires. You want a tire to blow out? No problem. Special effects will mount a shape charge on the inside of the frame, aimed at the tire. Just hit the button, and you have an instant blowout.

I was doing a chase scene driving an ambulance. Whether you know it or not, they are heavy. I asked for reinforced wheels and was told by the driver captain not to worry; the wheels were strong enough. Wrong. As I slid the ambulance around a corner, the left front wheel broke off. Traveling at a high speed, the wheel crashed into the area where the caterers had set up lunch. The only thing that kept some people from being hurt was a police motorcycle parked in front. Yeah, the company bought the demolished motorcycle, and I got heavy-duty wheels the next day.

One stunt I did on *White Lightning* almost introduced me to the Grim Reaper. The script called for Burt (me) to jump a car from a riverbank to a sand barge as it was departing. I wanted to jump the car as far as I could safely. Based on experience, I figured I could jump sixty or seventy feet if I hit my ramp at 75 mph.

I asked the boat captain to do a rehearsal for me. I had one of the stuntmen standing on the rear of the barge holding the end of a rope, which had a knot tied sixty feet in. I was standing on the edge of the jump ramp next to the barge, holding on to the same part of the rope. I would signal the captain to go, and time to a second how long it took for the knot to pass through my hands. This would tell me that the barge was 60 feet from the end of my jump ramp.

On the first rehearsal I told the captain to go. He revved his engine, but the barge didn't move for thirty seconds. Then it started creeping out into the river. When the knot went through my hand, I looked at my watch; 1 minute, 50 seconds. I thought, this ain't gonna be easy to time. The captain brought the barge back to the bank, and I asked him if that was the normal speed. He said that he could do it quicker, explaining that the barge had settled in the mud of the bank. The next time, he thought if he brought it in slower, he could get away faster. I told him to do it again, and the second time it took 40 seconds.

I decided I could figure my starting position with that time, but I wanted one more rehearsal. The captain obliged and repeated, with the same time. Next I made some practice runs to determine how long I would have to wait before I started my run after I told the captain to go. There was one other problem: because of the height of my ramp, I couldn't see the barge, so I told one of my stuntmen to stand off to the side with a red flag. If the barge had trouble getting away from the bank, he would wave me off.

We were all ready with our voice commands and flags, so I took my place and called the captain on the radio. I asked if he was ready, and he said yes. I told him that when I gave the signal to go, he should firewall that throttle. He said he would. My statement to the captain almost proved fatal.

I called camera and said, "Let's do it." On the radio I heard, "Camera's rolling; it's all yours, Hal." I asked, "Are you there,

Captain?" He answered, "Yes." I wanted him to be calm, so I told him I'd count down for him to start. I counted from 10 down to 1 and said, "Go!"

Looking at the second hand on my watch, at the predetermined time, I floored the gas and headed toward the jump. The stuntman with the flag didn't make any move to stop me. I knew the barge was more than eighty feet long and that there was no way to jump over it, so I decided to really give them a show. When the speedometer hit 75, I held the gas on the floor. But as I sailed off the ramp, I could see the barge was much farther out than it was supposed to be, and there was a good possibility I wouldn't land on it. If I didn't, I was dead. The river was swift and muddy, and I would have wound up in Louisiana.

The car was slightly nose-down when it hit the end of the barge between the front bumper and the front wheels, causing the car to jump up and forward and stop abruptly, so that it was teetering on the end of the barge. I looked out the window and saw water below me. Houdini couldn't have gotten out of that car any faster than me. I went out the window, leapt onto the barge, and passed out. They hauled me off to the hospital. Luckily, nothing was seriously wrong; I was just bruised and sore.

Back at the hotel I asked the other stuntmen what had happened. It felt to me like the barge was a hundred feet out when I landed on it. They had asked the captain why he was so far from shore; he told them he normally used only about 75 percent of the throttle, but I had told him to firewall it, and that's what he'd done. It never crossed my mind that he was operating the engine at 75 percent during our rehearsals.

I should have known better. Whenever you work with local people who don't understand the jargon of the business, you often have a misunderstanding. Plus, they're always nervous and trying extra hard to do a good job, so you can't blame them. Sometimes being a show-off paid big dividends. Had I not kept the gas pedal on the floor on my approach to the jump, there's a good chance they never would have found me in that deep, muddy water.

After *White Lightning* did big box office around the country, the studio did the only logical thing and made a sequel, *Gator*. In the movie, Burt's character has just gotten out of jail, and he's living in the Georgia swamps. The opening scenes take place there. The revenuers were after Burt for moonshining, so Burt had a boat chase to do. We custom-built fifteen wooden boats designed so that when I hit them broadside with my boat, they would shatter and split in half. We destroyed all of them.

When you do a car chase, you want the best equipment you can get, but you know from the *White Lightning* story that you don't always get what you want. This time I did. Burt both directed and starred in *Gator*, which helped me get what I asked for—namely, a rocket in a boat. I introduced rocket power to the movie industry. I'd used a rocket in a pickup truck to jump a canal for a commercial, and knew that when you need unlimited power, go for a rocket.

So I mounted a 1,500-horsepower rocket on the back end of a sixteen-foot boat, and the show began. I must tell you, we never used all the power we had. When I made the jump, I set a new world record for a speedboat: 138 feet. If we'd used all the horsepower, that boat might still be flying.

One time I made a quick U-turn and hit the rocket full power. It was so strong it blew a hole in the water so deep I couldn't see the shore. Afraid I was going to be swamped, I just held the firing button down. But the water became a ramp, and the rocket shot me out of the hole and fifty or sixty feet through the air. The "feds" were positioned in wooden boats. I ran over them, swamped them, and ran circles around them. Boy, was it fun.

Later in the movie, Jerry Reed, playing the heavy, was escaping in a pickup truck when Burt jumped in the back. As the truck sped away, Burt climbed onto the running board and was fighting with Reed through the window for control of the steering wheel. Then I took over, doubling Burt. As the truck approached an embankment, it leapt into the air and started to turn over. I tried to jump clear, but my momentum was the same as the truck's, and we landed within inches of each other. In the air, I knew it was going to be close, and I knew I would come out on the losing end trying to fight a pickup. Lucky for me, as the truck turned over and hit the ground, the right front fender dug into the sand, slowing the truck just enough that my momentum carried me past it...barely.

In between *White Lightning* and *Gator,* I worked on a movie with Burt called *Lucky Lady,* which was shot in Guaymas, Mexico. This turned out to be good and bad for me: good because I had a job, bad because I spent more money than I made. First of all, I wasn't the stunt coordinator on the movie, even though Burt was one of the stars, along with Liza Minnelli and Gene Hackman. The coordinator who ran the show didn't care for me, and the feeling was mutual. If it hadn't been for the fact that Burt was starring, you can bet I wouldn't have been on the show.

I knew going in that I wouldn't get to do stunt one if Burt didn't have to be doubled, and the truth was that his character didn't have much to do that required a double. I only went to the set if Burt was going to be involved in something where he might get hurt. One day I saw on the schedule a scene where Burt and Gene Hackman were going to be standing by a truck when a gas tank exploded. I wasn't on call that day, but I decided to go to the set anyway, to see how the special effects people were going to rig it. I watched them do the rigging and asked a couple of questions. They got downright angry and asked what the hell did I know about powder. I told them I knew enough to know that too much could launch you into space. They told me not to worry and went on their way. I was not intimidated the way I'd been years earlier, on *Little Shepherd of Kingdom Come*. I'd been around the business too long, and I sure didn't want my meal ticket, Burt, to get hurt.

Burt and Gene had more power than me, so after I told them I had some doubts about how it was rigged, I suggested they ask to see a rehearsal. Burt nonchalantly walked over to director Stanley Donen and asked where he wanted him and Gene to stand during the shot. Donen gave them a spot four or five feet from the explosives. Burt asked if he could see the explosion once, just so he felt comfortable enough to concentrate on the scene without worrying about his safety. Donen couldn't say no. If he did and something happened, there would be a problem. So he called the effects man over and told him they wanted to see the explosion once before shooting the scene. The effects man looked around for me. Our eyes locked, and I smiled.

The effects man went to the truck to hook up the wires to detonate the explosion. As he finished, I told him I thought it would be a good thing if he stood where the actors would be when they filmed it, to give them confidence. He just looked at me. Then he backed away from the truck, said "Fire in the hole," and hit the button. He wasn't just whistling Dixie. The fire wasn't in the hole, it was all over the truck and the spot where Burt and Gene would have been standing. Burt said, "I believe you overdid the black powder, not to mention the gasoline. I'd like to see another rehearsal."

The next time the blast was smaller, but still too big to put actors near it. I told Burt this, but he thought it would be okay, and besides, he didn't want the effects man to think he was a wimp. They did the shot and everything worked out. Later, Burt told me it got damn hot.

Another day I went to the set just to have something to do and to eat a free lunch. The stuntmen were debating a high fall out of a crow's nest atop the mast. It seemed that Donen wanted the stuntman to use the ladder leading to the crow's nest to slow his fall, so the camera could follow him all the way to the ship's deck, about forty feet below—meaning, no landing pads. Wow. If the stuntman missed grabbing one rung, it could ruin his day. Donen also had another great idea: the man should tumble head over heels on the way down.

The stunt coordinator was waiting for a volunteer, but nobody came forward. He damn sure wasn't about to do it himself. I thought, why not? So, I stuck my hand up. "I'm not officially on call today," I said. "You must have forgotten to put my name on the call sheet, so I decided to come out and have a free lunch. But since I'm here, I'd like to volunteer, if nobody's beat me to it."

He paused, probably thinking he might get to send this big-mouth home if I got hurt or worse. He said no one had been designated to do the stunt, so if I wanted to do it, that would be okay with him. I should go to wardrobe and get ready. I got into my bad guy wardrobe and reported back to the set. When they were ready to shoot, they told me to take my position. I started climbing the rope ladder. I reached the platform I had to fall from and looked down. It looked a lot higher from up here, but I couldn't back down now. Word would have been all over Hollywood that night that Needham had turned chicken. Remember, these were not the stuntmen I usually worked with. These guys didn't like me, and I had never sent one of them a Christmas card. They would love to spread a bad story about me.

I did the stunt, and it was a little hairy. Do you think one of them came over to me to say "Nice job"? Not a chance. But screw them. I knew it was—and knew that not one of them had volunteered to do it. It was a handful, but I managed to survive unhurt, and there went the coordinator's desire to send me home.

While we were shooting *Lucky Lady*, Burt had to fly to Tucson for a press junket to promote his latest movie. The studio sent a private jet to pick him up. He knew I wouldn't be working with him out of town and neither would his makeup man, Tom. He asked if we'd like to fly to Tucson and spend the night. What a good idea.

At the hotel Burt went to his room, and Tom and I went directly to the bar. Wouldn't you know, a couple of ladies dropped by, and we struck up a conversation. After some chitchat, they asked what kind of work we did. Tom said we worked for the sanitation department and that, in fact, he drove a garbage truck. Not to be outdone, I said he had the easy part: I had to throw the garbage in the bucket, which was much harder than driving the truck.

I thought it was time to bring in the big gun. I excused myself and went to the phone. I called Burt and asked if he would make a pass through the bar, say hello, and be on his way. Burt came by our table and asked if we wanted to have dinner later. Tom and I agreed we'd meet him in the lobby, and he left. The girls were in disbelief, though they weren't really sure. He *looked* like Burt Reynolds, he *sounded* like Burt Reynolds, but why would he be talking to a couple of garbagemen?

They asked, "Who was that masked man?" We told them he was just another garbageman. One of them said, "Not likely. That was Burt Reynolds." She said Tom and I were full of it. We fessed up, and the questions began and lasted late into the evening. Burt was a good sport and always ready to help a couple of buddies in need.

During the shoot, time dragged on—and my name never appeared on the call sheet, so I had to find a way to keep myself entertained. I was staying with Burt in a fourteen-room house just one block from the hotel where the company put most of the crew. It had a nice big dining room and a great bar, which I got to know very well. While in town, I met Bob, a real estate man from Greeley, Colorado, and Juan, a really nice and rich Mexican, and they both could be "forced" to have a drink. We became the Three Amigos in the hotel bar at night and would meet for breakfast each morning, take a few hours off in the afternoon, and then meet again that night in the bar.

One morning at breakfast, Bob proposed that we fly over to Cabo San Lucas, in Baja California, for lunch. Juan thought it was a good idea, and so did I. It turned out that my new friend from Greeley had a twin-engine cabin plane. We jumped in and buckled up, and we were off to Cabo. All the nice hotels had dirt landing strips. You could call them when you were twenty minutes out, and they'd send a car to take you to the hotel. Pretty classy. We landed and got our ride, had a few Bloody Marys, a bite to eat, and then it was back to the airstrip.

On the return, Bob told us the plane was weightless. He did whatever it was about flying that made you weightless: magazines, silverware, cups, and dishes were floating around the cabin. I thought it was fun. After a few minutes Bob spotted a fishing boat. He nosed the plane over and dove at it. As he approached, he made noises like a machine gun firing. He shook the stick as if the guns were making it vibrate, and exclaiming, "I'm a kamikaze!" Oh yeah, the Bloody Marys were kicking in.

Later, flying over land, he said he wanted to show us something. He was flying the plane no more than fifteen feet above the trees. When the trees disappeared, we were diving again, this time at a village a few hundred feet below, on the beach. Bob was on the machine guns again. Surprisingly, all the people were waving at us. Bob said the first few times he'd done that, they damn sure weren't waving; they were running for cover. By then my Bloody Marys had worn off completely, but after that, I could have used another one. I thought, if this fool doesn't get us on the ground soon, I might get my name in the papers after all. We landed safely, and, of course, we met up later at the bar. After a couple of drinks, the day's events seemed very funny.

One day Bob said he had to fly to Greeley, Colorado, on business and asked if I'd like to go with him. Why not? After all, I had worked only one day, doing a high fall, and gone to the set a few times out of boredom and to have a free lunch. Bob said we'd fly back the following day. I gave Bob's phone number to Burt's makeup man just in case the company needed me.

We were off to Greeley. When we arrived—you guessed it—the first stop was Bob's favorite watering hole. We were well into our cups when his phone rang. It was Burt's makeup man calling to tell me that I was on the call sheet for the following day at 7 a.m. I told him to hold, and I explained the situation to Bob. Though Bob's speech was slurred, he said getting back was no problem. I told the makeup man, "I'll be there...I hope."

We arrived at the airport to find it closed. Not a light anywhere. It was raining, and the night was pitch-black.

"What do you think?" I asked Bob.

"No problem," he replied. "I have landing lights, and I've done this many times."

"Drunk?" I asked.

He laughed as we climbed aboard. He fired up the engines, spun around, and headed down the runway. At first it wasn't too bad, but as we gained speed the rain became blinding. I couldn't see fifty yards in front of us. Bob kept the throttles to the firewall, and eventually we lifted off. I didn't say a word for five minutes, when Bob turned to me and said, "You can talk now. The worst is over." After an hour, Bob decided to take a nap. He set the automatic pilot. I asked if I could watch the gauges while he slept, and would he show me which were the most important. He said not to worry; he'd done this many times with no problems. However, if I saw a big city coming up, I should wake him. He laid his head back and zonked out. My eyes must have looked like an owl's scouring for prey as I scanned the horizon and watched the gauges. In due time I saw the lights of a city. I shook

Bob awake and pointed. He looked forward, mumbled "Right on course," and went back to sleep.

An hour later he woke up. He went back into the cabin, got a drink of water, washed the sleep from his eyes, and returned to the pilot's seat. "We're almost there," he said. The sun was just breaking over the horizon when we touched down. We jumped in his car and made a beeline for the location. On the set they told me Burt had to throw one punch at a stuntman, and the coordinator wanted me there in case Burt couldn't do it. I couldn't believe it. He had seen Burt do fights and knew it wasn't necessary for me to be there.

I found out later that he'd known I'd gone to Greeley, and there was a possibility that I wouldn't get back in time. Then he could point that out to the company and make me look bad. It was a scary ride, but we made it. In a sad footnote, Bob was killed three years later when his plane crashed making that same flight.

Stuntmen aren't bodyguards, but most of them will keep an eye out for troublemakers who want to challenge the actor they are doubling. They also try to watch for danger on the set, like the exploding truck with Burt and Gene on *Lucky Lady*. It's strange how actors like Burt Reynolds, who play all those macho parts, attract young studs who think that if they challenge them, it makes them the baddest of the bad. Guys thirty and older seem to need a little false courage, which usually comes from a bottle, or a little encouragement from their drinking buddies.

I learned this in Arizona while shooting *Have Gun — Will Travel*. After work and before showering, a group of the crew, including Richard Boone, stopped at the bar to wet our whistles. Boone was standing at the bar as a tall, lanky, thirtyish Arizonan approached him. The guy told Boone that he'd watched one of the episodes where Paladin (Boone) had whipped five men in a bar fight, and wondered how he'd pulled off such an amazing feat. He considered himself a good scrapper, but that fight scene was even more than he could do.

Boone said it was also more than *he* could do. In fact, he admitted that he didn't do his own fighting even on film. Boone pointed toward me and said, "That young man sitting at that table does all my fighting." Stunned that his challenge had been brushed aside so casually, the Arizonan looked at me. Not to be deterred from proving his manhood, he headed for my table. He arrived and started to say something. I stood up with a beer bottle in my hand. I really wasn't worried; I had three stuntmen at my table. I told him I had heard the conversation and that I was going to do one of two things: either he could join our table and I would buy him a drink, or I would part his hair with this beer bottle. He paused, then laughed, saying, "I believe you mean that, so I think I'll have a drink."

The guy not only had a drink, he had two or three. Talk of fighting never entered the conversation; he wanted to know all about the movie business. He seemed like a nice guy. When I told him I had to shower because I had a dinner date, he asked if we came in each evening after work. He wanted to know if he could join us the next day. The following night, he was a different man. He apologized, saying he'd been out of order. He then invited the entire company out to his ranch for a barbecue the following Sunday. We accepted, and ended up going javelina hunting on his property, which was big. What a nice guy. We became friends and stayed in touch for some years.

I got pretty good at spotting troublemakers. One evening on *Lucky Lady,* I was in the lobby of the hotel waiting for my amigos and overheard a kid about twenty years old tell his girlfriend and the other couple with them that he would get Burt Reynolds's autograph "or else." They headed for the dining room, where Burt, Gene Hackman, Liza Minnelli, and the director, Stanley Donen, were having dinner. I walked up to the young man and pulled him aside. I very quietly told him it was fine to ask for an autograph, but not to get carried away in his bravado to impress his friends, because I would be right behind him. He looked at me in total shock, as if to say, "Who is this guy?" As they proceeded to the table of stars, he glanced at me over his shoulder two or three times. I just smiled and kept following them. At the table, *the* most polite young man in the world said he was sorry to interrupt their dinner, but his girlfriend would really like their autographs. Burt signed her autograph book and passed it around the table for Gene and Liza. She handed the book back to the young man, who thanked them. As he turned to leave, he glanced at me. I winked, he smiled, and he went on his merry way.

But that was nothing compared to the time I helped Burt dodge a possible murder rap during the filming of *The Man Who Loved Cat Dancing*. I was the stunt coordinator and doubling Burt in the movie, and he was starring with Sarah Miles, who was married to *A Man for All Seasons* screenwriter Robert Bolt at the time. About halfway through the shoot, Sarah's business manager, David Whiting, came to visit her on location in Gila Bend, Arizona. Burt's birthday was coming up, so I had decided to rent a hall and celebrate with some barbecue, a little music, and a lot of booze. The Sunday morning I was preparing for the party, a crew member told me that David's dead body had been found the previous night facedown near a pool of blood in Sarah Miles's room.

When Burt showed up at the hall, I repeated what I'd heard. He asked what I was going to do about the party. I thought about it for a second and answered, "I'm sure not going to invite the dead man." Right or wrong, I forged ahead with the party. Needless to say, it wasn't much of a success, as everybody stood around drinking and gossiping about whether it was suicide...or murder.

The next morning the air was full of suspicion. Sitting by the pool on a rare day off, I started hearing rumors that the sheriff was going to arrest Burt for murder — something about some supposed love triangle. I raced out to the set to tell Burt and the director, Richard Sarafian, what was happening. We met in Burt's motor home. When Burt heard an APB might be put out on him, he was in shock. Sarafian was concerned about what his star was going to do. I suggested Burt go to Utah, the film's next location, so he could buy some time to hire legal counsel and stay out of the slammer while the law attempted to extradite him to Arizona. Burt agreed. How would he get there? I told him to lie down in the back of his motor home and hang on. I knew the way to Utah.

Burt was eventually called on to testify at the coroner's inquest, and he was cleared of all suspicion. The death was ruled a suicide when the coroner's jury found that Whiting had died as a result of a drug overdose. It was reported that testimony had shown him to be a manic-depressive and a manipulator who had threatened and attempted suicide previously in an effort to keep his position with Miles and her screenwriter husband.

But Burt's luck didn't get much better. We were shooting the last scene in *Cat Dancing* in a small canyon about a hundred feet deep. All the equipment had to be carried down piece by piece by the crew on a small footpath. In the scene, Burt was under attack. He had to run through the canyon, jumping over rocks, then dive behind a log for cover. As he rolled over and turned to face the camera, it was obvious he was in great pain. The crew and I ran to him to see what was wrong. He was holding his groin and gritting his teeth in agony. For sure, shooting was over for the day. The nurse on the set said we had to get him to the hospital. That's when everybody realized we had a problem: how to get Burt out of the canyon? The company called a medevac chopper and were told it had no equipment to extract him from the canyon floor, but they could fly out to transport him to the hospital.

I looked at the path to the top of the canyon. I told Burt if he could handle the pain and hang on to me, I would carry him out. He said, "I can handle it." I had the crew throw down a rope and get some men on the other end to pull us up. With Burt on my back and the crew pulling us, we started up the path to the waiting chopper. During the time it took to get up the hill my legs were getting weaker and weaker. I could feel Burt's grip around my neck slipping. I wasn't sure either of us would make it. As we reached the top, the crew and the medic put Burt on a stretcher and into the chopper. Burt was off to the hospital; I, on the other hand, was flat on my back trying to get some air into my lungs. Later, at the hospital, I was told that Burt had a hernia.

We had one day of shooting left at that location. I overheard the company bigwigs planning how they could shoot Burt's dialogue in close-ups and use me for all the running shots. This would allow us to move on to the next location and give Burt a chance to rest. I thought it was time for me to talk to Burt. As I entered his hospital room, I asked everyone to leave so I could speak to him alone.

I told Burt what the company had planned for him, and he asked what I thought. I said it was clear from the way you hung on coming up that hill, I know you can tough it out, but why? The company has insurance to cover these kinds of things, and I've heard that a hernia could be a problem if not properly treated. I suggested a trip home to his favorite doctor. The company wasn't happy with Burt's decision and knew all too well I had advised him to go home. Back in L.A., Burt had his operation and soon returned to location to finish the movie. I'm sure one of his happiest moments on *Cat Dancing* was when they said, "That's a wrap."

14

From the Outhouse to the Penthouse

Back when my ex Arlene and I split, I was talking to Burt on the set and told him I would have to find an igloo or a teepee when I got home from location. He had offered that I could stay at his house a few weeks while I found someplace to live. I moved in and had the upstairs all to myself. I started trying to find a place to live right away, but do you know how hard it is to get an appointment to look at a place between 2 and 6 a.m.? (Understand, the bars didn't close until two, and I had to be at work by seven.) After all, you have to have your priorities in order, and basically I really liked my new home.

Burt was seeing Dinah Shore, whom I'd met half a dozen times when she visited him on the set. Now that I lived at Burt's house, I would get to know her better. Wow, what a lady! She was pleasant, caring, and a genuine southern lady. Occasionally Burt would say Dinah was having some people over on the weekend for tennis and wanted to know if I would like to join the party. Although I didn't play tennis, I knew I would meet some nice people and that with Dinah cooking, the food would be wonderful. After a short period of time, I felt like I had known Dinah all my life.

At one point I chose to have some surgery done. The doctor was going to take out a chunk of my eyelids, so I didn't look like I was always sleeping. I asked if I should arrange to have someone bring me home; he told me it wouldn't be a big deal, and a taxi would be fine. The day of the surgery I took a cab to the doctor's office. He sliced off half a pound of excess eyelid and put me in a recovery room. When he returned, he said I was free to go. I asked if his secretary would call a cab for me. He said that wouldn't be necessary. As we exited into the waiting room, there was Dinah Shore, ready to take me home—or so I thought. When I asked what she was doing here, she said Burt had told her what I was doing and she thought I'd need a chauffeur. While driving me home, she made a wrong turn. When I pointed out her mistake, she said it wasn't a mistake, and not to tell a chauffeur the best way to get to a destination. I sat quietly, wondering what she was up to, and soon realized we were going to her house.

She parked and led the way to the guesthouse. Inside I found some of my clothes, my shaving kit, and my house shoes. She informed me that I'd be staying there until I recovered, and that between her and her housekeeper, she didn't think I'd go hungry. I began to hope my eyes would get infected and I'd have to stay longer.

After the bruising and swelling had disappeared, I went back to Burt's and got ready to go back to work. I had a late call to the set that day, so I slept in. When I went downstairs I was greeted by that unmistakable voice of Dinah's. She asked if I would like some breakfast. My mouth started to water, and I accepted the offer. I went back upstairs to shower. As I was getting dressed, I could hear Dinah singing. I could also hear the guys on the set, when I told them that Dinah had cooked breakfast and sung for me.

One Sunday a couple of my stunt buddies dropped by the house for a drink on the patio. We could see a number of homes that lined the hillside above us, and one of my buddies pointed to a house and said he thought we were under surveillance. I looked up and could see some girls at the edge of their patio using a pair of field glasses. Not to be outdone, I went in and got mine. As I focused in on the girls, they were waving, so we returned the wave. Then I held up the phone and, using hand signals, flashed my number. One of the girls exited the patio, and in a minute the phone rang. It was her. After a few niceties, I asked why didn't they come down for a drink. She told me to give them a few minutes and asked for my address.

The guys all agreed this was easier than barhopping. When they arrived, everybody introduced themselves and I asked what they would like to drink. I took the order and went to the bar. I discovered there wasn't any red wine, but I knew Burt had a couple of racks of wine in another room. Not being a wine drinker, I just grabbed a couple of bottles at random. The ladies were very complimentary, and as the party continued, I retrieved two more bottles. The conversation flowed easily. Some hours later they said they had to leave. Phone numbers were exchanged, with promises of future get-togethers. My buddies had to work the next day, so they said their good-byes and departed. I cleaned up the patio and put the empty bottles on the bar; I would throw them out tomorrow.

When I woke up the next morning, Burt was home. He asked if I'd had a good time the previous night, so I told him the story. He asked if we'd run out of wine. I told him there wasn't any at the bar so I'd taken some from his wine rack, which I hoped was okay. No problem, he said, but added it would be nice if I replaced what we had drunk. He suggested I take one of the empties with me, to make sure I bought the right kind. I grabbed an empty bottle and said I'd see him later. In my journey that day to numerous liquor stores, not one had that kind of red wine. Finally one proprietor told me I should go to a certain store that he was sure would carry it.

I drove to the store, presented the empty wine bottle, and asked if they had that exact wine. The guy looked at it and said, "Of course." Would I like a bottle? I told him I needed four. He moved to the back of the store and returned with four bottles, which he rolled up in bubble wrap and put in a bag. Bubble wrap? I may be in trouble. I asked what I owed. He moved to the register, punched in some numbers, and said $1,400 and change. I felt my knees get weak, and I realized Burt must be having a big laugh right about now. I handed the man my credit card.

As I entered the house, I saw Burt and said very casually, "I'll put the wine in the rack." When I returned, Burt smiled and said, "Pretty expensive night, wasn't it? I hope you got laid." I said, "No, I didn't, but I got her phone number. It'll probably be a one-time date now that she thinks that's our normal house wine and I order her some three-dollar-a-bottle stuff." But it didn't matter. I never saw them again.

Now, I know what you're thinking: those two rascals must have had a ball, with ladies all over the place and parties every night. Well, you're wrong. I saw Burt more on the set than I did at home. He was seeing Dinah, and he wasn't home too many nights. I was seeing anybody who was willing to go out with me, and occasionally I didn't come home, either.

One evening I had a date that I convinced to spend the night. We arrived at the house around midnight. Never being one to pass a bar, we had a couple of drinks and then went upstairs. About two hours later, a voice that was *very* close by said, "Anybody home?" I guess locking the door hadn't been the primary thing on my mind when I came home. I turned on the light to discover a naked man standing in the doorway, bleeding from fourteen stab wounds. Now there were three of us standing naked, looking at one another.

He lay down on the floor, and I put a pillow under his head.

He asked for a drink. I told him he probably shouldn't have any liquid in his condition. (Besides, he might have looked like a fountain with water squirting out of him.) I told my date to call an ambulance, and then go stand at the gate to flag them down. The house was set way back from the street and hard to find. Pulling on her dress, she said, "Not on your life! *You* go wait for the ambulance. I'll stay with him."

I was so concerned about his condition that I hadn't stopped to consider how he got that way. She called the ambulance; I waited a few minutes and then headed out toward the gate. As I opened the door, I heard a loud rustling in the bushes up the hill by the driveway. This was followed by a body rolling out. A man got up and headed for me and the door. He was only a few feet away when I jumped back inside and locked it. I yelled up to my date and told her to call the police. I armed myself with liquor bottles and patrolled the window area, the only place where he could break into the house. I heard the bushes rustling outside the window and moved over to see what was happening. I saw him disappearing down the hill, toward a doctor's house just below us.

Shortly after that, the gate phone rang. I answered, and it was the police. I hit the button and went out to meet them. There were two officers, one male and one female. She asked if I'd seen anything strange.

"Are you kidding me?" I said. "There's a naked guy up in my bedroom bleeding to death."

She said to the other officer, "That's him."

I interrupted. "No, I believe the guy you want just went down that hill."

She drew her weapon and disappeared into the brush. I couldn't believe her bravery. The other officer asked me to show him where the bleeding man was. I led the way. Upstairs, the officer radioed for an ambulance. I told him I had already called one. At that moment the gate phone rang. It was the ambulance. I met them at the door and led them upstairs. By the time they loaded the bleeding man into the vehicle there must have been twenty cops there. As they talked, I started to piece things together.

This gets confusing, so I'll try to keep it as simple as I can. Two men lived in a house just up the hill from Burt's place. A guy broke in and attacked them with a knife. One of the two men, after being stabbed six times, ran naked into the street, screaming for help. A neighbor called the police; the police called an ambulance, which took him to the hospital. The police were looking for the person who did the stabbing when they rang my gate phone, unaware that the second victim was in my bedroom.

The cops started asking us questions. I offered that I had all the answers, and it would be really nice if the lady could leave and not be involved—it could get messy otherwise. He knew she was probably married. The officer asking the questions said, "What lady?" and she was gone. One of the police drove her to a taxi stand. She *was* married, and it would have caused a heap of trouble for both of us had that nice officer not understood the situation. When the story later appeared in newspapers and magazines and her friends and family talked about it, I often thought of her having to stay mum, even if the media had the story all wrong.

The officer asked me to show them where the man had rolled out of the bushes and onto our driveway. We walked outside, and I pointed to the area. The officer trained his flashlight on the bushes and found a wallet with a picture identification and a name and address. I confirmed he was the man, and the officer called in and requested a stakeout on his house.

The questions continued until sunrise. Burt and I were scheduled to go to Tennessee that day. He was at Dinah's house, so I called and told him what had happened, and suggested he head for Tennessee because the street was jammed with the media. Why should he get involved? I said I would travel later that day and promised to keep him updated. I told the officer I had to catch a plane, but I would give him a key to the house and would pick it up when I returned. I also took his number, so I could check with him to see what progress they were making catching the guy, as I didn't want to come home until they did.

I met Burt in Tennessee. He was promoting a movie, but most of our conversation was about what had happened at the house. In my hotel room that night, I got a call from the officer whom I had given the house key to. "You're safe to come home," he told me. "We got him." Then he filled me in. The doctor who lived below Burt and me had come home from a vacation about eight o'clock that morning. He went to the closet to hang up some clothes and was flat run over by a man who ran out the door. The doctor called the police and reported what had happened. He told them he had watched the man run across Sunset Boulevard and head toward Santa Monica Boulevard, which was the direction of the address found in the wallet. Sure enough, he showed up at his house. The police surrounded it and started to move in. He saw them and made a run for it, but he was greatly outnumbered, and they caught him.

The officer said the guy was wearing a watch engraved to me from Burt and a jacket with a label that read "Designed for Burt Reynolds." He told me I was a lucky sonovabitch, because the guy had obviously been in our house, and that his MO was to break into a home, lace the milk, iced tea, and juice with a sedative, wait for the occupants to go to bed, and then kill them. The officer also said there was a good chance he'd been upstairs when my date and I came in, but we had chosen to drink alcohol rather than something in the fridge. He had probably heard us and decided to go on to greener pastures. We had gone to bed around 1 a.m., and the stabbing up the hill had happened close to 2, so when he fell down the hill, he was probably coming back to our house to hide. The next morning I told Burt what had happened, and he was relieved that we didn't have to go home with that nutcase on the loose.

When I got back to Los Angeles, the police told me I would need to testify at the trial. My response was: gladly, he should be put away. They also dropped some more news on me. This guy had been doing his thing for a long time, so long that the press gave him a name: the Skid Row Slasher. That was back from when he killed skid row bums, but of late the police said they knew he was operating in Hollywood and Beverly Hills.

At the trial I got to know all the detectives pretty well. On the stand, they asked my name, rank, and serial number. As I spoke, the Slasher was taking down all the details. This concerned me. Not that I thought he could do anything to me, because I knew he was going away for a long time, but I was worried that he might have a friend who would do him a favor. I told the detectives my concern, and they agreed. I also told them they couldn't protect me, so I would have to do it myself. Again, they agreed. The next day I made arrangements to acquire a 9mm Walther PPK.

After work, the detectives drank at a bar close to my office. I would join them a couple of times a week. The moment I came in, one of them would frisk me and then report to the others that they were safe, because I was armed. I got to know these guys real well over the next three or four years. As a matter of fact, I got to know many of the LAPDs as well as the L.A. sheriff's department officers.

The shadow of the Skid Row Slasher stayed with me. There was a lady who lived across the street from us. I swear she must have worked for a tabloid, because she watched our house like a hawk. As I drove out the gate, I would wave to her. I'm sure she wasn't watching me; she was waiting to see when Burt came and went, and with whom.

One night about 1 a.m. I heard a rap on my bedroom door. This was after the Slasher, so I was armed, not with my PPK, but with a sawed-off double-barreled 12-gauge shotgun loaded with buckshot. I grabbed the gun, cocked it, and waited.

Then a voice from the porch said, "Inside! This is the LAPD. Do you hear me?" I answered, "Yes." Then he told me to turn on the light so he could show me his badge. He did, and then asked if I was armed. Again I answered, "Yes." He told me to just be calm and not shoot. He wasn't in uniform, so he was going to step out so I could see him and see that he didn't have a weapon in his hands. "Don't shoot," he said. I told him to step out and that I wasn't scared or nervous. He moved out where I could see him. I had my doubts for a second about whether he was a cop or not, because he looked like a hippie. He then said his partner was going to come out where I could see him. He looked like a dope dealer. I asked why the hell they were knocking on my door. The first guy said that a neighbor across the street had called in to report seeing a man climb our gate and run up the driveway toward the house. They were aware of the Slasher incident, and had come to see if everything was okay. They said they thought I might be armed, which was the reason for all the precautions.

"Now that I'm wide awake, would you guys like a cup of coffee?" I asked. They said sure, why not. We spent the next few hours talking about the lady across the street who'd called in, but mostly about the Skid Row Slasher.

One day Burt walked into the house and said, "Roomie, take a ride with me. I want to show you something." We drove a short distance from our Hollywood Hills home to an area in Beverly Hills called Holmby Hills. We pulled up in front of a truly beautiful mansion, the kind movie stars live in. Burt hit a remote opener and presto, the big iron gate swung open. We rolled down the driveway to the garage, with a big swimming pool to our right. Below the pool was a tennis court.

Standing by the pool, Burt pointed to the guesthouse. The front door opened onto the pool deck. "That's your new home," Burt said.

"From the cotton fields of Arkansas to a mansion in Beverly Hills. You know, Burt, I deserve this," I said.

He laughed. "Let's look at the house."

We entered through the kitchen and walked into the formal dining room. We went through the large living room, the media room, and a downstairs bedroom, then upstairs, where Burt had designed his lair. It was unbelievable. I mentioned to him that he deserved it, too. I had no problem adjusting to life in Beverly Hills. To make sure I didn't feel out of place, I went out and bought myself a Ferrari.

After we moved, I happened to be flying home from New York, and wouldn't you know, first class had five stewardesses who should have been movie stars. In casual conversation, I asked one of them what they were doing that night, adding that I would consider it an honor if they would allow me to take them to dinner. She said, "All of us?" I said, "Sure. There's safety in numbers, and you can choose anyplace you like." She said she would ask the others. I came under scrutiny for a few minutes as they sized me up. The answer was yes, but they said that first they'd have to go to Santa Monica to their hotel to change. I told them they could change at my house, and I'd take them to their hotel after dinner. I then told the group to meet me in front of the terminal. One asked how they would all get to my house, and I told her to leave it to me.

They appeared in front of the terminal with their roll-on luggage, and I escorted them to a stretch limousine. Drinks were in order as we made our way to the house. Not once did anyone ask what I did for a living. I had used the limo service often, so the driver knew where to go. When he pulled up to the house, I hit the gate opener I carried in my briefcase. He pulled down to the garage, where we unloaded. I led the way to the guesthouse. Burt and his girlfriend, Sally Field, were out by the pool. As we passed, I said to Burt, "Hi, Roomie." Sally said, "Hi, Hal."

I greeted her and kept going. The girls were tripping all over themselves. Inside the house they all rushed to the window to confirm their suspicions. One turned to me and asked, "Is that Burt Reynolds and Sally Field?" Trying to act surprised, I moved to the window, turned back, and said, "Well, I'll be. I believe it is!" Okay, who are you, they said, and why do you live here? While we ate dinner, I answered rapid-fire questions for three hours. Then I took them to their hotel. They agreed I was a super guy and that they'd had a wonderful time. I said we should do it again sometime, gave them my number, and told them to call next time they came to town. The next day Burt said I should have a forty-passenger bus pick me up in the future. That way I could invite *all* the stewardesses.

More often than not, if you're making pretty good bucks in Hollywood, you need a business manager—especially me. I thought an investment meant buying a Ferrari. I was making good money and spending it as fast as I could. Then I met Laura Lizer, who was as smart as she was good-looking. She worked for a business management firm that represented a lot of stars, writers, producers, and directors. She happened to be married to a producer with whom I shared a suite of offices, and when she decided to open up her own management company she set up shop in those same offices.

I became her first client. She ruffled my feathers at our first client–business manager meeting when she had the audacity to put me on a budget. She took over my bank account, paid all my bills, gave me a couple of credit cards and a few dollars in cash, and warned me that she would be monitoring my credit card statements. The upside was that within a short time I would see a difference in my net worth.

Soon after, she told me we needed to buy some investment property. I suggested a bar; she said definitely not, because I'd give away everything to my friends. She had found a fourplex that would be a good first investment. She knew I could make the down payment and let the tenants make the monthly payments and pay for the upkeep. As I kept making more money, she kept buying property. But she did set a rule: "one for you, one for me." Every time a sizable check came in, we would trade off on who got to buy what. She would send over papers for me to sign, and when I'd ask, "What's this?" she'd say, "You now own an apartment building in Las Vegas" or "some land in Utah." She'd rathole money without my knowing about it until I signed more papers.

If it hadn't been for Laura Lizer, there's no telling how far in debt I might be. I surely wouldn't have the financial security I enjoy today or been able to share my financial success with my family. When I got my first profit participant check, I couldn't believe it. It was more money than this cotton picker had ever seen. I came up with a bright idea. In all the years I had stayed at Burt's house, I'd never paid a dime in rent. I thought it was time. I told Laura to get me $25,000 in hundred-dollar bills, take the wrappers off, and put them in a briefcase.

At home that evening, I asked Scotty, the houseman, if the boss was in and had two minutes to spare. I found Burt lying in bed, watching the fish tank and the TV. He said, "Hello, Roomie, what's up?" I said, "Burt, your business manager, the government, nobody knows about this." He said, "About what?" I told him I had come to pay my rent. I opened the briefcase, dumped the cash on his bed, and said goodnight. At the door I turned around to see Burt playing with the money, throwing it up in the air. Burt had way more money than I did, but like me, he never saw it in cash or even in check form, because it all went to his business manager. Like most stars, he hadn't known what $25,000 in cash looked like.

15

Smokey and the Bandit Is Born

While shooting *Gator* in Georgia, something small happened that changed my life forever. The driver captain on the movie came to me one day on the set and said he had brought some Coors beer from California, and that he would drop off a couple of cases in my room. At that time you couldn't buy Coors east of the Mississippi River. I thanked him but didn't mention that I didn't drink much beer. Two cases of Coors appeared in my room. I put a few bottles in the fridge and forgot about it. Some days later I noticed that the fridge was empty of Coors, so I restocked it. As days went by, the beer again disappeared. I don't claim to be a detective, but it was pretty obvious that someone with a passkey had been raiding my fridge. A good guess was a hotel employee; better yet, how about the maid?

One day when I didn't have to work, I set a trap. I counted the beers in the fridge and went to breakfast, figuring by the time I got back the maid would be there. That's the way it worked out. As I returned, she was making up my room. I left for a few minutes and returned to verify my suspicions. I counted the bottles; there were two missing. I tried to figure out why. How important was it to acquire Coors beer? I had read an article about Coors being transported on Air Force One. The driver captain had bootlegged a number of cases to Georgia. The maid was stealing two bottles at a time. This must be serious stuff. Bootlegging Coors would make a good plotline for a movie.

Over the next several weeks I scribbled out a script that I titled *Smokey and the Bandit*. What I wrote and what we filmed are worlds apart, but the basic plot remained the same: the Bandit was hired to bootleg a truckload of illegal Coors beer, with the law in hot pursuit. My plan was to try to put together a low-budget film for $1 million and get Jerry Reed, who had played the heavy in *Gator*, to star in it. My secretary, Kathy Shea, typed it up, and I took the script home and asked Burt to read it. He reported back that the idea was good, but the dialogue was horrible. If I could find a writer to polish the dialogue and get a studio to commit to it, he would star in the movie in a six-week window he had in his schedule, and I could direct. At that time Burt was the number one box office star in the world. This shouldn't be a hard sell; every studio wanted to be in the Burt Reynolds business.

I called James Lee Barrett, a good friend who was a terrific writer and very much in demand. He'd written *The Green Berets*, *Bandolero!*, and *The Undefeated*. I thought if I could get him to put his name on it, I would have a slam dunk. Burt Reynolds starring in a James Lee Barrett script? No problem. Again I was wrong. At every studio I approached and asked if they wanted to do a Burt Reynolds movie with a James Lee Barrett script, the answer was always yes. Then I would drop the hammer: the director was Hal Needham. I got accustomed to the hems and haws before they threw me out. But I refused to let rejection get me down. I just kept knocking on those doors.

I guess word got around that I had Burt in my pocket and a Barrett script in my hand, and I was looking for money. I got a call from a producer named Mort Engelberg, who worked for Ray Stark, who had produced big hits like *The Way We Were*, had a studio deal, and could make things happen. I went in for a meeting with Engelberg and Stark. There were no hems and haws; they knew I was going to direct. We got right down to basics. Would Burt do the movie? Was any money owed on the script? How much would it cost to shoot? I gave them their answers, and they said they would get back to me. I knew Stark could get it done if he wanted to, and I felt good about the meeting.

The next word I got was: it's a go. Universal Studios would bankroll *Smokey and the Bandit* for $5.3 million. Universal figured it was a good risk, even with me directing. After all, Burt and I were good buddies, and Burt had directed two films that he starred in. They figured he would see that I didn't get on the wrong trail.

There are perks to being a director. As a stuntman, most of the time I would have to park a block away from the studio and walk. Now I could drive onto the studio lot and pull into my own parking space right in front of my office.

But on my second week on the job, when I returned from lunch, my parking space was occupied. I decided to make sure this person didn't do it again, so I parked my car directly behind theirs, and left a note on the windshield as to where my office was located. An hour or so later my secretary came in to say there was a gentleman who would like to see me. When she told me his name, I recognized it as a director I had worked for on various TV shows. I told her to send him in. As he entered, he stuck out his hand and congratulated me on getting a director's job and thanked me for all the stunts I had done for him. Then he asked if I would do him one last favor. I said sure, just name it. He said, with a smile, "Move your damn car so I can go home!" As he backed out, he gave me a thumbs-up.

Burt and the studio wanted to punch up the comedy dialogue, so they hired a couple of comedy writers. Screen credit for writing a script is determined by the input of each writer. Therefore each writer wants to change as many things as possible, to enhance their chance of a better screen credit.

My first meeting with the writers went something like this. Me: "Don't change the name of the movie, don't change the name of the characters, don't change the action that is written... just jazz up the jokes. A little." Them: "Okay." A week later they came to my office with their version of the script. The first thing I saw was that the title had been changed. On the first line of the script, I saw that Burt's character had a new name. I had a tooth- pick in my mouth. In anger, I yanked it out—along with the cap on my front tooth. I threw the script in the wastebasket, picked up my tooth cap, and as I left for the dentist's office, told them they were fired.

I was to be paid a salary plus own 7 percent of the profits. As deals were made for the actors and producers, the studio wanted to renegotiate my deal. Universal was being asked to give up more percentage points than they were willing to. Because *Smokey* was to be my directorial debut, I was the low man on the totem pole. Every time the studio had to give up more points, I was asked to take less. What's the old saying—100 percent of nothing is nothing?

I didn't have an agent at the time; my business manager, Laura Lizer, was negotiating on my behalf. I told her to hang as tough as she could but not to blow the deal. When the dust settled, I ended up with 3 percent instead of 7. I thought she'd made a great deal. I also think my relationship with Burt helped in the nego- tiations. No, I know it helped. Most first-time directors never get profit participation.

When we got to casting, the decision was made to go after Jackie Gleason to play the sheriff chasing the Bandit. It was during a time when Jackie hadn't been working much, so we thought we had a chance, and sent him the script. A few days later he called and asked what made me think he would do this script. I told him I'd written it and was going to direct it, and that nothing was etched in stone, but I thought there was a very funny character in the sheriff with him playing the part. He replied that he would get back to me — and the rest is history.

Another major part that needed to be cast was the leading lady. Engelberg, Stark, and Universal all wanted Sally Field, who was best known then for *The Flying Nun*. I had worked with Sally on *The Way West*. She was cute and perky and a good actress. I had no objection, and it wouldn't have mattered if I did, because the decision was made. This would be the beginning of Burt and Sally's romance, and I think you saw them fall in love on-screen. One scene in particular really showed their chemistry. Bandit has parked his Trans Am by a covered bridge for a break in the action. She asks him, "Do you ever take that hat off?" He replies, "Only for one thing." She says, "Take your hat off."

The last major character to be cast was the Snowman, the Bandit's accomplice. Burt had done two movies with Jerry Reed, *W.W. and the Dixie Dancekings* and *Gator,* and I knew that he had a knack for comedy and was a country-and-western music star. So Jerry, you're Snowman, not the Bandit as you and I had talked about. Actually, Jerry wasn't the last character to be cast; that was Fred, the basset hound who rode in the truck with Jerry. We had prepped the movie and moved to Atlanta. Even though I'd already hired a Hollywood Fred and his trainer, before we started shooting, the PR department thought it would be great press to invite the locals to bring their dogs to a park on Sunday and have Burt judge which dog would play Fred in the movie.

Between six hundred and seven hundred ladies showed up with dogs (many of them, we later found out, came straight from the pound). Burt took one look and decided to let the audience be the judge. We put ten at a time on the stage. Burt would hold his hand over each dog, and the one that got the most applause would transfer to the next group. It took a couple of hours, but once the basset hound took the stage, the contest was over. Burt said, "Hal, I don't know what you're going to do with the Hollywood dog and his trainer, but you have to cast the basset hound as Fred." *Thanks, ladies!* Fred stole every scene he was in.

I should have been nervous, but I wasn't. I figured if this thing went into the toilet, I could always do stunts and direct second unit and make a living. But I had one more obstacle to overcome that I hadn't anticipated. I had picked all the locations and made a shooting schedule to fit the $5.3 million budget. Two days before we were to start shooting, Universal sent a hatchet man down to Atlanta to inform me that my budget was being cut by $1 million. Wow, what a shock! Burt was getting paid $1 million, so that left me with $3.3 million to make the movie.

My assistant director and I spent thirty straight hours revising our shooting schedule. The cut meant that we had to shoot extra pages each day, and the new schedule looked nearly impossible to achieve. You know, it's hard to remember that your objective was to drain the swamp when you're up to your ass in alligators. That's exactly where I was, so I went to work draining the swamp.

On the Sunday before we started shooting, some of the cast and crew were hanging around the pool. As I passed by, Jerry Reed came bounding up. It had been agreed that Jerry would write and sing the movie's theme song. I said, "Hey, Jerry, you've had the script for a while; any ideas on the music?" He told me he was working on it.

That same day Jackie called and said he had a few questions about the movie and wondered if I could come over to his hotel to discuss things. An hour later I rang his doorbell, wondering how this was going to work out. The Jackie Gleason we all knew answered the door dressed in slacks and a sports jacket with a red carnation in the lapel. I stuck out my hand and introduced myself.

Invited in, I took a seat, and we made small talk for a few minutes. Then I told him I had been working all day and sure could use a drink. He apologized, and we moved to the bar. He fixed the drinks, and we toasted to a good shoot. I told him how much I'd enjoyed watching him on *The Honeymooners*. I think he had a story about every episode, and we drank a toast to each one. That's a lot of episodes. Finally I told him I had to get up early for the first day of shooting. As I headed for the door he said, "Now, don't you be late." I promised I wouldn't and said goodnight. On the way back to my hotel, I wondered what he'd wanted to talk to me about, because not one word had been said about *Smokey*.

The next morning I arrived on the set and found Jackie sitting in his chair, legs crossed, wearing the same clothes as the night before. He might not have taken his clothes off, but he had removed his shoes, because now they were on the wrong feet. As I approached he said, "Hi, Pally," raised his coffee in a salute, and tipped over backward. He got up laughing and said it was time for him to get dressed and made up. As I got to know him better, I learned that all he wanted was company and a drinking partner.

I made two movies with Jackie, *Smokey I* and *Smokey II*. To the day he died, I don't think he ever knew my name. When things were hunky-dory, he called me "Pally," and when he was unhappy, it was "Mr. Director." He told me he would always be on time but he didn't like to sit around the set and wait to do his first shot. I tried to do it his way, but one day on *Smokey I* we had a problem. Jackie's call was for 11 a.m. He was there and ready for us, but we weren't ready for him. He snapped his fingers, and his man Friday went to his motor home and returned with a scotch and soda. Okay, so he's having a drink. But the shooting problem continued to get worse, and so did Jackie. By the time I was ready for him, he was a little under the weather, but as usual ready to give it a go.

This scene was the one where he caught the governor in a motor home with some hookers. I had to shoot it from various angles because Jackie was having trouble remembering his lines. If you saw the movie, I guarantee you wouldn't ever suspect he'd had a drink. Now that you know, if you see it again, you might get just a hint that he'd had one or more.

My mother was a Southern Baptist lady who was always looking for ways to spread the word of the Good Lord. I figured I could use all the help I could get, and thought it would be a good idea to have her ask for a blessing from the Man Above before I began to shoot the movie, so I flew her in. Prior to our first shot, I gathered the cast and crew. We bowed our heads as Mom prayed for the safety of all involved and the success of our endeavors. In the future she would do this on every movie I directed.

After Mom's prayer, we were waiting for the first scene to be lit when Jerry approached with his guitar. He sat down and said, "Listen to this and see if you like it." He sang "East Bound and Down" and waited for my reaction. As a country-and-western music lover, I was blown away. It had everything we needed for the movie: gettin' down the road truckin' music, it told the story of the script, and it was perfect. My pause made Jerry blurt out, "Okay, you don't like it. I'll come up with something else." I said, "Don't change a word!" He didn't change a word when he recorded it, but made the song more powerful and moving by adding a five-string banjo. We laid it into the soundtrack, and I loved it.

A few days into the shoot we had some bad luck when Burt got sick. We had to rearrange the schedule again. I knew Burt well and could see he had to suck it up to work four or five hours a day. He hung in there and worked when he could. We changed the schedule daily, according to how he felt. So much for Universal thinking Burt would be their watchdog over me.

The brighter side of things was Jackie Gleason. When I told

him nothing was etched in stone, he took it as gospel. I would say three-quarters of what he said in the film, he came up with on his own, starting with "sumbitch," which he called everybody. When his son wrecked the car, he called him a "tick turd." When his son did something stupid, he said, "There was no way—no way—you could come from my loins. The first thing I'm gonna do when I get home is punch your momma in the mouth."

One day when we were shooting a scene with Burt and Jackie in a coffee shop, Jackie came over and said, "Pally, I got a good one for you." Who am I to argue with the master? I asked him to tell me his idea.

"When I leave Burt at the counter, I'm going to the men's room," he explained. "When I come out, I want the camera to follow me as I leave the coffee shop, and then outside, I'll have a zinger for you. And one more thing. Get a waitress pretty big across the beam and have her follow me outside."

I did as the master asked and set up a dolly shot to follow him from the men's room to the parking lot without a clue as to what was going to happen. I called "Action," and out came Jackie, cleaning his glasses with toilet paper. As he put his glasses on, the toilet paper got hung up on them, and forty feet of toilet paper trailed behind him as he exited, followed by a waitress with a *very* broad beam. We continued the scene outside. As Jackie left with the toilet paper trailing behind him, the waitress said, "Oh, Sheriff," which made him stop. She reached up, took the toilet paper off his glasses, and returned to the coffee shop.

Jackie asked me to do a close-up on him for the tagline. I've talked to many people about this scene, and very few know what Jackie says, because the audience is laughing so loud. As he turns and looks at the waitress, his line is "Nice ass"—as only he could say it.

After we finished shooting, Universal sent me across the country on a promotional tour. On my return to the studio, I was told they wanted me to see *Smokey* again. I asked why, and they told me they had sweetened the music. In the projection room I was flabbergasted. They had added a bunch of brass that ruined "East Bound and Down." I yelled, "Stop the film!" and asked why they'd added the brass. The studio thought it made the song better. Knowing I had Burt on my side, I decided to get a little loud and bossy. I said, "Take it out." They said I was making a mistake.

I think Jerry Reed would agree with my decision to take out the brass. His most famous song at the time was "When You're Hot, You're Hot," which was his theme song when he did concerts. After *Smokey* was released, his new theme song was "East Bound and Down." It was the number one song on the country-and-western charts for sixteen weeks.

After the release of *Smokey,* I flew to Nashville to visit Jerry. He told me he and his band had a concert over in Kentucky and asked if I'd like to make the three-hour trip with them on their bus. Sure, why not? It was a chance to visit and tell success stories. At the concert, Jerry got me a front row seat. The applause was deafening when he and the band came onstage. Everyone was screaming "East Bound and Down." Jerry promised to get to it later, and the band went through their regular setlist. Not a person in the auditorium knew who I was and they could care less, until Jerry told them he had a friend in the audience: the director of *Smokey and the Bandit.* He introduced me; I was an instant celebrity. Then he did "East Bound and Down," and the place went crazy. Take that, Universal.

After all the problems — Burt being sick, my budget being cut, the studio messing with the music — releasing *Smokey and the Bandit* taught me an interesting lesson. Universal decided to go big-time and give the movie an exclusive engagement at Radio City Music Hall in New York City. Are you kidding me? *Smokey* wasn't made for New York, Philadelphia, or San Francisco. In my mind it was targeted for the South, Midwest, and Northwest. But they went ahead and booked it at Radio City, where it fell flat on its face. It didn't even make enough to pay the Rockettes.

Smokey was jerked from the Music Hall, and a new attack plan was made to put some bucks into promotion and release it in the South. Now you're talking. In the South the movie went through the roof, and using those box office numbers as a promotional tool, *Smokey* was released nationwide. The shocking part to me was the staggering business at the box offices in New York, Philly, and San Francisco. I guess it was a movie for everybody.

The studio brass estimated that *Smokey* could make $50 million, but I said I thought it would make more than $50 million. At that point, I was promised a red carpet anytime I came to the studio if it grossed more than fifty. To date it has grossed over $300 million—and I have yet to get the red carpet treatment. But that 3 percent I got turned out to be a good deal. Had my business manager and I demanded the original 7 percent I was promised, the movie might never have been made. After the success of *Smokey,* my profit participation only went up on future movies I directed.

While prepping *Smokey,* I saw a picture in a magazine of a Pontiac Trans Am that gave me a product placement idea. I could picture Burt Reynolds behind the wheel with Jackie Gleason on the chase. I called Pontiac and asked if they would like to have the car in the movie. They asked how many I thought I would need. Knowing the Trans Am was going to take a beating, I asked for six. We negotiated down to four, and I also asked for four Bonnevilles to use as Gleason's sheriff car and settled for two.

The bridge jump in the movie wiped out one Trans Am. Jumping the fence into the ball field took care of the second. Jumping curbs and driving through ditches and down embankments pretty well trashed the other two. Using parts from the cars that would no longer run, we managed to make it to the final day of shooting. When we got ready to shoot the last scene, car number four just flat-out wouldn't start, so we used another car to push it into the scene. I was surprised the cars lasted as long as they did, considering all the abuse we put them through. When *Smokey* was released and became a blockbuster, Trans Am sales went through the roof. If you wanted a black Trans Am, you had to wait a minimum of six months.

By the time we were ready to shoot *Smokey II,* I was on a first-name basis with Pontiac. How many cars would I need? I asked for ten Trans Ams and fifty-five Bonnevilles: five for Gleason, and fifty for Gleason's Canadian law enforcement buddies who'd come down to help him catch the Bandit. I wanted twenty-five painted red and the other twenty-five painted white. Pontiac's only questions were where and when. I gave them the start date and the location, Las Vegas, and they said, "No problem." The cars were shipped by rail to Vegas. The only stipulation was that at the end of the movie shoot, I had to return every car to Pontiac so they could put them in the crusher. They didn't want them sold to fans or the public, for fear of lawsuits. If one were in an accident, a good lawyer could argue that the cars had been used for stunts and were no longer safe for the street.

A question I get asked quite often is, "How many cars did you wreck on *Smokey*?" My answer is, "About twenty-five on *Smokey I* and in the neighborhood of seventy on *Smokey II.*"

At the time, I was taken to task by the critics for using real products in my movies. Now product placement in movies has grown into a multimillion-dollar industry.

It was no thanks to the critics that *Smokey* became a box office smash. They panned it even after it became a hit. They said things like "Dull"; "Gleason played a buffoon"; "Burt walked through the movie"; and as a first time director, "Needham had failed miserably." One Texas critic said that after he saw the movie, he walked out into the lobby and heard someone behind him say, "That's the best movie I've ever seen!" The critic turned around to see a nine-year-old boy, and added, "That's my review of *Smokey and the Bandit*." I saved that one.

Now let me jump forward to *Smokey II*. What the same critic said about *Smokey II* was that "Needham failed to capture the magic that was in *Smokey I*." Critics are a strange lot. They write what they think their readers want to read, and heaven forbid they write a glowing review of a popular movie like *Smokey* and lead their readers to think they're not sophisticated or knowledgeable about the arts.

To say the least I was upset at some of the reviews and wanted to show that the critics didn't have the faintest idea what the folks liked to see. I knew they read the Hollywood trade papers that are considered to be the industry bibles, *Daily Variety* and *The Hollywood Reporter*, so I took out a center spread, double-page ad. On one page I quoted some of the negative reviews under the headline "Here's what the critics said about *Smokey and the Bandit II*." On the opposite page I put a picture of me sitting on a wheelbarrow filled with cash, in front of a Wells Fargo Bank, with hundred-dollar bills stuck in my shirt and in my belt, posing with my arms out as if to say, look who's laughing now. The headline for that page read "Here's what the people said: *The biggest opening week in the history of the film business!*"

I didn't have to worry about making critics mad; they gave me bad reviews on every movie I made. (Although in one *Smokey and the Bandit* review, the *Washington Post*'s critic, Gary Arnold, compared me to Frank Capra!) In my career I directed ten feature films at a total cost of $110 million that today have grossed $1.4 billion and counting. The only movie to outgross *Smokey I* the year it came out was *Star Wars*.

If critics are so smart as to what people want to see in a movie, why the hell aren't they producers, writers, or directors? If you want the lowdown on a movie, listen to the word of mouth of people who have seen it. Don't be swayed by what a critic writes. Before the critics were so harsh with their reviews of *Smokey and the Bandit,* they might have spoken to Alfred Hitchcock. When asked to name his favorite movie—in an answer later verified by his daughter—Hitch answered, "*Smokey and the Bandit.*"

16

Ain't Nobody Can Fly a Car Like Hooper

After the success of *Smokey,* the Hollywood studios thought I knew what I was doing, and they knew Burt was big box office. Together we might pull off another box office smash hit. But in between *Smokey* and deciding which movie Burt and I would shoot next, I directed a little movie called *The Villain.* The critics said *The Villain,* a comedy Western, was a salute to the sagebrush Westerns. I thought it was more like the Roadrunner cartoons, with Kirk Douglas playing Wile E. Coyote and Ann-Margret and Arnold Schwarzenegger together playing the Roadrunner.

Ann-Margret played Charming Jones, a country girl traveling to another town to pick up some money for her pappy, who had arranged for a friend, Handsome Stranger, played by Arnold, to escort her and the money home safely. In her opening scene she's very flirtatious with some guys on the train, but when she meets Arnold, she becomes obsessed with getting him in the sack. Arnold, oblivious to her advances, proceeds with his obligation to her pappy to get her and the money safely home. Kirk Douglas, playing Cactus Jack, is hot on their trail, trying to get both the money and Ann-Margret.

One day Kirk asked about a scene we had shot that he thought hadn't worked as well as it could have. He wanted to shoot it again, so I said, "Why don't you come to the dailies, and we'll look at it and make the decision together."

He asked, "You don't mind if the actors look at the dailies?" I said no, knowing he'd be shocked when he walked into the room and saw all the cast and crew there.

We were showing dailies at a small theater. I had a seat on the aisle and a seat saved next to me for Kirk. He came in, and I called his name. As he made his way to where I was seated, I knew he was trying to figure out who all these people were. He sat on the step next to me, not in the seat I had saved for him. When he realized this was the crew, he asked if I did this all the time. "Sure," I said.

The dailies started, and when the scene Kirk had questioned came on, the crew roared with laughter. When the lights came up, Kirk smiled and said, "I think that works fine." He never missed dailies after that, and he thought inviting the crew was a great idea. Kirk later wrote me a letter saying he'd had more fun on *The Villain* than on any movie he had ever worked on.

Arnold played the do-gooder, Handsome Stranger, to the hilt. We became pretty good friends, but I made one of the biggest mistakes of my life concerning Arnold. After we wrapped the movie, Arnold sent me a script he was going to star in and wanted me to direct. I read the script but just didn't get it, and told Arnold he'd be better off with a different director. The script was called *Conan the Barbarian*...and the rest of his very successful movie career is history.

Back when Burt and I were shooting *Lucky Lady*, Warner Bros. had given him a script called *The Stuntman*. Burt asked me to read it and give him my opinion. Since it was about a stuntman, he thought I would have a little insight that a screenwriter might not. After I read it, I told Burt that if he did this movie, every stuntman in Hollywood would stop talking to him, and possibly even put out a hit on him. The stuntman lead was the most obnoxious, bigmouthed, no-talent character I had ever seen written. I don't think it was my opinion that made that script disappear, but I never heard about it again until after *Smokey*. I believe Warner's thought if they rewrote the script to Burt's liking and hired me to direct, it had possibilities. The studio brought the idea to us, changed the title to *Hooper,* and we went to work.

Burt and I had as much input as you could have without dictating the script. Playing a stuntman offered Burt unlimited stunt opportunities. One day he could work on a Western, and the next day he could be a spy in a foreign country. Because there didn't have to be any continuity, *Hooper* would have every stunt I could dream up — a motorcycle sliding under a moving semi, car jumps, fights, explosions, and high falls.

For his role, Burt decided to dress like me. He had wardrobe match my clothes, and he also incorporated many of my trademark one-liners, such as "If you're waitin' on me, you're backin' up." In a bar scene, Burt took a line from a story I'd told him from my army days. Burt is getting ready to fight Terry Bradshaw and his gang. Bradshaw says, "There are fourteen of us and six of you." Burt replies, "We'll wait while you go get some more men."

I got to film some great stunts, including A. J. Bakunas doing a world-record high fall of 250 feet from a helicopter into an air bag. I also blew up half of Alabama along the way. We had a special pickup truck built for *Hooper*. Burt was to be driving backward, passing beer to another vehicle, when a cop stopped him. In order to go as fast as we wanted backward, we rebuilt the truck so the back wheels would steer. We locked the front wheels so they wouldn't turn, and put a horizontal steering wheel in the truck bed a couple of inches high. This way, a hidden driver could lie on his stomach, looking through a screen that had been incorporated into the tailgate, and zoom on down the highway.

The morning they showed it to me, we were shooting on the back lot at Warner Bros. and I decided to take it for a little test drive. I thought it would be funny to drive it past the guard shack, which I did. Soon I was on the city streets. I was looking for a place to turn around when I saw a motorcycle cop parked at a cross street. As I passed him, I could hear him coming in hot pursuit. I pulled over to the curb and stopped. When he turned off his engine, I called out, "Officer, I'm in the truck bed [it had a bed cover]. If you'll open the tailgate, I'll try to explain."

The officer unfastened and lowered the tailgate. As I crawled out, I was looking into a face I knew. He said, "Holy shit, Needham. What are you doing?" I said, "Escort me back to the Warner's lot and I'll tell you." He flipped on his red lights and away we went. As we pulled onto the set, it got very quiet. He walked back, let me out, and told the crew they had to watch me a little more closely or I might harm myself. Then he got on his bike and left.

Later, the officer told me he hadn't known what to think when he first saw the truck on the street. When I pulled over and parked, he thought it might be a hidden-camera episode. Then I told him about the crew's shock that he had escorted me back to the set without giving me a ticket. Of course, I didn't tell them we were friends. Am I lucky? Los Angeles probably has seven thousand police officers, and I got pulled over by one I knew.

For the film's locations we found a complex in Alabama that had been a POW camp in World War II and later a college dorm, and was scheduled for demolition. Perfect—but let us destroy it for you. We were told that the salvage value of each building was ten grand, and if we were willing to pay the price, we could have it.

I took my special effects man, Cliff Wanger, to the location and pointed out the buildings I wanted to destroy. There were so many on one street, my crew named it Damnation Alley. In the scene, Burt and Jan-Michael Vincent were to drive down the street with buildings exploding on both sides of them. It would be dangerous to put effects men on the street to set off the charges because of flying debris, so Cliff rigged trip wires across the street—when the car hit a trip wire, it would trigger the explosion of a building, or two or three. If one failed to explode, you'd never know it, as there were so many that would. This was going to be the master shot of all master shots. I had thirteen cameras placed all around the area with a major stunt set up to happen right in front of each one of them—all while the world was being blown up in the background. The final camera would be positioned in a chopper with me, because that was the only seat in the house where you could see the whole thing unfold.

We planned to shoot at two in the afternoon, but on a shot this elaborate, everything has to be perfect. With one problem here and another over there, the day was slipping away. We couldn't leave all those buildings armed to the hilt with explosives overnight. We couldn't get enough guards to watch them; even that would be scary. So we had to shoot it. I was in the chopper, waiting for word that all was ready, when I looked down and saw my prop man entering Damnation Alley on a bicycle. Before I could get anyone to signal him to stop, he hit a trip wire and one building disappeared from the face of the earth. He was knocked off his bike but immediately got up and looked around to see if anyone had seen him. Then he threw his bike under a building and ran like hell.

It was getting late when word came that everything was finally ready. We rolled the cameras, and when I called "Action," that's what I got. The scene had so much going on that, even knowing the sequence of events, I couldn't follow what was happening. But I did know that when Burt's car reached the takeoff position to jump the bridge, it was over.

When I called "Cut," it looked as if a Berlin bombing raid had just ended. So many buildings were burning, I couldn't count them. I checked by radio with each camera position to see how the shot looked to them. Everyone was positive. I called my assistant and said, "I guess that's a wrap." The chopper pilot asked where I wanted to go. I told him I wasn't a firefighter, and since it would take two hours to get things under control down there, he should take me to the motel parking lot.

I waited for the crew to arrive—where else but in the bar. As they came stumbling in, they looked like they'd been fighting a forest fire. Finally the prop man who'd accidentally blown up the building came in and sat at the table next to mine. I asked him if he'd retrieved his bike after the shot was over. He said, "Damn, Hal, nothing gets by you. I thought I had committed the perfect crime. How'd you know what happened?" I told him I was the eye in the sky: the chopper. Then I told the story to the other crew members, and they had a good laugh. By the time the bar closed, I'd run up a good-size bar tab trying to thank the crew for a job well done.

In another stunt Burt had to slide a motorcycle under a moving semi, between its trailer wheels. Once he had passed under the truck, he had to get the bike upright and hit a curb, which would send him over the handlebars. Stan Barrett was going to do the stunt. An expert rider, Stan had no problem sliding under the truck, but he saw hitting the curb and flying over the handlebars as a problem. If his feet or legs got caught on the bars and pancaked him facedown onto the pavement, there was a good chance the motorcycle would land on him. Every stuntman on the set had an idea about how to rig the stunt. Stan listened to them and then turned to me and asked if I'd ever done anything like it. I told him yes, I'd done a similar stunt on an Ann-Margret/Joe Namath movie titled *C.C. and Company*.

That scene called for a bad guy on a motorcycle to hit a parked convertible. The impact threw me (doubling the bad guy) over the car to the ground, and then the motorcycle flipped upside down, landed in the front seat, and exploded. I had placed a ramp against the car door, with a four-by-four at the top of the ramp that would throw the bike's front end into the air. A cable attached to the front axle would stop the forward movement of the bike, jerking the front wheel down and causing the bike to flip upside down and land in the front seat. Special effects would then trigger the explosion. It was a first for me. Effects and I agreed it should work. When the front wheel hit the four-by-four, sending it skyward, the cable took effect, jerking it down as the back end came over and the seat hit me in the backside, throwing me forty feet.

Stan said he would go get dressed while I had the stunt rigged. When he returned, I showed him the setup and assured him the handlebars wouldn't be a problem. Without a word he climbed on the bike and said he was ready. It looked spectacular and worked like a charm.

I also had a little fun with the director character in *Hooper,* whom I modeled on Peter Bogdanovich. I had worked for Bogdanovich on *Nickelodeon,* doubling Burt, and he was the most arrogant know-it-all I have ever been with on a set. In one scene on *Nickelodeon,* a hot-air balloon was supposed to lift off and go directly away from camera one hundred yards, then make a right turn. Balloons were the first thing man used to get airborne, and from that day forward there has never been a way to guide or turn them except for Mother Nature's breath. A hot-air balloon will go the way the wind blows, which is the reason balloonists have a chase vehicle.

I told Peter the problem with trying to turn a balloon. His reply was that Burt had told him I was the best stuntman and stunt coordinator in the world and that I could do anything. "Make the balloon turn," he said, and walked away.

This was really a job for special effects, but Burt had unknowingly dropped it in my lap. I didn't know of any fan strong enough to blow a hot-air balloon from fifty yards away, so I came up with a plan. I would run a small, very strong cable connected to the balloon directly away from the camera about 150 yards and hook it to a winch with an operator and a radio. I would hook a second cable to the balloon and run it off to the right side 100 yards, and also hook it to a winch with an operator and a radio. As the balloon lifted off, I'd tell the first operator to take up on his winch, pulling the balloon directly away from camera. When Peter wanted the balloon to turn right, he would signal me, and I would tell the first winch to stop and the second operator to take up on his winch, causing the balloon to turn right.

They rolled the camera, and the balloon lifted off and moved straight away. Peter said "Now," and on cue the balloon turned right and the shot was over. Not a thank-you, nothing. Days later we were shooting the exterior of a whorehouse. The scene called for guys crashing through windows, crashing through doors, and falling from balconies. Peter said he would give $1,000 to the person who came up with the funniest idea of a way for someone to exit the house.

I fastened a cable about eight feet long inside a second-story window. Then I ran it up my pant leg and fastened it to a harness underneath my red flannel underwear and to my suspenders. As I fell backward out of the window, I'd be upside down, and my pants would slip up to my ankles and make it look like my suspenders had gotten hung up and were supporting me. As I hung upside down in my red long johns with my pants around my ankles, the crew broke up. They thought it was funny, and I thought I'd made an extra grand. Peter wanted to know whose idea that was. Still upside down, counting my money, I said, "Mine." He said set up the shot again, leave your stunt out, and let's just do the things we agreed on. Obviously, he didn't think it was funny.

Another time, Burt was standing on a rock ledge about thirty-five feet high, with a bushy oak tree about ten feet below him. Peter wanted me to fall into the top of the tree and then climb down. I said, "Are you kidding me? One of those limbs could take out an eye, punch through my rib cage, or possibly *really* injure me." He saw no humor in my response. He said that was the way it was written, he'd shot all the lead-in scenes, and that was what he wanted. I looked it over and said, "Okay, I'll do it, but tell Warner Bros. to get their checkbook out." I knew I had to hit the limbs from the side so they'd bend with me. If I came straight down on them, I could get seriously hurt. I did the shot and never heard him say "Nice job." And yes, Warner Bros. ponied up, because I charged ten times the going rate for the stunt.

So when I directed *Hooper*, I modeled the pompous director on Bogdanovich and wrote the dialogue accordingly. I had him say things like "Films are tiny pieces of time, and we captured it." Then I told Robert Klein, who was playing the director, to find out everything he could about Bogdanovich. Every time we shot a scene, I would say to Robert, "Here's what Bogdanovich would do," and Robert did it. The Bogdanovich attitude—no excuses, just give me the shot I want—is okay for actors, but it could put a stuntman in harm's way, so you have to be sure of your ability and be aware of the danger.

When I finished editing *Hooper*, I had a lot of stunts that hadn't made the final cut. What a waste, I thought. My next thought set a trend. It became my trademark, and it's called "outtakes." I showed a songwriter my outtakes and asked if he could write a song around them. He did a terrific job; the song is "Hollywood Stuntman." We cut the outtakes so the lyrics matched the action on the screen. It worked so well that two or three TV series were produced using outtakes. I was the first director to do this. I never again put the words "The End" at the conclusion of my movies. I'd let the screen go black for a few seconds and start the end credits accompanied by outtakes.

Over the years, I've had a whole bunch of people tell me how much they enjoy this. It lets them know how much fun we had doing the movie. I've been in theaters where the screen went black and people stood up to leave, and then heard a lot of folks who knew what was about to happen shout "Sit down!" That makes me feel good.

17

Breaking the Sound Barrier — 739.666 Miles per Hour!

I hate to leave a job undone. Three years had passed since I'd driven the Rocket Car: Project SOS—speed of sound—and SOS in a land vehicle was still out there calling. I decided I would buy the car and finance the effort myself. I asked Bill Fredrick if he still wanted to try to put a land vehicle through the sound barrier, and he told me the only thing stopping him was money. How much did he think it would cost? He estimated about half a million dollars. I said I'd get back to him.

My next stop was Laura Lizer. She wasn't thrilled with the idea and thought buying real estate was a better way to go, but she would earmark $1 million for it. We talked about getting a sponsor and how to approach the overall project.

CBS had covered my attempt to break the barrier when I drove 620 mph; maybe the network would be interested in another show. I set a meeting with CBS and made an offer they couldn't refuse. It wouldn't cost them a cent; all they had to do was commit at least one hour of coverage, or more if warranted. Why would I give CBS the show? Because now I could approach a company for sponsorship and guarantee them an hour of network airtime. (This was back when there was basically only network TV.)

Through some connections I set a meeting with Budweiser in St. Louis. I presented them with my plan. I could guarantee at least one hour of airtime, though realistically I thought we could stretch it to two hours or more. I explained that the car was forty-one feet long and we would call it the Budweiser Rocket, creating a very colorful moving billboard. After a few hours of negotiation, we agreed to these terms: Budweiser would pay me $250,000 to put their name on the car for a one-hour TV show. If we broke the existing land speed record of 622 mph, they would give me another $250,000, and finally, if we managed to break the sound barrier, they would give me an additional half a million. We had a deal.

I felt confident the land speed record was within reach. If Bill could stay on budget, I could at least break even — and if we broke the barrier, I could make half a million dollars. But there was one small issue: who's going to drive? I needed someone who was committed to seeing it through even if the going got tough, and I knew it was going to get tough. I went through the list of possible drivers. Over and over, like cream, the name that kept rising to the top was Stan Barrett. I knew that if Stan committed to drive the car, he would give it his all. Because of another commitment he had made, to God, his faith was strong and his word was his bond. I asked Stan if he'd like to drive the car. He answered with four words: "When do we start?"

I made a deal with Budweiser that they would pay him $50,000, and I matched it. After my ride in that monster, I knew he was being underpaid, but I reasoned that he could do a lot of endorsements and that it would open doors to future opportunities. When I told him this part, he only said two words: "I'm ready."

We moved the car to the Bonneville Salt Flats, in Utah, to begin our attack on the barrier. The site is a vast plain of thirty thousand acres that is amazingly flat. Stan made a few runs to get the feel of the car, and things were looking good. He became more confident with every run, and we boosted the power each time, until he hit 638.637 mph. Wonderful! We had just exceeded the existing land speed record and had half a million dollars coming from Budweiser. But there was a major problem. We couldn't go any faster on the salt flats. A lack of winter rain had made the salt very thin, and the two-and-a-half-inch metal wheels had broken through the surface, causing the car to tricycle on that run. When the rear wheels broke through the salt, it forced the rear of the car to go airborne for a hundred feet at a time.

Stan was fortunate to survive. It was scary watching it. I have no idea what it must have felt like inside the car, but it was obvious we had to find more solid terrain to run on. A dry lake would be ideal. Where would we find one long enough?

Fortunately, I'd met General Chuck Yeager while doing the U.S. Air Force survival film. Yeager was a fighter squadron wing commander who was also the first man to break the sound barrier, in the Bell XS-1 experimental plane named Glamorous Glennis, for his wife. We had become friends and stayed in touch. When CBS agreed to cover the SOS project, they wanted a knowledgeable color commentator. I called Chuck and he agreed to come aboard. He gave the project real credibility, and he came up with the solution to our location problem. With his air force connections, Chuck got permission for us to run on the dry lake at Edwards Air Force Base, in Mojave, California, which was an emergency landing strip for the space shuttle. It was 22 miles long and as smooth as glass, perfect to land a space shuttle or run a rocket car. So we set up camp at Edwards.

We could only run on weekends, so as not to interfere with the air force's regular operations. They would have a safety officer assigned to us to control the press, the visitors, and the fifty people in our group.

We began our assault on the sound barrier making two runs a

week: one on Saturday and one on Sunday. The expenses were really adding up because of the travel, motels, catering, and delays. Then we blew a nozzle on the rocket, which caused the power thrust to be off-center as Stan took another heart-stopping ride. That delayed us while we built a new one. Though the delays were costing bucks and time, the sound barrier seemed doable.

With the new nozzle Stan ran 690 mph. The problem now was, that was all the power this rocket had—48,000 horsepower. We figured we needed to build a new rocket with 12,000 more horsepower and we'd have to reconfigure the car. But that was financially out of the question. What to do? Again Chuck Yeager came to the rescue. He had fired many, many Sidewinder missiles from beneath his fighter-jet wings, and he suggested that if we attached one Sidewinder to our rocket car, to be fired about half-way through the run, it would supply enough power to get us through the barrier. The general went to the powers that be, and they allowed us to buy six Sidewinder missiles—without the warheads, of course. The Sidewinder was a solid-fuel rocket. Unlike the liquid-fuel rocket in the car, which could be shut off simply by Stan taking his foot off the accelerator, once he fired the Sidewinder there was no turning it off.

We mounted one of the Sidewinders on the car just as a test. Stan took his place behind the wheel and from a dead stop fired it. Everyone was shocked except Yeager. He knew that when Stan fired that baby, he'd be hit with 15,000 pounds of thrust. After the test run, Stan could hardly explain what it felt like. He said it had thrown him back against the headrest so hard that he had a headache. He was concerned that if he fired it during a run and something went wrong, he couldn't turn it off. Yeager explained that he would be going 550 mph when he fired the sidewinder, so the kick from the added power would be much less severe. Still, there was no way to turn it off. As I knew he would, Stan said, "Tie a new one on, and let's do it."

On the next run we didn't use the full power of the car's rocket, though we did fire the Sidewinder halfway through the run. Stan was damn sure the fastest man in the world, reaching a speed of 714 mph. After checking all the telemetry readouts, it was clear that the car had reacted as expected.

We had one more shot. Now we would turn the power to the max and pray for Stan to break the sound barrier. Stan had gone almost 100 mph faster than me. I couldn't imagine the buffeting he was experiencing in the cockpit, but I was concerned. The barrier wasn't worth Stan's life. That night I told him if he wanted to quit, I'd tell the press I had pulled the plug and that we were going home. Stan looked at me as though I had lost my mind, then said, "We're too close to quit, and when I signed on it was for the ultimate, the barrier or whatever happens." I don't know how much he slept that night, but even with the help of a half dozen scotch and sodas, I didn't sleep at all.

We showed up the next morning at 5 a.m. It was twenty degrees, which was good. Cold is your friend, because the air is thicker, and therefore the speed necessary to break the barrier drops substantially. That morning Stan would have to run 731 mph to achieve the barrier. As the sun peeked over the horizon we all gathered by the side of the Budweiser Rocket Car and bowed our heads while Stan said a prayer. Then we strapped him in and closed the hatch.

To get the rocket motor warm, you have to give it a little fuel, which causes it to belch white smoke. It was an eerie sight with the sun silhouetting the car and the smoke engulfing it. I wondered what the next moments were going to bring. I wouldn't have to wait long, as the countdown to ignition began. It was the longest ten seconds in history. Three, two, one, ignition!

Stan hit the accelerator, and in the first second was doing 140 mph as the total 48,000 horses pushed him across the dry lake faster than man had ever gone before in a land vehicle. At the 1.5-mile marker, doing 550 mph, he unleashed the 12,000 horses in the Sidewinder. Seconds later he went through the speed trap with the rear wheels a foot off the ground, an effect caused by the airflow over the fuselage as it penetrated the sound barrier. Stan had just become the first man to break the sound barrier in a land vehicle. Official speed timed by the U.S. Air Force: 739.666 mph.

On his way to the sound barrier, Stan set numerous speed records, including acceleration from a dead stop any distance up to two miles, which still stands today. The air force did a flyby with a jet as a salute from one Mach Buster to another.

To say there was a celebration that night is putting it mildly. Although I didn't drive the car, Stan Barrett's achievement fulfilled my dream to break the barrier. He had completed the job I started three years earlier. Lizer had been right to put aside $1 million for the project; the final tally was $1.1 million. It cost me a hundred thousand, but so what? We made history. CBS aired two one-hour specials, and Budweiser got lots of publicity.

After it was all over, I had a history-making car stored in a garage that I was paying rent on every month. Did this make any sense? Not to me. I'm not the sentimental kind. I had some offers from car buffs and collectors who wanted to buy the car, but Lizer had a better idea. "Let's donate it to the Smithsonian and take a tax deduction," she said. "Then the world can see it on display." I agreed.

If you try to donate anything to the Smithsonian, be prepared to certify everything about the donation, because they only want documented originals. Lizer gathered all the bids from the collectors, and with U.S. Air Force documentation, off to the Smithsonian it went. They estimated its worth at $2.5 million, which I took as a tax deduction over the next three years. So the Budweiser Rocket Car ended up making me a couple of bucks. Today the Budweiser Rocket Car, as well as General Yeager's Bell XS-1, Glamorous Glennis, is on rotating display in the Smithsonian's National Air and Space Museum in Washington, D.C. Both are recognized as firsts: General Yeager's in an aircraft, and Stan Barrett's in a land vehicle.

18

The Real Cannonball Run

By 1980 Burt Reynolds had done a number of action movies involving car chases, including *White Lightning, Gator, Smokey and the Bandit I* and *II,* and *Hooper*. Some critic made mention of that fact, which made Burt want to choose films of another genre. In fact, Burt declared that he wasn't going to drive a car in a movie over 35 mph. Here's what happened to change his mind.

When I drove the rocket car, one of the CBS commentators was Brock Yates. We spoke the same language: speed and racing. After my rocket car run, Brock and I saw each other often at various NASCAR races, which Brock also announced.

We crossed paths at Watkins Glen International racetrack in New York State, and over a drink one night Brock told me how he'd started the cross-country Cannonball race, which had its starting line at the Lock, Stock, and Barrel restaurant in Darien, Connecticut, and its finish line at the Portofino Inn in Redondo Beach, California.

The race had been run a number of times. The drivers would disguise themselves and their vehicles to be less conspicuous, as if that were possible, racing from coast to coast at a hundred-plus miles an hour. The vehicle covering the distance in the shortest amount of time was the winner, and the prize was a trophy and bragging rights until the next race. The only rule they had was that there were no rules.

After Brock had told me about all the crazy people who drove in the race, it got me thinking. "That sounds like a great, fun movie," I said. "What if next time you run the race, you and I drive it together? We'll give every racer a tape recorder and pen and paper, and they can record the outrageous things that happen to them along the way. Then, along with past incidents, we'll compile everything into a script and look for a studio that also thinks it's exciting, funny, and unique enough to make into a movie." Brock was game.

The race date was set. Brock and I had a tough time trying to decide what to drive. Then one or both of us came up with the idea of an ambulance. We would give it as realistic a look as we could on the outside and put a 440 wedge engine under the hood, with a big Holley carburetor and a B & W tranny to handle the torque. We had ambulance driver uniforms made for us and discussed the idea of having a patient on board. Brock's pretty wife, Pam, volunteered. Then we thought, if we have a patient, why not a doctor, just in case we get stopped? It might make a police officer think a little more before he hauled us off to jail.

In the Saratoga, a bar on Sunset Boulevard, I was telling a group of regulars how Brock and I planned on winning the race. All I needed was a doctor. Then I heard a voice say, "Count me in." It was Lyle Royer, a young, adventurous lad who had no idea what he had just volunteered for. But he was a doctor, and that's what counted.

I bought a Dodge van, ripped out the interior, and semi-equipped it to look like an ambulance. It had red emergency lights on the roof and "TransCon MediVac" painted on the side. Besides the 440 wedge engine, we added two extra gas tanks capable of carrying ninety gallons. Then I mounted three filler spouts, one for each tank, so we could fill them quickly. Our team was ready.

The first car in the cross-country race left the starting line at 9 p.m., followed every fifteen minutes by the next in line. We left Connecticut at 1:45 a.m. and headed west with Brock driving. The traffic was bumper-to-bumper. I told Brock we wouldn't win at this pace, so I hit the red lights. Now I knew how Jesus (or was it Moses?) felt when he parted the Red Sea. The cars ahead moved to the side of the road, and we left New York City in our wake.

Around 3 a.m. I got behind the wheel and had it to the floor between 140 and 150 mph. Outdriving my headlights, I wished the detour sign would have been two hundred yards earlier. The detour made a slow turn to the left, and with no other choice, I decided to go for it. The van went into a broadslide, and just as I got control of it, the detour turned to the right. Now we were in a right-turn drift. One more small turn, and we were back on the highway. It was very quiet in the van. Nobody said anything for a minute. Then, as though nothing had happened, Brock started telling me where to turn at the next highway.

Around 4 a.m. we were blowing through New Jersey, gobbling up miles in record time. I looked in the mirror and saw headlights way, way back there. Brock told me to back off to about eighty and see if they got any closer. Sure enough, the car closed the gap and turned on its red lights. We pulled over.

Brock and I, both dressed in orange-and-white ambulance attendants' jackets, got out and walked back to meet the police. One officer asked, "Where are you heading? It's a long way to a hospital in that direction."

Brock casually replied, "California."

"Why?" the officer asked.

"That's where the patient has to go," I said.

The officer looked confused. "Why California?" he asked.

"You'll have to ask the doctor. We're just drivers," Brock said.

Brock and I led the way to the ambulance door and opened it. Pam lay strapped to a gurney with an oxygen mask on and IV needles taped to her arm. The Doc, who was wearing a white coat, handed the officer a clipboard with a UCLA Medical Center form filled out. The officer looked down at it, obviously confused by the jargon. The Doc explained, "She has a lung disease."

The officer appeared suspicious. "Why didn't you fly her?"

"She couldn't tolerate the altitude," the Doc said impatiently. "We can't even take the northern route . . . too high. Have to head to the south."

We could see them mulling over the dilemma. If they delayed us and something happened to the patient, it would be on their heads—which is what Brock and I were counting on. Finally one said: "Okay, go ahead, but keep your speed down. Emergency or not, you're going way too fast. You're endangering half the state."

After they left, we jumped in the van and Brock turned to Lyle and said, "Nice going, Doc" as I mashed the gas and asked that engine for all it had.

Things were going well. We were averaging 90 mph, thanks to gas stops that went like this. At a small gas station with a gravel driveway I smoked in, brakes locked up, creating a cloud of dust that engulfed the van. By the time the dust settled, Brock, Pam (in her hospital gown), and the Doc were in the restrooms. I had stuffed a gas nozzle in each of the filler pipes and was checking the oil as a young attendant came out of the station and stopped about halfway to the van. He looked first at me and then toward the restrooms. When Brock got back, he took over my chores and checked the transmission fluid. It was my turn for the restroom.

When I returned, we waited for the pumps to shut off,

indicating that it was time to pay and go. I'd brought $5,000 in twenties so we wouldn't have to wait for the attendant to add all three pumps and then get change. I'd look at a pump, and if it read $25 I'd call it $30, and do the same with the other pumps, so the attendant could easily see he wasn't getting cheated. Then I'd count out twenties until he smiled. We jumped in the van and left the way we came in, in a hurry, leaving the attendant in a cloud of dust. Total pit stop time: 5 minutes, 20 seconds.

We kept the CB radio on the entire time, listening for any trouble ahead. When we reached Missouri, we knew from the chatter that a rodeo had just ended and the highway we were on was about to come to a crawl. We broke in on the CB chatter and informed anyone listening that we were headed in their direction, so be on the lookout for an ambulance. The CB squawked, and a voice came on saying, "This is Officer [Somebody], and I just copied your last transmission and will assist you through traffic." As we approached the traffic, the cars in our lane were stopped. Those in the oncoming lane were idling on the shoulder, so we took that lane and roared ahead. At the entrance to the fairgrounds, a traffic cop was holding back the cars trying to get on the highway and signaling us to come on through. On the CB we thanked one and all and put the pedal down.

I believe we were in Arizona. It was nighttime, and traffic was light. The highway was straight as a line drawn with a ruler. Up ahead we could see a truck convoy. We contacted them on the CB and told them we were coming up on their back door. We said we were a "meat wagon" and asked how many were in their convoy. The answer was ten, and they would increase their intervals so that if we had to we could duck in to avoid an oncoming car. I told them I'd turn on the red light just for a moment, then turn it off to let them know we weren't a smokey. I flashed the red light on and off and asked whether they could see it. The answer: "Bring on the meat wagon."

We were about three hundred yards from the last truck when I keyed the mic and asked the leader how the traffic looked out his front door. He said he could see five miles, and traffic was as clear as the weather. Brock swung into the oncoming lane doing 140. It didn't take long to pass all ten truckers. The lead trucker said, "Son, you must be in some kind of hurry. You be careful now, or I might have to call a meat wagon for *you*." I thanked them for their help and concern, and signed off.

Brock has better hearing than me, plus he was driving when he said the transmission was slipping. We pulled into a gas station and checked the fluid. No wonder it was slipping; we were out of transmission fluid. We dumped in a few cans and hit the road. About an hour later even I could hear the transmission, and it didn't sound good. At the next gas station we filled the reservoir again, and I bought a case of fluid to go. By this time we were in California. How much could it leak in the next two hundred miles to the finish line? We filled it every twenty miles. The last time we did it, the oil was coming out of the bottom almost as fast as we poured it in the top.

Finally, just outside Palm Springs, the TransCon MediVac shook, rattled, then stopped. We tried every gear, even reverse. Our race was over. A kid came by with an eighteen-wheeler pulling an empty flatbed. We made him a deal, and he hauled us across the finish line to a big ovation. We didn't win the race, but using all the recordings and notes taken by the Cannonballers and thanks to Brock's quick mind, he wrote an exciting and funny script. He gave it to me and said, "Okay, do your thing. Get us some money and some stars, and let's make a movie."

Back in Hollywood, I got a call from a famous producer named Albert "Al" Ruddy, who had produced *The Godfather*. I've worked on 310 feature films and 4,500 television episodes. I've had thousands and thousands of call times on movies, TV shows, and commercials. And I have *never* been late. I always allowed for traffic delays, a flat tire, or a fender bender.

The first time I was supposed to meet with Al Ruddy, who produced my *Cannonball* movies and *Megaforce*, was at Nate & Al's, in Beverly Hills. He called and told me he wanted to talk about the *Cannonball* script, financing, and all the details that go into putting together a movie. I told him, just give me a time and I'll be there. He suggested 8 a.m. for breakfast, and I said that I'd see him at eight.

I walked into Nate & Al's at 7:45 the following morning. Escorted to a table, I had a cup of coffee and a cigarette. (At that time you could smoke in a restaurant.) At ten minutes after eight, I decided that Mr. Ruddy thought his time was more valuable than mine, so I decided to leave. I paid my check and headed out the door. There I met a tall, smiling Al Ruddy. He asked, "Mr. Needham?" "Yes," I replied. He said, "Al Ruddy," and stuck out his hand. I shook hands with him, looked at my watch, and informed him that it was 8:15 and we would have to meet another time. He should call me to set up a date. I left.

Now, Ruddy is not your typical Hollywood producer. He's personable, well mannered, funny, and *always* late... but not with me. Every time we had a meeting after that, he'd point at his watch as he arrived and show me how many minutes early he was. He was also the one who created the phrase "There's real time... and then there's Hal Needham time."

Ruddy was on time for our second meeting at Nate & Al's, and we got down to business. He told me that he knew I had control of the *Cannonball Run* script and that he would like to produce it. I said that was all fair and good, but we would need some money. He said that was no problem. He knew a producer in Hong Kong named Raymond Chow, who had produced all of Jackie Chan's movies in the Far East and wanted to break into the American film market. Ruddy said Chow had plenty of money and wanted to go "big-time" on his first film. He knew the story line and wanted Burt Reynolds to star.

I told Ruddy that Burt had vowed he would never drive a car more than 35 mph in a movie. Ruddy said he knew I shot fast, so we could lay out a schedule and bunch Burt's part into twelve to fourteen days, and he'd be done. I told him that this movie wouldn't work at 35 mph. Unconcerned, he said that if we could shoot Burt in fourteen days, pay him $5 million, and make him a profit participant, he might change his mind. At this time no actor had been paid $5 million for a movie, so I thought Ruddy had a good plan.

I really like Ruddy. He's a great producer and a good friend. The man could get along with the devil and probably get him to finance a movie. We hung out together and could occasionally be talked into having an adult beverage. One day, after leaving the studio, we dropped by my office, where I just happened to have a fifth of Royal Salute scotch. Now, here's a scotch you don't want to dilute with anything, except maybe one ice cube. I opened the bottle and poured a couple of glasses. Ruddy and I sipped the scotch and planned the *Cannonball* shoot. Something strange happened: the more we drank, the better our ideas sounded. With the bottle empty, we decided to head home. Ruddy is tall, but he managed to squeeze into the passenger seat of my Ferrari.

Speeding along on Ventura Boulevard, everything was shipshape—until I noticed a flashing red light following me. I pulled over and met the officer at the back of my car. He asked to see my driver's license and then asked if I'd been drinking. The one thing I never do is try to BS a police officer. So I fessed up and said yes. He asked how much I'd had to drink. I told him about half a fifth. He said I didn't act drunk, but he wanted to know why I didn't let my passenger drive. I told him he might have noticed my passenger hadn't gotten out of the car, and that was because he drank the other half of that fifth. The officer actually laughed and asked, "If I let you go, will you stop at that coffee shop on the next corner and have some coffee?" I told him not only would I have some coffee, but also I would pitch a teepee and spend the night. He handed me my license and told me to "slow this thing down and have a good night." Back in the car, Ruddy asked why I wasn't going to jail. I told him it must be my lucky day.

Ruddy and I laid out a shooting schedule to wrap Burt's scenes as quickly as possible. It looked as if we could do it in twelve days, but to be on the safe side, we allowed fourteen. So with the script in hand, a fourteen-day shooting schedule, and a $5 million quote, I went home to tell Burt. The conversation went something like this. I told Burt the movie was called *The Cannonball Run,* Al Ruddy was going to produce—which meant it wouldn't be a schlock movie—and I could shoot his part in fourteen days.

Burt interrupted me. "Roomie, I told you I don't want to do any more movies about fast cars." I told Burt I understood, but Ruddy had a pretty convincing idea. "How about five million dollars and a percentage of the profits?"

Burt paused. "I know all about you and that crazy Brock Yates and your loony race across the country," he said. "I've told people and I'm telling you now, I've *always* thought it would make a helluva movie!"

By now Ruddy had put out the word around town that he was going to do a big movie. It was going to be fun and games and action, I was going to direct, and Burt was going to star. The phone lines lit up, and Ruddy worked his magic. Ruddy, Burt, and I sat down and began spitballing about who we could get to play the Cannonballers in the movie. We looked at the notes from the race and started to devise a list of teams similar to the real ones. First up was Dom DeLuise, who would be Burt's partner in crime. Burt suggested Farrah Fawcett as the patient in the ambulance, and I think I know why... because he was dating her.

I had doubled Dean Martin in a couple of movies, and we'd become good friends. Ruddy said he would call him. If we got Dean, we thought maybe we could get Sammy Davis, Jr., to be his teammate. Their cover was posing as Catholic priests. They drove my Ferrari in the movie.

We got Jack Elam to play the doctor. I'd worked with him a number of times, and so had Burt. He loved to play cards. He was offered a series at Warner's, but they wouldn't allow him to play cards on the set, so he refused to take the part until they changed their rule. Jack could play cards all he wanted to on our set.

Burt asked, "What if we could get Roger Moore to play... Roger Moore?" We did, and we gave him the Aston Martin and some Bond-like dialogue to go along with it. He couldn't help being somewhat British, and it worked perfectly.

Jackie Chan came with Raymond Chow's money, and that was just fine with me. We hired an English teacher to help him learn his lines. He was funny as hell and incredibly agile, and I knew he would be a big star.

As a favor, Peter Fonda made a guest appearance in the desert fight scene. Terry Bradshaw and Mel Tillis would team up in a stock car. Soon we also had Jamie Farr as the sheik, Jimmy the Greek setting odds in Las Vegas, Bert Convy as a game-show host, Valerie Perrine as a female cop, and even Bianca Jagger as the sheik's sister. We needed a couple of good-looking actresses to drive a Lamborghini: How about Adrienne Barbeau? And, I suggested, Tara Buckman...because I was dating her.

The Cannonball Run was shot in thirty-two days for $15 million, which was a pretty good value for the cast we had and our schedule. Bunching up Burt's scenes and skipping everything else meant we would have to start shooting in Atlanta, move to Las Vegas to shoot the Western states and the desert, to Los Angeles for the end—and then double back to Atlanta to shoot the scenes not involving Burt. It was an extra expense, but you do what you have to do to make it work.

A few days into the shoot, we had a big mishap. The scene was the start of the race. We were shooting at the motel where we were staying. It was a night scene, and the cameraman brought in a twenty-ton truck crane. He hung a bunch of lights on it to light the parking lot where we'd positioned all the cars that were in the race, plus some exotic cars as background. It was the first shot of the night. The operator raised the crane arm with the attached lights and swung it to one side to place the lights over the parking lot. As the rig's weight shifted, the outriggers (the legs that balance the crane) sank into some mud, and down it came. The crane arm landed on a Ferrari — not mine — which was suddenly only three feet high, about $12,000 worth of lights scattered across the parking lot, and the crane lay on its side. The only good thing was, nobody got hurt.

My assistant director asked what we should do. I told him that first of all, we needed another crane to pick that one up and get it back on its wheels. We needed to order more lights to replace the broken ones, and we needed to try to calm down the owner of the Ferrari, who'd come running out of the upstairs bar where he was having a few drinks. And we needed to wrap shooting for the night. He said we could probably be ready by midnight and get in four hours of shooting, but I thought safety was more important than the schedule. I had the best crew money could hire, and I treated them as such. I knew they would bust their butts to get back on schedule. They were not only my crew but also my friends. Unlike many directors, I ate what they ate, I stayed where they stayed, and I partied with them.

The next night, with a new crane and new lights, we were ready to go. I gathered the crew for a little pep talk. I told them that the scene had been scheduled for two nights of shooting, but provided the crane didn't tip over again, I believed that by the time the sun came up we could finish both nights' work. With a group response of "Let's do it," we started. We broke for dinner at 11 p.m. Trying to save time, we only took thirty minutes instead of the usual one hour. I looked at what we had shot so far and what was left to shoot and knew we had no problems. After dinner the crew scurried about moving lights and cameras, and the actors got caught up in the energy and never missed a beat.

When I next looked at my watch, it was 12:45 a.m. and we had only two short scenes to do. The motel had a big bar upstairs that closed at 2 a.m. I told my secretary, Kathy Shea, to go up and tell them to be prepared to stay open late. Straight up 2 a.m., we finished. I told the crew to take all the time they needed to wrap the equipment. But the bar was open, and the drinks were on me.

It was the fastest company wrap in history, and every crew member—about seventy in all—took me up on my invitation. The party got into full swing and the mood was so festive that Dean and Sammy took the stage and belted out a couple of songs. Dom got up and did what he always did—kept the crew in stitches. Farrah was her beautiful, bubbly self. Onstage, Burt told the crew how great they were, and I knew I was back on schedule. I was right that we could do two nights' work in one. When the sun came up, we were still partying.

Another thing that made my crew trust me was that I was always up front with them. I never took advantage of their hard work, but rather, tried to reward them for it. Every crew member had access to the shooting schedule, so they knew whether I was ahead or behind. One day we had finished shooting by eleven, so it wasn't even lunchtime yet. I told my assistant director to break for lunch and then wrap the company. Ruddy, being the good producer, wanted to know what I was doing, wrapping so early, because we still had a half day that we could shoot. I told him the crew wasn't dumb. They knew we'd finished the work scheduled for the day, and if I started shooting tomorrow's scenes they'd say,

"Why did we bust our butts to finish so quickly only to be rewarded by shooting tomorrow's schedule?" So we wrapped.

I went to look at another location, and by the time I got back to the motel, about two that afternoon, the crew was in and around the pool, as were a lot of the local ladies. A few empty drink glasses and beer bottles were sitting around. As I walked by, one guy called out, "Thanks, boss. Maybe we can finish at ten tomorrow?" Another voice said, "What if we shoot long days for a week and get two or three days ahead of schedule, and have a big party?"

I knew directors who would only allow the cameraman, camera operator, and the script supervisor to look at the dailies. Not me. I invited the entire cast and crew. I set up a bar and buffet for everyone, because I wanted my crew to share in every way they could. There's no mystery to making movies. Why not let everyone see the results of their hard work? Thanks to my crew, I was always on schedule and on budget.

After I finished editing *Cannonball Run,* Ruddy had a private screening at the Beverly Hills Hotel one Sunday evening, and he wanted me to attend. I said, "No way. I have a NASCAR race to attend." By now I owned my own NASCAR team, and it was coming to California to run at Riverside in the last race of the season. My driver, Harry Gant, was second in the point standings. Terry Labonte was first, but the point margin was small, and the championship could go either way. I couldn't wait for the green flag to fall. Wouldn't it be nice to win the NASCAR championship?

As the green flag was waved, I felt lucky. I just knew Harry was going to win. It was head-to-head between Harry and Terry. I was on the crew radio listening to every word Harry was saying about how the car was running, until I heard the two words I didn't want to hear: "She blew," meaning the engine had blown up. I felt worse for Harry than I did for myself. Harry would finish second in the championship standings.

On my way home after the race, I passed the Beverly Hills Hotel. A quick glance at my watch told me I still had time to make the screening. I whipped a U-turn and pulled up to the door. As I approached the concierge desk after my day at the track, I realized I wasn't dressed for the occasion—or any other occasion at the Beverly Hills Hotel. I marched in and inquired where the screening was taking place. The concierge looked at me and asked if I was an invited guest. I assured him I was.

Following his directions, I proceeded to the screening room. As I opened the door, I was confronted by a doorman who asked if he could help me. I knew I was about to have some fun, so I told him I had come to see the movie they were going to show; Mr. Ruddy had invited me. He said, "Wait right here," and went to a lady sitting beside Ruddy. He whispered in her ear, and she looked back at me. Then she got up and came back to see who this person was trying to bust into the screening. She asked if she could be of assistance, and I told her I'd like to talk to Al Ruddy. Again, I was told to wait. She whispered in Ruddy's ear, and he turned to see who she was talking about. Recognizing me, he stood and yelled, "Needham, get your ass down here!" When I reached his seat, Ruddy gave me a bear hug and introduced me to the lady messenger. She owned the hotel and was very apologetic for not recognizing me. Ruddy said that without all my gold chains around my neck, he wouldn't have known me either.

Sitting behind Ruddy was Sammy Davis, Jr., and next to Sammy was a blonde dressed to the hilt and lookin' good. They didn't call her Dani Diamonds for nothing. There was ice hanging from her ears, around her neck, and clamped around both wrists. Sammy, with his big, broad smile, greeted me warmly, saying he was glad I could make it. I suppose he noticed I couldn't keep my eyes off the blonde, so he introduced me. "Hal Needham, this is Dani Janssen." I recognized the name Janssen, as in the actor David Janssen, whom I had doubled one time as a stuntman. I also knew he had passed away a few years earlier. With the introductions complete, they started the movie.

Afterward we moved to a banquet room for cocktails and the usual BS about how good the movie was. With stealth and determination, I managed to corner the blonde for a quiet conversation. In my country boy style, I persuaded her to let me call her. The next day I phoned and asked if she had plans for Friday night. Would she like to go to a cocktail party? She asked where and when. I told her that it was at Sean Connery's and gave her the address. She told me that it was in her building, and yes, she would go with me.

Dani Janssen and I soon became an item. One columnist called us "the cowboy and the lady." The romance blossomed, and eventually a wedding was planned. We got married on the Western Street at Universal Studios. It was a cowboy wedding. The street was decorated as though a movie was going to be shot. There were checkered tablecloths, mason jars for glasses, and Texas barbecue unmatched in Hollywood. Burt was my best man. We rode in on matching black horses with silver saddles. Dani arrived in a horse-drawn carriage with a driver dressed in tails. We invited a few close friends, about six hundred.

That wasn't all. Movie and country-and-western star Mel Tillis came up to me and said, "Hal, I didn't bring you a gift, I just brought my band." His bus was parked around the corner. The guys set up and provided entertainment throughout the evening. Mel sang a couple of his hit songs, and most everyone exercised their vocal cords that night. Not only did Mel and his band perform, so did Burt, Mike Connors, Glen Campbell, and Tanya Tucker. Rod Stewart was there with Alana, but I don't remember if he sang. Anyone and everyone who could carry a tune, and some who couldn't, sang. As the night went on and the booze took effect, that included about half the people there.

I moved out of Burt's house and into Dani's penthouse in Century City. The mortgage was a lot, but she was a hell of a lot prettier than Burt. Things were rosy. I had a new bride, new movies to direct, and my race team was running good. I took Dani to the NASCAR races, and she was an instant hit. One day, as she passed a crew member from another team, he said, "Lady, when you walked through that gate, the ants just fell off the flagpole and died." She loved the good old boys and their southern humor.

Before I met Dani I wasn't someone who attended many Hollywood parties, but she did. We averaged two or three a week when we were in town, which was fine, but after a while it got old—same people with the same Hollywood stories I knew by heart. There was one exception. Early in those partygoing days, we were at Swifty Lazar's Academy Awards party, and Dani introduced me to the great director Billy Wilder. He asked how I'd gotten into the stunt business. I told him I had worked on a movie on which the director had done the stunt to prove that the stuntmen were asking too much money. (The movie, of course, was *The Spirit of St. Louis,* and he had been the director.) He smiled, and I saw the same twinkle in his eye as the day he'd stood on that airplane wing. I told him if he was any kind of a sport, he would come up with the five or six grand he cost me. He wasn't really trying to save the company money, he said; it just looked like a fun thing to do.

My next meeting with Wilder was a couple of years later, at the Cannes Film Festival. I had gone to promote *Cannonball Run II.* One evening I was in the hotel bar alone. Billy came in, saw me, and came over to my table. We closed the bar that night and a few others. I thought I had stories, but my stories paled in comparison to his.

Billy had obviously looked at some of the movies I directed. He wanted to know why they were less than a hundred minutes long. I told him the theaters could have an extra showing per day if the movie was shorter than one hundred minutes with the same staff plus an extra audience buying popcorn and drinks. He said that for a tree-climbing, wing-walking farm boy, I was reasonably smart.

Back in Hollywood at the parties, I would find my drinking buddy Billy Wilder, who disliked the parties as much as I did. We would find a corner near the bar and tell each other stories. As Dani and I arrived, I'd tell her I would be with Billy in the corner, and when she got ready to leave, to let me know. As time went by, my partygoing got to be less and less. Dani had had her fill of good-old-boy humor and grew to hate the tight schedule we had to keep, leaving Friday night, spending two days at the races, and traveling home Sunday night. She attended the races less and less; I guess she figured that cowboys and Beverly Hills ladies didn't gel as well as she'd thought they would. After five years we separated, then divorced. We stayed friends, and still talk on a regular basis.

The Cannonball Run made so much money that a sequel was inevitable. Burt was again the lead, and many of the original *Cannonball* actors returned, including Dom DeLuise, Jackie Chan, Dean Martin, and Sammy Davis, Jr. The leader of the Rat Pack himself, Frank Sinatra, also came aboard. With Dean and Sammy already cast, that only left one remaining Rat Packer to be persuaded to join them: Shirley MacLaine. *Cannonball II* would be the last movie they would all appear in together. These great actors were joined by Sid Caesar, Charles Nelson Reilly,

Susan Anton, Catherine Bach, Telly Savalas, Jack Elam, and many other stars. With this marquee cast, you couldn't go wrong.

Burt, Dom, Shirley, and Marilu Henner would run the race in a limo disguised as a military vehicle. Dean and Sammy would swap their religious garb for police uniforms as they competed in a plain jane police car—not coincidentally because my red Ferrari, which they'd driven in the first *Cannonball*, had been stolen from right under my nose. I had a big picture window in my office that overlooked my parking space. During prep for the movie I headed out to my car one day to go to a lunch meeting. In the parking lot I looked at where I'd parked the car that morning. What the hell? That's my parking space but where is my Ferrari?

I called the cops and gave them the details. They were as shocked as I was that somebody would steal my car, considering where it was parked. I picked up a rental.

The following day I got a call from the police. They had good news and bad news. The good news was that they'd found my car. The bad news was that it was trashed. It seems an LAPD chopper had been doing its daily flights over East L.A. when they spotted a red Ferrari in a dirt lot doing donuts, figure eights, and other car-damaging maneuvers. When they saw the license plate—1-4-HAL—they radioed in to the ground unit. The police knew I wasn't going to be very happy. The insurance company wasn't very happy either. It was totaled.

The stunts and jokes were endless as the Cannonballers raced from coast to coast. It was so hot in Vegas that one of my crew fried an egg on a manhole cover and made it into a sandwich. He said it tasted better than what was available from the catering truck.

Bobby Berosini's orangutan, which had just starred with Clint Eastwood in *Every Which Way But Loose*, played the role of the limo chauffeur for Cannonballers Mel Tillis and Tony Danza.

We actually used three orangutans; each had its own specialty, depending on what the scene called for. What surprised me about these critters was how sensitive to heat they were. They couldn't stand on hot pavement, so they were brought to and from the set in wheelchairs. Carpet would be laid down for them to stand on. If it was going to be more than twenty minutes before camera was ready, Berosini would wheel them back to their luxurious, air-conditioned Greyhound-type bus, where they would eat, drink, run around, and play until they were needed. The luxury bus also transported them to and from location. For sure they were treated like the stars they knew they were.

We shot a dangerous and spectacular stunt on a city street just two blocks from the Las Vegas Strip. Pilot Don Lykins, flying a CASA-212 Turboprop cargo plane, dropped down on a city street doing 90 mph, with minimal clearance over power lines. As the wheels touched the pavement, a parachute deployed from the rear clamshell doors, extracting a high-tech Mitsubishi driven by one of the two stuntmen who were doubling Jackie Chan and Richard Kiel. Lykins then firewalled the throttle, and with the plane now three thousand pounds lighter, lifted off, just barely clearing the power lines in his flight path. The Mitsubishi released its chute, spun a 180 to escape an approaching police car, and sped down the highway. This stunt was nothing compared to getting the necessary permissions from the Las Vegas city fathers, not to mention the FAA.

In *Cannonball Run II* the Mafia was trying anything and everything it could to kidnap Prince Abdul Ben Falafel, played by Jamie Farr, for ransom. Falafel raced in his Rolls-Royce. After many inept attempts, the goons came up with the idea of attaching a very big magnet to the bottom of a very small chopper to clamp onto the speeding Rolls-Royce and lift it up, up, and away.

Don Lykins also piloted the chopper. We did eight takes of chopper approach shots, which included dipping down and flying sideways with the chopper struts and magnet dragging on the highway, as well as bouncing off the tops of brush on the roadside. The final maneuver would be Lykins flying two inches above the Rolls-Royce at 70 mph. The updraft created by the Rolls made the chopper unstable, but with Lykins at the controls, we got the shot. This would later be cut into close-ups of actors Abe Vigoda and Alex Rocco flying the chopper, and a close-up of Jamie Farr reacting to the clunk of the magnet as it attached itself to the roof of the car.

Months earlier, back in Hollywood, we had prepared for this moment. We took the body off a three-quarter-ton pickup truck, built a roll cage to support the chopper, and then put a fiberglass Rolls-Royce replica body on the truck and attached the chopper to the roll cage. In the movie we would cut to a shot of the welded double for the Rolls and the chopper, which disappeared into a tunnel. With the camera placed at the tunnel exit, we hear a humongous crash as Jamie and the Rolls emerge sans the chopper.

How do you get Frank Sinatra to do a cameo? It helps to have a smart, deal-making producer like Al Ruddy, who, after enlisting Dean and Sammy, convinced Frank that it was a chance for the Rat Pack to perform together once again. Now that you have Frank, how do you pay him for one day's work? Frank suggested that $100,000 be donated to the charity of his choosing. He had a deal. He even flew in on his own jet.

I was concerned about having Frank for only one day. Would he be on time? Would he be difficult? The answer: he was the first person on the set. By the time I got there he was out of makeup and having a cup of coffee. He joked with the cast and crew, which made for a fun and calming atmosphere throughout the day.

I knew Frank collected model trains, so I had told the set decorator to get a rare model train and run a track along the wall behind the chair Frank would be sitting in during filming. As

Frank came onto the set, he walked directly to the train to have a look. I approached and asked what he thought of it. He said it was unique. I asked if it would fit into his collection and said I hoped it would, because we were shipping it to his house. He smiled and thanked me. It turned out to be the last feature film Frank Sinatra appeared in.

19

NASCAR and Setting Trends

Inexperience had never stopped me in the past, so once I decided to build a NASCAR Winston Cup race team, I took a trip to Charlotte, North Carolina, the hub of NASCAR. Although I had raced stock cars locally in Southern California, I had no idea how the big boys operated. I got to know Humpy Wheeler, who managed Charlotte Motor Speedway. I told him I could get Stan Barrett, the fastest man in the world, to be my driver. He listened to my plan to start a race team and warned me that it was tough to start a team with a rookie driver. I probably wouldn't win a race for years, so I should try to find a veteran driver. Humpy added that it would also be difficult to get a sponsor with a rookie driver. I said, not if I go outside the regular group of sponsors that every team competes for. I also told him that Burt Reynolds would be my partner, so with Burt and me as car owners and Stan, the first man to break the sound barrier in a land vehicle, as our driver, I believed we could get a tremendous amount of publicity. After all, that's what a sponsor is looking for.

What I really needed was an experienced crew chief to run the operation. Humpy suggested I contact Travis Carter, who at the time worked for legendary car driver and now car owner Junior Johnson. I met Travis, and we made a deal. Travis began hiring his crew and was eager to build a big shop. To save me some money, Laura Lizer suggested that we take over an existing building and see how things worked out. Travis moved the operation into a shop that was so small he claimed the crew couldn't all be in the shop at the same time. Travis built a few cars, and we headed to Daytona to test them. Everything went well until Stan lost control in turn four and kissed the wall. No big deal. I'd seen the King, Richard Petty, hit the wall numerous times, so let's just repair the car and move on.

As money was evaporating rapidly, I worked on getting a sponsor. I knew a guy named Bob Kashler who'd introduced me to some corporations that were involved in product placement in some of my movies. I told him to work on a sponsor for the race team. Some weeks later he called and said, get ready, U.S. Tobacco is interested, and they're coming out to meet us and discuss the possibility of them sponsoring the team. I told Bob to bring along our proposal, but Bob said all he had at the ready was a proposal written for Arby's. Just bring the Arby's proposal, I said, and I'll tell them that instead of selling roast beef sandwiches, we'd be selling Skoal.

When the U.S. Tobacco corporate jets landed at LAX, Bob and I were waiting with five limos. I met Lou Bantle, a smallish guy with a twinkle in his eye and a no-bullshit attitude, who was chairman and CEO of U.S. Tobacco, and marketing VP Garnis Hagen, a tall Texan dressed the part, with a broad, friendly smile, who was responsible for setting up this meeting. There were eight U.S. Tobacco executives in all. I handed them keys to their hotel rooms and loaded them into the limos.

We proceeded to a famous steak house atop a high-rise with a great view of the city lights. Bob was sitting on one side of Lou, explaining that because this meeting happened so fast, all he had was a proposal that said Arby's. I was on the other side, talking about how much PR the team would get with Burt Reynolds as my partner and how I intended to have the fastest man in the world as our driver. I added that as a bonus, I planned on putting U.S. Tobacco products in my future movies. By the end of dinner we'd sold them our sponsorship package. The team would be called the Skoal-Bandit, to capitalize on the popularity of *Smokey and the Bandit*. No race car ever before had had its own name, and it turned out to be a stroke of genius.

We tested at tracks that were on the schedule for future races. Travis suggested that we hire a veteran driver to go with us, to help Stan get a setup on the car, since Stan was a rookie and had never seen or driven on these tracks. Travis had a friend he thought could help us out, Harry Gant. Although Harry had not raced that much with the big boys, he was well known for his skills in the Busch series, and Travis liked him. We tested and raced for six months, and as I promised Lou at our first meeting, we got tons of PR.

Stan was doing a great job running between tenth and twentieth place, but I wanted our car to run with the big boys up front. I suggested to Travis that we run two cars and hire Harry Gant as our second driver. Travis thought it was a great idea. I made a deal with Harry, and we became a two-car team—against the advice of other team owners, who said a two-car team never works. Today there are a number of teams that have four or five cars, so in that regard we were trendsetters.

I set other trends: PR trends. I suggested to Lou Bantle that we hire some cheerleaders and call them the Bandettes, like a football team's cheerleaders. He thought it was a bad idea, but by now you know I never listen to people. So I hired some cheerleaders from the Atlanta Hawks basketball team. Then I had my Hollywood costume designer put together some skimpy, sexy outfits, and we were off to the Coca-Cola 600 at Charlotte Motor Speedway. Humpy Wheeler always put on a great prerace show. I asked if I could introduce my Bandettes onstage. He thought it was a great idea, and he was right. With over 100,000 screaming, cheering fans, the Bandettes were a hit—so much so that Lou Bantle hired models for every racetrack, put them in the sexy costumes, and had them pass out Skoal samples.

Another trend I set that's become the norm in NASCAR is painting the truck that hauls the race car around the country. As I looked at all the trucks lined up in the garage area I noticed they all looked interchangeable except for their colors. I had an idea. I would have a moving billboard traveling thousands of miles a year, with my sponsor's name on it. On both sides of the truck I painted a picture of the Skoal-Bandit race car up on the banking of a racetrack. On the rear doors we painted a rear view of the race car with a sign that read "You are following the Skoal-Bandit Race Team." The first day we drove the truck into the track, Richard Petty came over to me and said, "I don't know how your car's running, but you got two laps on the field with the paint job on your truck." Within a year every truck was painted in a similar fashion.

When I first became a car owner, pit crews wore whatever they wanted, which was mostly jeans and T-shirts. I wanted my team to stand out, so I asked the sizes of each team member and had uniforms designed and tailor-made, to the tune of $750 each. Of course, each member had to have at least four. I coordinated the colors to match the car, which was green and white, and put the words "Skoal-Bandit" on the trouser legs and on back of the shirts. I also included decals of secondary sponsors and the crew member's name. At the first race with the new uniforms, the news media mobbed our pit to take pictures. You also didn't have a hard time spotting our pit from the grandstand or the corporate suites. The press we got from that little idea was tremendous, and Lou Bantle thought it was another inspired move. Watch a NASCAR race today, and you'll see that every team lined up in front of their pits during the opening ceremony is wearing custom-made uniforms.

To make sure my guys were in shape to fill out those uniforms and be agile when they went into action as Harry Gant brought the Skoal-Bandit to the pit for service, I built a gym in the shop. To make it more enticing to work out, I told the crew they could exercise on company time. Pit stops are extremely important; a race can be won or lost on the speed of a pit stop. Let's say Harry came into the pits running fifth, with only a few laps until the end of the race. If the pit crew was fast enough to send him back out on the track in first place, it could mean a win and a big payday.

When U.S. Tobacco saw what I was doing, they hired a sports medicine company to evaluate the efficiency of the pit crew. They positioned four cameras to record each crew member as they performed numerous pit stops. The sports medicine technicians would then study the film and establish how the position and actions of each crew member could be modified to save precious time. Over a period of two months, we shaved off critical seconds. We were the first to do this. In my NASCAR days, pit stops were in the 16- to 16.5-second range. Today they average 13 to 14 seconds. New technology makes a difference.

NASCAR chairman and CEO Bill France, Jr., and I had become good friends. I called to ask him if I could put a telemetry system in my race car. He said yes, though he had no idea what I had in mind. My Budweiser Rocket Car was extremely high tech. The car had a telemetry system with twenty-three readouts that measured yaw, pitch, lift, down force, exhaust temperature, wheel speed — and just about anything else you'd want to know about while the car was making a run. An onboard transmitter sent the signals to a receiver and printer in the semi parked at our base camp, so we could gauge the performance of the car in real time as well as have a printout to study later.

Once the system was installed in the race car, we could measure the rpm's of the engine, driveshaft, and wheels. It would tell us to the pound how much weight was on each wheel at any given moment; the temperature outside the car, under the hood, and in the throat of the carburetor; or anything else we needed to know to get maximum performance and perfect the car's handling. It would definitely give us an advantage.

When I told Travis that NASCAR had approved our using the system, he was in shock. But not as big of a shock as the NASCAR inspectors were in for at the next race, in Talladega, Alabama, when during the prerace inspection they wanted to know just what the hell that thing was! It took up the entire area behind the driver's seat. I explained what it was and that I had permission from Bill France to use it. It took a couple of hours to get things straightened out, and we were good to go.

The race started, and Harry radioed Travis and told him how the car was handling. Travis could verify what Harry was telling him by the telemetry transmission sent to the TV monitor and could then plan what changes he needed to make when Harry made his first pit stop. CBS, which was televising the race and was aware that something unexpected was happening, placed cameras on our pit crew and must have interviewed Travis half a dozen times about how the system worked.

The system was working fine—until the engine blew up. NASCAR told us to leave "that thing" in the shop; they didn't want to see it again. Next time I saw France, he warned me never to ask to put anything on my car that NASCAR had not pre-approved. Okay, so we couldn't use it when we raced. But it worked wonders when we tested. A number of teams today use telemetry when they test. It proves beneficial to get a better setup on the car for race day.

There are a lot of people behind the scenes on a race team. Eventually a personality conflict and a difference of opinion on how to run things became evident between Stan Barrett and one of the key team members. Stan grew very unhappy and chose to go his own way. I was faced with a dilemma: do I throw all that money down the tube or go with Harry Gant as my driver? Lou was impressed with Harry and willing to move forward with him as the Skoal-Bandit. I agreed with Travis that we needed a new and bigger shop. He found a location he liked, so I bought the land, and we built a fancy new shop with new cars and a lot of new personnel.

Harry had a couple of nicknames — "Handsome Harry" and "Hurrying Harry" — but eventually the one that stuck was "the Skoal-Bandit." He scored a number of second-place finishes, and his popularity grew. The only driver more popular than Harry was the King, Richard Petty. Skoal wasn't hurting either; it had grown from the tenth most recognized tobacco product to number three. Lou, I told you we could do it! Lou Bantle was a great supporter of the team. Lou and many of his executives showed up at so many races that the corporate jet could've made its way to any racetrack without a pilot.

Despite the fact that prior to working with our team Travis had never held the position of crew chief, Humpy Wheeler was right about him. He had the right stuff. Nobody expects a new team to come out strong; it takes time for the team chemistry to gel. The first year we held our own, finishing respectably. The second year, Gant drove like a man possessed and finished second in four or five races. Soon enough, another team tried to hire Travis away from me. I believe I was paying him $60,000 a year, and the rival team was offering him $75,000. At that time, that was top dollar for a crew chief. To keep Travis, I made the decision to pay him $100,000. In two years' time, Travis had achieved two goals: he'd gone from being a member of a crew to being a crew chief, and he was the highest-paid crew chief in NASCAR.

In the meantime, I was having a ball flying from L.A. to wherever the race was, thirty or more times a season. I would leave the set of whichever movie I was directing in L.A. on Friday night, normally fly to Atlanta, and arrive at seven or eight in the morning. I was on a first-name basis with all the airline gate attendants. I would tell them I was going to be asleep on a bench and asked if they would wake me so I didn't miss my next flight—to the airport nearest to where the race was being held. After a while they'd ask which bench looked the most comfortable, so they wouldn't have to look too hard to find me.

One of the guys on my team was Johnny Bruce, JB for short. Travis assigned him the chore of picking me up at the airport and delivering me to the track. He always had some Chivas Regal and soda in the van to make the trip more enjoyable. JB used one of the team vans that had "Burt & Hal's Skoal-Bandit" painted all over it. JB looked a little like Burt and sported the same mustache. As we drove to the track, people would think we were Burt and Hal, going to the races. Sometimes ten or twelve cars would be following us. Both single, JB and I became a team. We missed very few bars or parties on the race circuit, and believe me, there were plenty of both. NASCAR fans are the partyingest group I have ever met. Hell, they spill more booze than most groups drink.

By 1984 the Skoal-Bandit team was on fire. Harry was winning races and scoring lots of top tens. And he was running in the championship race against his top two competitors, Dale Earnhardt and Terry Labonte. I hatched a plan to get Skoal some more PR. I called a press conference in a tent, where I had two toy race cars sitting on a table, one that looked like Dale's and one like Terry's. Incense was burning, and atmospheric smoke floated out from beneath the table. I proceeded to stick pins into the cars. The story made all the race magazines and newspapers—because Earnhardt's engine blew up halfway through the next race. Personally, I didn't think my voodoo act had anything to do with his engine blowing.

The PR was so outstanding that I came up with a new voodoo

plan. I hired an actor from Atlanta, flew him to Charlotte, and dressed him in a top hat and tails. He wasn't just any actor; he was a black Shakespearean actor. I told him that as I walked through the garage area, he should follow six feet behind me. When I stopped at Dale's car, I wanted him to move close to the car and stare at it. Then we would do the same thing when we came to Terry's car. He did exactly what I asked. As we passed Richard Petty's car, his crew chief, Dale Inman, was sliding under Richard's car just as he caught a glimpse of my voodoo doctor. He immediately slid back out and stared at the guy.

By the time we reached the other end of the garage area, the speakers were blaring "Hal Needham! Report to the NASCAR trailer!" The officials in the trailer looked at me as if I was crazy. Then one of them told me, "If you don't get that guy out of here, there might be a riot." I thanked the actor, rushed him into a limo, and put him on the next flight back to Atlanta. Though my well-being might've been in jeopardy, the PR was bigger than ever before.

The following weekend our truck was parked right next to Earnhardt's. When he saw me, he said, "Don't leave." He went into his truck, returned with two shock absorbers, and formed them into a cross, saying, "I got you covered, Needham!" And then he laughed.

There were twelve races a year where I could fly to Charlotte International Airport and from there take a helicopter to the track. My secretary found a pilot, Cress Horn, with his own chopper, and he agreed to fly me to the track, spend the night, go to the race with me, and then fly me back to Charlotte after the race. We did this for seven or eight years, and the stories are endless. First of all, he put dual controls in the chopper so I could learn to fly. I got so I could handle it pretty good. At one race, Ken Squire, the race announcer I knew from CBS's rocket car coverage, asked if he and his producer could get a ride to Charlotte with us. I told Cress that once he cleared traffic, he should let me fly while he turned around and started talking to Ken and his producer. Once airborne, Cress took off his headset and turned to talk to Ken. After a few seconds, Ken asked in a panicked voice who was flying the chopper; Cress told him that I was. Ken, now beside himself, said he would feel much better if Cress would take the controls.

Another time, my secretary made arrangements for us to land the chopper in the parking lot of the motel where we had reservations. They told her they would put yellow tape around one corner of the lot for us. We arrived at the motel at around six that evening to find a spot marked with yellow tape that had trees on one side and the building on the other. Cress had only about ten feet of prop clearance. No problem, he said, and sat it down.

Before he could kill the engine a police car appeared. Cress said, "Oh shit." I got out and went to meet the officer, who said, "Mr. Needham, we'll keep an eye on your chopper to make sure nobody messes with it." I thanked him and motioned for Cress to kill the engine. Cress and I had dinner and then went to the bar for a nightcap. The manager came by and asked if we could move our chopper to the front parking lot because it was difficult to control the "looky-loos" in the back, and the police would be better able to watch it out front. I said, "Sorry, pardner, but my pilot barely shoehorned it into that area sober." I added that it would be pushing the envelope for him to try to get it out while drunk, and the manager agreed.

The next morning a crowd had formed around the chopper that included the nice police officer from the previous evening. I asked if he'd spent the night, and he said yes; during race weekends they had to work twelve-hour shifts. I slipped him a hundred-dollar bill and said we'd be back that evening. Guess what? So was he, and he was also there Sunday morning when we took off.

Darlington, in South Carolina, was considered a track too tough to tame — and so was its landing area, for any chopper that might fly in. It consisted of a dirt field so dry you had to wait five minutes for the dust to settle before you got out. On our second trip there, Cress was complaining about the dust clogging up the filters and getting the chopper so dirty you couldn't read the numbers on it. I suggested we look for a better landing site. As we approached the track I told him to circle so we could have a look at the area. Directly across the highway from the track I saw a backyard big enough to land in. There was a guy in bib overalls standing in the middle of the yard, watching us. I pointed to the spot and asked Cress, how about that yard? He asked if I knew the people who owned it. I told him no, but if you'll put her down there, I'll introduce myself. He banked around and headed in. As we got closer, the guy in the overalls backed away, giving us room to land. I told Cress not to kill the engine until I gave him the signal.

We touched down, and I got out and approached the man, greeting him with "Howdy, pardner." He was too shocked to answer, so I continued with "What's the chance I can land my chopper here for a couple of days?" He said it wasn't his property; it was his momma's. I asked if his momma was around. He pointed to the house, where I saw a seventy-year-old lady heading toward us. "Howdy, ma'am," I said. "I was asking your son about landing my chopper here today and tomorrow." She said she didn't have insurance for a chopper. I assured her I had plenty of insurance. She paused and said, "Well, I guess you can, then."

I signaled Cress to kill it. We had a new landing spot. The man looked me over and asked, "Ain't you the guy that owns Harry Gant's car, the Bandit?" He shook my hand and said it was a pleasure to meet me. I thanked him and moved to Mom with a hundred-dollar bill in my hand. She said, "No, no, there's no charge." I stuffed it in her apron pocket and went to the track.

After the race I went to our truck that hauled the race cars and equipment and got six Skoal-Bandit T-shirts and six hats. Back at the chopper, I gave them to my new fan in the overalls. He thanked me, and we took off, vowing to see him in the morning. And so the next morning, and for as long as I owned the race team, as we would approach the yard, he and his momma would be waiting for us, waving us into our landing zone.

At one race, we had reservations at a motel where I'd never stayed. It had an address on a highway, so Cress figured we could just fly low down the highway, find it, and land. It took a while, but we found the motel, tucked away on top of a hill surrounded by trees, with no place to set the chopper down. We circled and spotted another motel under construction where there was plenty of room to land, but not a soul in sight. It looked pretty good, except we would have to walk down the hill to the highway and about a quarter of a mile to our motel driveway, and then up the hill with our luggage. We talked it over and decided to go for it. We landed, and while waiting for the engine to cool down so it could be turned off, I looked down the hill and couldn't believe my eyes. Here comes a taxi. As he stopped, the driver said, "You guys need a taxi?" I said, "You've got to be kidding me." He said that he saw us land and knew we weren't staying at the construction site, and he thought we might need a ride. On the way to the motel I asked how much we owed him. I think it was three or four dollars. I took out a fifty and tore it in half. I handed him one half and told him to be here in the morning at seven, and I'd give him the other half. That guy, with his quick thinking, probably owns the company by now.

Every trip had a chopper story, but I'll quit for now. I not only hired Cress and his chopper to go to the races but also used his services as a camera chopper anytime I needed an aerial shot for my movies. He went on to become one of the most successful chopper pilots for movies in the Southeast. He now owns U.S.

Helicopters and has a fleet that he supplies to TV news stations throughout the country.

When I built my team, NASCAR was known as a southern sport. It all started when the moonshiners all had hopped-up cars so they could outrun the feds with their loads of booze. Once bragging rights came into play as to who had the fastest car, the only way to settle the argument was to have a race. It might have started small, but it's huge today. There are racetracks across the country, and some can accommodate in excess of 200,000 fans. Not to mention the hundreds of small tracks, known as bullrings, from coast to coast. The sponsorship money to run a team when I started was between $1 million and $1.5 million. Today I'm led to believe it's between $12 million and $15 million. Drivers today make more than it cost to run the entire team when I started.

Every race is televised from start to finish and reruns are shown during the week. NASCAR racing has become one of the biggest audience participation sports in the United States. And why not? With action like forty-three cars running 190-plus mph inches apart, there's bound to be a wreck with the possibility of wiping out half the field.

I loved going to the races and watching Harry Gant drive my Skoal-Bandit car and seeing all the fans in the stands at the tracks. I wasn't the only one in love with NASCAR racing, so I thought, why not make a movie about it? I'd have a built-in audience. A deal was put together for me to direct *Stroker Ace,* starring Burt Reynolds and Loni Anderson. It was the story of a happy-go-lucky NASCAR driver. Since I owned a NASCAR team myself, the story really appealed to me. Universal agreed to bankroll the movie, so off we went to shoot in the South, the heart of NASCAR. We shot most of the movie at Charlotte Motor Speedway, but to give the flavor of following the NASCAR circuit, we also shot at Atlanta Motor Speedway, in Georgia; Daytona, in Florida; Talladega, Alabama; and Darlington.

While reading the script, I realized that product placement could cut a big chunk out of the budget if I played my cards right. The challenge of putting together the kind of deal I'd done with CBS and Budweiser to break the sound barrier kept me up at night, until I figured it out. I started scouting locations during the week, and on weekends I'd go to the races and watch my team compete. At the tracks I went from one corporate suite to another. I knew most of the chairmen and CEOs of the companies that sponsored race teams, so I asked them to supply a replica of their race car, a truck to move it from one track to another, a driver to drive the car in the movie, and a pit crew with uniforms—and I didn't want to see a bill for anything. I guaranteed them as much screen time as I gave my own car.

Twenty-two sponsors came aboard for the run of the movie, and I estimate it cost each sponsor about $50,000. I also got Goodyear to supply all the tires I needed, plus two men and a truck to do the tire changing and haul the extra tires from track to track as we changed locations. Last but not least, the chairman of Union Oil lived in the same building I did. At dinner one night I made him an offer. For $100,000 worth of gasoline, I'd make sure Union Oil signage was prominent throughout the movie.

My plate was full, directing movies and battling to win a NASCAR title. Harry Gant and Travis Carter were winning races and scoring championship points. Harry had a terrific fan following; Skoal was happy as its sales mushroomed; and I was still sleeping on benches at the Atlanta airport, waiting for my flights.

At one race, it was the normal routine: catch a 10 p.m. flight out of LAX, arrive in Atlanta about 6 a.m., and sleep on the bench a couple of hours until JB picked me up. We drove to the track to watch Harry's Winston Cup practice and qualifying, followed by the Busch series race, and then went to see what kind of trouble we could stir up Saturday night before the big race on Sunday. Harry finished in the top five on Sunday, and all the teams and fans headed home, except for us. We had rented the track the following day to practice. When we got back to the hotel on Sunday night, the bartender had only one customer to keep him company. She looked so good I decided to join in the conversation. Three or four drinks later, she and I decided to drop the bartender from the proceedings by going to my room. We got some drinks and headed upstairs.

Having been at the track all day, I decided a cold shower would pep me up. While in the bathroom, I heard glasses breaking and stuck my head out to ask if she was okay. No problem; she had just dropped the tray with the drinks on it. I told her to order some more. I finished showering and returned to the room. She was standing there with one glass about a third full, and she suggested that I could finish that one while we waited for room service and she went into the shower. I propped myself against the headboard, finished the drink, put the glass on the nightstand, and settled back, waiting for the lady to emerge from the bathroom.

The next thing I knew, my phone was ringing. I fumbled to reach it. Now, I've had some hangovers, but this one was a doozy. It was Travis Carter, wanting to know what was the holdup. I was a half hour late, and everyone was waiting for me, but Travis knows I am *never* late.

Confused, I managed to get dressed and start down the hallway, but I was ricocheting off the walls and totally out of control. In the van my crew gave me a hard time all the way to the track. I was trying to put last night into perspective. I didn't remember the lady ever coming out of the bathroom. What did I do, other than make a fool of myself? The bartender must have poured a helluva strong drink. Never before had four drinks had such an effect on me.

At the track Harry was running laps and Travis was timing him, but I couldn't have cared less. My head was throbbing, my hands were shaking, and all I wanted to know was how long this day was going to drag on. I looked to see what time it was, but my Rolex Presidential wasn't on my wrist. Must have left it at the motel—but hold on! My rings were missing, and I never take them off, even with a fuzzy mind. I discovered that my wallet was also gone. I quickly figured out that the lady was no lady, she was a thief, and that third of a drink she'd given me was a Mickey. I also knew she'd made a good haul. My rings were way more expensive than my eighteen-grand Rolex. I pulled JB aside and told him he had to drive me somewhere. In the van, he asked where we were going and I said to the police station.

On the way I explained what had happened and then I repeated the story to two detectives. They told me there was a ring of women known as the Rolex Queens who worked big sporting events and were very good at picking their prey. Looking at a Rolex's second hand, they could tell at a glance if it was real or fake. A real Rolex second hand sweeps around, and a fake one jumps from second to second. They also told me I could forget about recovering my loss; the Queens were usually from out of town, and the minute they made their haul, they headed for the airport and were gone. I filled out a report and thanked them.

We returned to the track, and I told the crew what had happened. At first they were shocked, but as the day went on they found some humor in it, and by drinking time that night it was downright funny to all of us. Back in Hollywood, I was talking to producer Al Ruddy about a movie and mentioned my loss. Along with the stupidity, he also saw some humor in my story. The next day he presented me with a Movado, saying he wanted me to be on time. That was the biggest chunk of gold I ever wore, and expensive. With my new Movado I managed to get to the set on time, and I made all my flights to the races with no problem.

In those days NASCAR normally ran two races at the same track each year. When the time came for the second race at the track where the Rolex Queen had relieved me of my jewelry, we were staying at the same hotel, and as a joke each and every one of my crew volunteered to chaperone me in the evenings to keep me out of trouble. It was Saturday night. The bar was jammed with race crews, fans, and me. I struck up a conversation with a lady who had a problem. She was stranded for the night; her flight had been canceled, and she had to wait until morning to get to her destination. She had a room but no way to get to the airport the following morning. I told her the hotel had a shuttle, but she told me it didn't start running in time for her to catch her flight. I estimated that thirty dollars should take care of the taxi fare, but just to be sure, I peeled off a fifty and gave it to her. She asked for my address so she could repay me, but I told her not to worry about it.

A couple of drinks later I excused myself and went to the restroom. I returned and finished my drink. She suggested we go to her room. I was smarter now. I didn't suggest we take any drinks with us, and I promised myself I wouldn't even have a glass of water when we got to her room. To get taken twice would be *really* dumb.

In her room, she turned on the TV and found a station showing highlights of that day's race and the lineup for Sunday's event. She told me to have a seat; she'd only be a minute. Then she disappeared into the bathroom. Watching TV was the last thing I remember until six in the morning, when I woke up alone in the room, without my Movado and with another whopping headache, knowing exactly what had happened. Here's how I put together the evening. When I'd gone to the restroom in the bar, she'd slipped me the magic potion and then suggested going to her room, where I went to la-la land. Good timing on her part.

I pulled myself together and took a taxi to the police station. When I asked the cabbie what I owed him, I discovered I had no money to pay him, so I asked him to wait and take me back to the hotel. In the police station, I asked for the detectives to whom I'd reported the first incident some four months earlier. I knew their names, because they had contacted me a few times with additional questions. One of them came out and greeted me, commenting that he'd told me to drop by when I was in town but hadn't expected it to be this time of day. I asked if he still had the report I'd filed a few months ago. Sure, he said. Why? I told him to duplicate it with today's date and save himself some time, because it had happened again.

In his office I told him my story, and then he told me I was one lucky man. These women were very dangerous. If the person they slipped the Mickey to had health problems, he could die. There had been a dozen or more incidents reported in his town alone, and so far so good: no fatalities. He warned me to be more careful, and I went back to the hotel, borrowed some money from JB for the cabbie, and went to the race. The joke of the day was the crew asking me what time it was.

Fast-forward. The race season ended, and I threw a big party for the crew. I was sitting with Harry when a lovely lady walked by. I turned and told Harry I thought I'd ask her to dance. All he said was, "Let me hold your watch."

My ten years in NASCAR ended when I sold the team. My camera-car business, Camera Platforms International (the Shotmaker and the Lightmaker), was about to require my attention for the next few years—but I love racing, and my interest has never waned. Whenever there's a NASCAR race on, you'll find me kicked back in my La-Z-Boy in front of the TV. My La-Z-Boy sits in a den that probably looks a lot like yours. It's a comfortable place with stuff I like. I have some posters from the movies I directed, my saddle and spurs, memorable awards, and lots of pictures signed by friends. (I even put some of them in this book.)

You know, I've been lucky to have done what I loved at every point in my life. When I was trimming trees, I loved doing it. When I was jumping out of planes in my paratrooper days, I loved it. And how could I ever forget showing John Wayne how to throw a punch?

I was always learning everything I could about the job at hand, and then pushing the envelope. Looking back, one thing is just as true of my career in movies as it was in NASCAR: nobody ever gave me anything but an opportunity, and I worked hard to be prepared and at the ready to take advantage of new prospects and maybe have a little fun at the same time. I was helped by imagination, dedication, and the good work habits I learned as a kid on the farm. It just never crossed my mind that I wouldn't succeed at something, once I came up with the idea—even with a few wagon crashes or broken bones along the way. And each time I fell farther or crashed harder, I found the rewards far outweighed the effort it took to get there.

It's difficult to explain how I felt when I'd done a spectacular stunt and the cast and crew would applaud and it would be the buzz of the day. Or if I made a suggestion to a director or an actor and the suggestion turned out to be just what the scene needed. After I started directing, I'd go to see one of my movies and sit in the back of the theater to watch and listen to the reaction of the audience. I would actually get goose bumps thinking, *I did that!*

In 2001 the World Stunt Awards were established to recognize and honor outstanding achievements in the world of movie stunts with the Taurus Award. Arnold Schwarzenegger was awarded the Taurus Honorary Award for his contribution to action movies; John Woo received the Action Movie Director Award, and I was the recipient of the World Lifetime Achievement Award. The ceremony aired on ABC as a two-hour special.

I worked in the world of stunts from 1956 until I directed *Smokey and the Bandit*. I've been thrown, run over, and busted up more times than I can count. Looking back, movies and I had a pretty volatile relationship, but there's nothing like working for weeks or months—even years—to get it done and do it right. The payoff is on the screen. Even today, with all the new technology used in movies and stunts, they still need people—real people—crashing cars, doing high falls, and generally getting it done with the same kind of adrenaline rush I've felt throughout my career, and my life.

Do It Well

Back in 1959 my mom had a car accident that left her with a limp. She could get around but was in constant pain. She worked in a restaurant as a cook and was always on her feet yet never complained. But then, she had never complained in St. Louis, where she'd worked two jobs sixteen hours a day, trying to raise my sister Gwen and my brother Jim. I had contributed $20 a week of the $45 take-home I made climbing trees, but it was her dedication and hard work that kept us together. Then there were the years in Arkansas when she got up before daylight to work in the field, chopping and picking cotton, then stayed up long after nightfall, canning food and sewing up the holes in our clothes by the light of a kerosene lamp before going to bed.

By 1961 I had married Arlene and adopted her three children. I had enough work to pay the mortgage on our new home, make payments on our two cars, and put food on the table. My life was good, but I was concerned about Mom. Arlene and I talked the situation over and agreed that if we watched our pennies, we could buy the half-acre lot next door and build a house for Mom. I told Mom the plan and she said no, as I knew she would. But we built the house anyway. With a little persuasion, she moved in. Now I had a wife, three kids, my mom, two mortgages, two car payments, and two stunt horses to feed.

After a couple of months Mom got restless. She didn't have anything to do but watch the kids occasionally when Arlene and I went out. As a faithful Southern Baptist, she devoted much of her time to the church, but she wanted to work. I asked her what she thought she could do on a part-time basis. The only trade she knew was cooking, and that meant standing on her bad ankle. She mentioned that a couple of the ladies at church were having trouble finding a housekeeper who was good and trustworthy. Mom took the job two days a week. I said, "If it makes you happy and you can do it, give it a go."

As my career flourished, I made sure Mom wanted for nothing. Laura Lizer made sure her bank account never ran dry. Mom was now cleaning houses four or five days a week, and giving every dime she made to the church, because that was what made her happy.

One Christmas I bought her a new Cadillac Seville, and parked it in her driveway with a big blue ribbon around it. My sister had taken her to breakfast while the car was being delivered. When they returned, Mom got out and I said, "Merry Christmas." She walked around the car and said, "I always wanted a new Chevrolet." Oh well, so much for all the money Cadillac spent on advertising.

I gave her enough credit cards to fill her wallet. Mom had never had a credit card in her life. I told her she couldn't spend all the money I had, so she should throw caution to the wind. I never regretted telling her that, but believe me, she learned how to use those cards.

Every Christmas thereafter, I would send Mom on the trip of her choice. I also sent my sister Gwen to accompany her. Mom had never been out of the country and was getting up in age, so I'd make arrangements for them to be part of a tour once they reached their destination. Fearing the long flights would be hard on Mom, I'd book them on the Concorde. One time, in Czechoslovakia, they were visiting a high-end crystal factory when a glass caught Mom's eye. She told Gwen she'd like to buy one, but it was very expensive. Gwen said, "Hal won't care. Buy a set." So Mom did. She rode in gondolas in Venice, saw the Sphinx and the pyramids from the back of a camel in Egypt, had her ears pierced at age seventy-four, and bought herself diamond stud earrings in Amsterdam. She bought a Rolex in Switzerland, toured St. Peter's Basilica, walked the Spanish Steps, and visited the Colosseum in Rome. She took in the view of Paris from the Eiffel Tower, rode through the Alps in Austria, and watched the changing of the guard in London. Her favorites were Israel and the Holy Land. She saw it all.

Mom died in 2004, at age ninety-seven. The last two years of her life, her health deteriorated rapidly but she never lost her mental capacity. The last time I saw her, she told me she was ready to go home and wished the Good Lord would call her. Two days later she died. For the last forty-two years of her life, Mom never wanted for anything. I was happy to be able to support and repay her for all the years she had worked two and three jobs, never complaining and never once accepting welfare or unemployment benefits as she struggled to support and raise me and my brothers and sisters.

Mom had set the bar high with her work ethic, so in my early television and movie career, I watched the people who became successful and knew how they got there. This also gave me the answer to a question I'm often asked: "Who was your favorite actor to work with?" No contest: the answer is the Duke, John Wayne. Duke was dedicated. He knew every job on the set and could do most of them. He wasn't afraid to get his hands dirty. He always looked out for his crew and treated people with respect. But he also knew about hard work and wasn't afraid to tell someone the truth if he felt they weren't putting forth enough effort.

Truth be told, the Duke reminded me of my stepdad, Corbett,

who died in the summer of 1959 of a heart attack. He also was a dedicated man. He had to be: he married my mom, who already had three kids, during the Great Depression. One day Corbett gave me a chore to do on the farm we were sharecropping in Arkansas. He wanted me to plant some corn, which meant digging a small hole, dropping in a kernel of corn, and covering it up. I did about two-thirds of the field and, deciding it was time to take a break, I leaned against a tree and fell asleep. When I woke up, it was getting dark. Knowing I couldn't finish the job, I dug a big hole, dumped all the seed corn in, covered it up, and went to the house.

Two weeks later Corbett took me for a walk in the cornfield and pointed out that some of the planting I'd done was growing well. Then he pointed to a part that hadn't grown at all. He walked me to the place where I'd emptied the bag and covered it up. Sure enough, every kernel had sprouted. Corbett didn't give me a whipping; he never did.

"Come here, Hal," he said. "Sit down. I'm going to tell you something I want you to remember as long as you live."

He said:

When a job is once begun,
Never leave it 'til it's done.
Be it great
Or be it small,
Do it well
Or not at all.

Acknowledgments

A Big Thanks to Little, Brown and the *Stuntman!* team: Publisher Michael Pietsch and Editor-in-Chief Geoff Shandler, thanks for being fans. My editor, John Parsley, a man of his word. The two Heathers (Rizzo and Fain), Carolyn O'Keefe, Laura Keefe, Amanda Tobier, Valerie Russo, Lathea Williams, and Brittany Boughter, for their enthusiasm, great marketing, and PR. Jacket designer Allison Warner, copyeditor Ben Allen, and Sarah Murphy, tireless editorial assistant to John Parsley.

Penny Copen Fender, Director of Communications for the Elevation Group of Companies.

To my agent, Howard Yoon, who made things happen from Day One, and Gail Ross at the Ross Yoon Literary Agency.

Nobody influenced me more than my hardworking mom, Edith, and my stepdad, Corbett. They taught me the importance of good work habits, honesty, and to fess up when I was wrong.

And to my loving wife, Ellyn, who put her life on the back burner to help me tell the story of mine.

Index

About the Author

HAL NEEDHAM's career has included work on 4,500 television episodes and 310 feature films. He directed 10 features, including the classics *Smokey and the Bandit, Hooper,* and *The Cannonball Run.* He set trends in movies (the first director to show outtakes during end credits) and NASCAR (the first team owner to use telemetry technology). His Skoal-Bandit race team was one of the most popular NASCAR teams ever—second only to that of the King, Richard Petty. Hal set Guinness World Records and was the financier and owner of the Budweiser Rocket Car (now on display in the Smithsonian's National Air and Space Museum), the first land vehicle to break the sound barrier—traveling at 739.666 mph. The highest-paid stuntman in the world, he has broken fifty-six bones and his back (twice), was the first human to test the car air bag, and has fought for the respect and recognition that stuntmen and stuntwomen deserve for their contribution to the world of moviemaking. His many awards include an Emmy and an Academy Award.